1520

The Field of the
Cloth of Gold

About the Author

Amy Licence is a journalist, author, historian and teacher. She has an MA in Medieval and Tudor Studies and has published several scholarly articles on the Tudor dynasty and Richard III. Her books include *Cecily Neville* ('This insight is so rare and so valuable' PHILIPPA GREGORY), *In Bed with the Tudors* ('A fascinating book examining the sex lives of the Tudors in unprecedented detail' THE DAILY EXPRESS), *Anne Boleyn* and *Living In Squares, Loving In Triangles: The Lives and Loves of Viginia Woolf and the Bloomsbury Group*. Amy has written for *The Guardian*, the *Times Literary Supplement*, the *New Statesman* and *BBC History Magazine* among others, and has appeared on BBC radio and television.

1520

The Field of the
Cloth of Gold

Amy Licence

AMBERLEY

This edition published 2023

Amberley Publishing
The Hill, Stroud
Gloucestershire, GL5 4EP

www.amberley-books.com

Copyright © Amy Licence, 2020 2023

The right of Amy Licence to be identified as the
Author of this work has been asserted in
accordance with the Copyrights, Designs and
Patents Act 1988.

ISBN 978 1 3981 1541 5 (paperback)
ISBN 978 1 3981 0047 3 (ebook)

British Library Cataloguing in Publication Data.
A catalogue record for this book is available
from the British Library.

Typesetting by Aura Technology and Software
Services, India.
Printed in India.

CONTENTS

Is it not fitting that my pen should take part
In writing out the artificers of this Triumph,
For such great and exalted acts
Not even the warlike Caesars ever accomplished.

Clement Marot,
Ballad of the Field of the Cloth of Gold

INTRODUCTION

The year 2020 marks the 500th anniversary of the meeting between Henry VIII, King of England and Francis I, King of France. They came face to face in a French valley midway between the towns of Guines[1] and Ardres in the modern Pas-de-Calais department of northern France. Today, a minimalist stone plinth marks the spot where thousands of attendees feasted, danced and jousted. Dressed in cloth of gold, crimson satin and yellow velvet, or in the servants' livery clothes of Tudor white and green, and Valois black, white and tawny, they converged in the 'golden valley' between 7 and 24 June 1520. Due to the quantities of glittering material used in their costumes and tents, it would go down in history as The Field of the Cloth of Gold.

Modern retellings of the period have tended to relegate the event to the status of a glorious party. Undoubtedly there was a party atmosphere, with fabulous costumes, temporary palaces and tents, dazzling props, masked dancers and chivalric feats. At a distance, these epitomise the glamour of the Tudor period, condense it into a short summer's lease, and present it as a glittering historical bauble. In many ways, the Field of the Cloth of Gold represents the perfect simulacrum of the Tudor experience. It was the long-awaited meeting between two European giants, alike in dignity and ambition; it was the height of Tudor spectacle and pageantry, and it was the most expensive display of magnificence of which either king would ever conceive. It shines across five centuries as a stand-alone moment amid the turbulence of international politics, reformation and national redefinition. As such, it makes for a full and rewarding micro study of Anglo-French spectacle. But it was also far more than this.

In terms of its scope alone, the Field of the Cloth of Gold was a phenomenal feat of logistics. The convergence of Francis' court upon Ardres was less of a Herculean labour than the task of transporting at least 5,800 English individuals across the Channel in the space of days, and arranging for the movement of around 3,200 horses, although some animals were sourced afterwards. Ships had to be found and supplied, accommodation arranged in existing or specially constructed buildings, and all those mouths had to be fed, whether human or equine. Many different materials were required for the construction of Henry's temporary playground, for his two-storey glazed pavilion, hung with gold, his jousting lists with symbolic 'tree of noblesse' and his two chapels adorned with crosses, candelabra and icons, as well as the ovens and offices of the kitchen, stable and wardrobe. Where possible, items were constructed off site and transported to Guisnes, but significant building work took place around the event, in the preceding weeks and whilst the courts were present. Fortunately, many of the lists of instructions, payments for supplies, wages and descriptions of the camps survive in contemporary sources. Thus, we know just how many strawberries were consumed and how much the painters were paid for adorning the banqueting house with roses. It is possible to deconstruct, meal by meal, timber by timber, how this historical moment was created.

Of course, the Field of the Cloth of Gold did not occur in isolation. It arose out of the international political climate of the 1510s and influenced subsequent Anglo-French and Imperial foreign policy. However, it is remarkable for the singular lack of politics discussed at the event. Those two weeks in June did not include any negotiations or discussions about strategy or policy, or even any new treaties. Apart from the ratification of former agreements, the emphasis was entirely upon entertainment.

Yet every discussion, every meal and every event was loaded with political significance and transformative potential, none more so than Henry's choice to sandwich the event between two meetings with Francis' main rival, Emperor Charles V. Anxious to influence his uncle, Charles sailed to England in late May, and met Henry between Gravelines and Calais in mid-July. However, this was an open secret. It did not make the Field of the Cloth of Gold the 'most portentous deception on record' or 'little more than an immense charade', as two historians have labelled it.[2] It was more the 'mock international chivalric court festival par excellence' described by Professor Sydney Anglo, and if any side was disadvantaged in 1520, it was more Charles than Francis, whom Henry preferred, and defended. It is true, though, that this balance did not last beyond twelve months, but even in its brevity, the event exposes a truth of international relations in a rapidly shifting world.

If anything, the Field of the Cloth of Gold is metonymic of the fragility and transience of temporal life, rather than its splendour. It was a motif which surrounded the pre-Reformation guests in daily life, through the expression of *memento mori* art, poetry and architecture. Reminders of death were painted on the walls of churches and cadaver tombs featured stone-carved bodies riddled with pain or worms. The proximity of unexpected and premature loss was a feature of early sixteenth-century life against which no amount of status could protect. This Catholic imagery was usually macabre in mood, but as the Bishop of Rochester, John Fisher, observed in November 1520, the wealth of the Field of the Cloth of Gold was overlaid with a veneer of weariness and the golden tents were destroyed by the weather. Its fleeting luxury was as powerful an allegory for mortality as the meagre skeletons of the ecclesiastical mural of the dance of death. Francis' palace of pleasure, supported by three ship masts lashed together, was blown down, as was Henry's banqueting hall. Even the famous pavilion in Guisnes, painted in trompe l'oeil effects to simulate brick and tile and set with glazed windows inside a wooden frame was built and gone within a space of weeks. The Genoan secretary Gioan Joachino wrote 'You would be surprised to hear of its architecture, but you would be more delighted to behold such a structure, built to last a day, and no longer. It appears to be that which it is not, and it is that which it does not appear to be.' In comments like these, the temporality of life was allied with the motif of playful deception, masques and disguise, so beloved of Henry's court. It may feel an uneasy juxtaposition today, of the oxymoronic carnival with the morbid, of play with death, of magnificence with dust, but this was a familiar early renaissance mood. It is precisely this which typifies the concept of 'merry England' of popular culture: a pre-Reformation gaiety fringed by darkness.

On 25 June 1520, the courts withdrew from Ardres and Guisnes, leaving the towns to restore order, and the blaze of splendour became a memory. There is a degree of pathos in the attempt to mimic a state of architectural permanence which implicitly acknowledges that friendship does not last forever. The meeting of the kings blazed like a comet upon the tail of which Henry and Francis tried to ride for as long as possible. And yet, when its light had dimmed, and only the memory of it remained, its standard had still been achieved, as much as any victory on the battlefield. The ideal of perfect chivalry and friendship, as unsustainable as the summer, had been realised. So much so, that five centuries later, its legend lives on.

I

THE WORLD IN 1520

By 1520, Europe was dominated by cathedrals. Their gothic and romanesque arches formed a Catholic network from France's Amiens and Avignon, to Spain's Zamora and Zaragosa, defining not just the landscape, but all the rites of passage of human existence. Their painted aisles rang with song and prayer, their many saints' shrines glittered with jewels, and the scent of their incense floated out into the air. It had been that way for centuries, since the spread of Christianity across Europe, and the dominant narrative continued in the curlicued archways and stained glass of churches completed in the early sixteenth century. In the 1510s, they rose at Wittenberg, Salamanca, Venice, Gdansk and Moscow, captured in the vaulted ceiling of King's College Chapel, Cambridge, and the southern transept of Metz Cathedral.

A Venetian visitor to England at the turn of the century wrote that 'there is not a foot of land in all England, which is not held either under the king or the church and many monasteries also pay acknowledgements to the king for their possessions.'[1] The church defined people's lives in the western world, from the moment they woke, until they slept at nightfall, from before birth, until burial and beyond, in perpetual mourning chantries full of flickering candles.

Outside the churches, the other big landowners were the rulers of Europe: Kings, Princes, Dukes, Counts and the Emperor.

Set alongside rivers and royal hunting parks, the great palaces of the age were undergoing a transformation. The Chateau d'Amboise and its ornate gardens had been remodelled along Italianate lines, and provided a final home to Leonardo da Vinci, who died in its grounds, in 1519. On the banks of the Thames, Thomas Wolsey, England's only Cardinal, lavished 200,000 crowns upon his fairy-tale Hampton Court, just five miles downriver from the newly completed Richmond Palace with its long galleries of sculpture and art, panelled windows, octagonal towers and ornate decoration. In Granada, Charles, the new king of Spain, had begun to dismantle the intricate architecture of the Moorish Alhambra for a scheme of modernisation, while in Malines (Mechelen) in the Netherlands, his aunt Margaret expanded the Hof van Savoye into a renaissance ideal. It so impressed the young Anne Boleyn in 1513 that she would use it as the model for London's Whitehall Palace twenty years later.

Through the corridors and tiltyards of power strode Europe's larger-than-life rulers, in their slashed sleeves, handmade armour or masque costumes sparkling with gold. International politics and warfare were now a young man's game with the recent deaths of Emperor Maximilian, Louis XII of France, England's Henry VII and Ferdinand of Aragon ushering a new generation into power, who still had their spurs to win, and their peers to outshine. In 1520, the English throne had been occupied for eleven years by the now twenty-nine-year-old Henry VIII, a man known internationally for his physical beauty, his pleasure-loving court and the expensive wars he had waged against France. The French king for the last five years was the elegant but sybaritic Francis I, aged twenty-six, who continued the Hapsburg-Valois wars against the newly appointed Emperor, Charles V. At sixteen, Charles had become King of Spain and at nineteen, he had beaten Henry and Francis to win the Imperial title. His vast realm stretched from the Netherlands to Spain, encircling France entirely inside what was known as the Hapsburg Ring. Rivalry between the three men was intense, as they veered between attempts to outshine each other personally, and pair up for mutual advantage against the third. It was a politics of emerging identity and masculine ego, with the art of warfare and renaissance style as the backdrops against which their youth and fortunes would compete.

In 1500, the world population was somewhere between 425 and 500 million, which is around one sixteenth of that recorded in the census of 2001. Of the three kings concerned, Charles ruled over the largest territory, combining around 16 million subjects in the Holy Roman Empire, with 8,550,000 in Spain, giving him power over 5-6 per cent of the entire known world. France was next, with almost 4 per cent, represented by 16 million individuals, while the small island of England, described in 1500 as 'sparsely populated', contained slightly under 3 million, with 60,000–70,000 of those living in London.[2] The majority of people didn't live in cities, though, but in smaller towns, villages and hamlets spread across the countryside. Secular wealth was held by a small, privileged elite, and transferred by birth, marriage or death, with most people belonging to the middling and lower classes, with little opportunity for advancement. However, the new renaissance ideal of the *homo novus*, or self-made man thriving on his wits - and the new reformation ideal of a direct personal relationship with God - forefronted the individual, allowing the sons of a blacksmith and a butcher to transcend their class through education and become chief ministers to Henry VIII.

This was an era which questioned the scientific limits of understanding. For centuries scholars had understood that the earth was spherical, after the eighth-century monk, Bede, explained it through the differing lengths of daylight, and by 1500, Amerigo Vespucci was mapping out the stars. The first empirical confirmation that the world was not flat began in the summer of 1519, when the Portuguese explorer Ferdinand Magellan and his crew set out on their circumnavigation of the globe, mapping out their route across the Atlantic, Pacific and back through the Indian Ocean.

Pioneering was dangerous: Magellan would not return home, being killed by natives in the Philippines, and his crew would be branded traitors for landing in Spain, Portugal's rival. Time was changing too, literally, when in 1515, Pope Leo X summoned astronomers and theologians to recalculate the Julian calendar, as it was now ten days out of synchronicity with the sun. Polish astronomer Nicholas Copernicus was invited to assist, but declined, because he believed a reform of astronomy was required before the length of the year could be standardised. Increasingly, astrologers were rejecting the fixed, Aristotelian model of the universe in favour of a heliocentric view, with da Vinci's belief that 'the sun does not move' but that the planets did instead, as affirmed when Copernicus completed his review *On the Revolution of the Heavenly Spheres* in 1543. All the while, some of the oldest clocks in Europe ticked away inside English Cathedrals, in Salisbury from 1386 and Wells from 1392.

Spain and Portugal dominated the race to discover the New World. In the 1490s, explorers Christopher Columbus and John Cabot had established a range of small settlements on the coast of America but had not pushed far inland, so that cartographers struggled to represent the shape and scale of this new-found isle.

The earliest surviving globe, Behaim and Glockenden's *Erdapfel*, or 'earth apple', created before 1492, does not show any land across the Atlantic, but only five years later Cabot's expedition landed on the coast of North America. He was funded not by the leading European powers but by Henry VII, and upon his return, Cabot was feted in London, dressed in silk and given a £10 reward. In 1500, America was first recorded on a map by Juan de la Cosa, and first named as such by cartographer Martin Waldseemüller in 1507. Through the early sixteenth century, Spanish and Portuguese conquistadors claimed the Caribbean islands and waged war against the indigenous population. Then, in 1519, Hernan Cortez reached Mexico and launched his first attack upon the Aztecs, decimating their population in the ensuing two years.

When it came to discovering the East, explorers were guided by myth as much as fact. The popular fourteenth-century work, *The Travels of Sir John Mandeville,* had been published in Westminster in 1494 and was translated into almost every European language by 1500. Detailing fictional travellers' tales by an anonymous author, it repeated the popular confusion that an additional continent existed, named Cathay, and cited by Marco Polo, but which was later understood to be China. When the Portuguese landed on China's south coast in 1513, they were still unsure which country they had reached. Australia would remain a complete unknown in European circles until the Dutch arrived in 1606, but Portuguese explorer Vasco da Gama had established trade links with the Vijiyanagara Empire in India before 1500. In a factional Russia, Ivan III had trebled the size of the Grand Duchy of Moscow, but the country would not be united under one Tsar until 1547, and although furs were traded, no formal English connection was made until the foundation of the Muscovy Company in 1553. The Turkish Ottoman Empire, marking the border of the civilised world in the east, was starting to play an increasing role in European politics and, from his succession in 1520, Suleiman I acted as a buffer to Charles V extending his territories further.

Culturally, it was a time of rapid advance. The first printing press was established in Mainz, Germany, followed by Paris in 1470, Spain's Segovia in 1471, Utrecht in the Netherlands in 1473 and London in 1477. By 1500, there were estimated to be 1,000 presses operating in Europe, which had produced 8,000 books or *incunabula*.[3] With printing centres in London, Oxford and St Albans, books were being produced in England at such a rate that they would become fixtures in most middle-class homes. In the last decade, Michelangelo had completed the ceiling of the Sistine Chapel, and Raphael had painted the *Sistine Madonna*. Baldung had produced his *Three Ages of the Woman and Death*, Matsys finished *The Money Lender and His Wife*, and his portrait of the reformer Erasmus, Durer had drawn his *Rhinoceros* and Titian's *Assumption of the Virgin* was finished.

Medicine was still a male preserve, caught between the ancient Galenic system and more modern innovation. In 1518, Henry issued a charter to the English Royal College of Physicians, enabling them to license approved practitioners, regulate them and punish those operating without. The same year, a case of the dancing plague occurred in Strasbourg, when 400 people felt compelled to dance in the streets continually for a month, often without rest or food, many dropping from exhaustion or suffering heart attacks. The most convincing explanation was that the people of Strasbourg were the victims of mass psychogenic illness, or 'mass hysteria', induced by a belief in the 'curse of St Vitus', who would punish sinners by making them dance.

Religion was changing too. While the Catholic church had always had its critics, the first phase of a more serious reformation had been set in motion in 1517, when Martin Luther nailed his 95 theses to the door of All Saints' Church in Wittenberg. Two years later, the reformer Zwingli preached for the first time in Zurich against the veneration of saints, and a copy of Erasmus' vernacular translation of the Bible was approved by the Pope. In 1520, Luther published three of his most significant works, including *On the Freedom of a Christian*. It was too early for the term 'Protestantism' to be attached to these changes and many of those questioning established practices still considered themselves to be Catholics in search of reform.

A Venetian, who had visited England in around the year 1500, sent home a detailed description of the country and its people, whom he found to be intelligent, martial and well-dressed gourmets. Both men and women of all ages, he wrote, were 'handsome and well-proportioned', and wore 'very fine clothes and were extremely polite in their language'. There was a confidence, or arrogance about them, though, being 'great lovers of themselves and of everything belonging to them; they think that there are no other men than themselves, and no other world but England.' Along with this went a pronounced xenophobia, an 'antipathy to foreigners', whom they imagined 'never come into their island but to make themselves masters of it, and to usurp their goods.' Perhaps, as a result, the English had a 'very high reputation in arms' and, as the Venetian believed, were greatly feared by the

French. Yet they were clever too, 'gifted with good understanding and very quick at everything they apply their minds to'. Most of all, they loved to eat, taking 'pleasure in having a quantity of excellent victuals and also in remaining a long time at table', but were also devout, attending Mass 'every day' and saying 'many Paternosters in public'.[4] England was also proud to retain a small area of northern France, as a remnant of the old Angevin Empire. The Pale (or region) of Calais, extending from Wimereux to Gravelines, had been taken by the English after the battle of Crécy in 1346, and provided a useful foothold across the Channel for trade and invasion.

In 1516, one Englishman had set out an extraordinary vision of a perfect world. Thomas More's *Utopia* was derived from the Greek eu-topos, meaning equally 'nowhere' and 'a good place'. On his imaginary island, located in the New World, a sort of proto-communism governed a society of equality and accountability. People all learned an essential trade and lived in large family units, overseen by one individual, with shared meals, no privacy, or private property and access to warehouses where they could request what goods they needed. A hereditary prince ruled, but had no distinguishing clothing or crown, signalled only by a sheaf of corn carried before him, assisted by elected officials and very few laws. The tract criticised kings who started unnecessary wars and wasted large sums of money; religious diversity and tolerance were encouraged in Utopia, but the patriarchal system was still in place. It has been suggested that this ideal world was a either satire of the England which More knew, or a vision for a new, ideal way of life.

Diametrically opposed to More's Utopian political philosophy was Niccolo Machiavelli's *The Prince*, in circulation from 1513, but not printed for another twenty years. Far from the tolerance, humility and community advocated by More, Machiavelli defined a Prince's power as obtained, and exercised, through perfecting the art of war. It might be necessary for a Prince to give the appearance of being merciful, humane, honest and pious, but in reality, he should be ruthless, unforgiving and cruel, commanding respect only through his military and religious victories. Ferdinand of Aragon, Henry VIII's father-in-law, was cited by Machiavelli as an exemplary ruler for his recent subjection and persecution of the Jews and Moors in Spain. Although literary historians have argued that *The Prince* might just as equally be a satire to expose contemporary corruption, as it is a manual for political success, its content is diametrically opposed to that offered by More, and exposes the conflicting nature of the contemporary renaissance influences upon figures like Henry, Francis and Charles. The Field of the Cloth of Gold would blend elements of visual and material culture, military feats, national identity and Princely ideals. Venetian ambassador Nicholas Sagudino declared that 'Two such courts as those of France and England have not been witnessed for the last fifty years.' On a warm day in early June, 1520, these two courts would unite to create the most extravagant spectacle of the century.

THE ENGLISH

Henry VIII in later life, with Mary and Will Sommers, the King's fool. Artist unknown.

2

HENRY VIII

The young Henry VIII had acquired a well-deserved reputation for dancing. As a ten-year-old at his brother's wedding, he 'flung off his coat and cavorted around in his doublet and hose',[1] enjoying the admiration of his parents and courtiers. Dancing was the prince's 'favourite daily exercise', in which he performed 'wonders', leaping 'like a stag' and acquitting himself 'divinely'.[2] From his youth, Henry loved to perform, dazzling his audience with his skill and endurance, stealing the limelight, shedding gold spangles from his costume as he threw himself into the moment. In 1513, during a lull in his invasion of France, the victorious king stayed up until the early hours with the court of Margaret of Savoy, dancing in his bare feet and shirt sleeves. Seven years later, Henry was still the partying gourmand who personified merry England, but approaching thirty, he was inching towards dramatic change.

Henry had been born in 1491, at Greenwich Palace. His father's financial and military successes meant that the young prince's childhood was one of comparative calm, learning, hunting and entertainment in the royal nursery at Eltham Palace, and at court in Westminster, Greenwich and Richmond. His prospects changed in 1502, upon the death of his elder brother, Arthur, when the exuberant, red-haired boy found himself promoted to heir to the throne, and later invested as Prince of Wales. The loss of his mother the following year left a further mark upon the boy, as his father's character darkened, and their relationship became more complex. Yet the country was at peace, and the Richmond coffers were overflowing by the time the old king breathed his last in April 1509, and his son succeeded as Henry VIII.

The new reign dawned with expressions of genuine enthusiasm and optimism. The mood was one of chivalric glory and celebration, of relief and joy, of parties and pleasure. The plaudits of the poets in 1509 seem too genuine, too frequent, for historians to conclude they were merely following convention in their flattery of a new king. Instead, they welcomed what they saw as a golden age, ruled over by an unparalleled man of the renaissance, as beautiful as an 'angel'. Chronicler Edward Hall wrote of the people's 'great reverence, love and desire'[3] for Henry's kingship, Lord Mountjoy hyperbolised that Heaven and Earth were rejoicing, as 'everything is full of milk and honey and nectar' and that Henry was not inspired by 'gold, or gems or precious metals, but virtue, glory, immortality', for his character was 'almost divine'.[4] Thomas More, writing seven years before *Utopia* in verses composed for the coronation pageant, promised that such a king would free them from slavery, 'wipe the tears from every eye and put joy in place of our long distress'.[5] The Spanish Ambassador concurred that the English were 'very happy and few tears' had been shed for the old king: 'instead people are as joyful as if they had been released from prison.'[6] When Henry wrote to Ferdinand of Aragon that his people's joy was 'immense' and their 'applause most enthusiastic'[7] he was witnessing the expressions of hope in more than just a new reign, but a new era, a new century. More than this, he was the embodiment and the spirit of this new age. In the euphoric summer of 1509, England was looking to this 'perfect model of manly beauty'[8] to create a new world for them.

One of Henry's first acts was to marry his brother's widow. Catherine of Aragon was six years his senior, regal and beautiful, and a match between them had been proposed for years. Henry acted swiftly, keen to maintain the Spanish alliance, and perhaps also from inclination. The new king explained that he had taken 'into consideration the high virtues of the Princess Catherine'[9] and that the match had been his father's dying wish. Catherine came from a large family where the women had proven themselves fertile, at a time when it was crucial for a queen to provide heirs. Perhaps there was also a chivalric element to the feelings of a young man fond of reading historical romances and playing the role of the ardent lover in masques, in rescuing a princess who had spent many years in distress. Hall gives a more cynical explanation, that Henry was moved 'by some of his counsail that it should be honourable and profitable to his realme' to marry Catherine who had 'so great a dowrie', lest she should 'marry out of the realme, whiche should be unprofitable to him'.[10] Whatever his motives, Henry married Catherine quietly at Greenwich Palace on 11 June 1509. The speedy marriage was probably timed to allow for their joint coronation, which took place two just weeks later.

Around 4pm on the afternoon of Saturday, 23 June, Catherine and Henry left the Tower of London to ride through the city streets to Westminster. No expense was spared: £1,749 8s 4d was spent on Henry and £1,536 16s 2d on Catherine, and their entourages. The new king went first, riding a horse draped in damask gold, dressed in a crimson velvet robe edged in ermine, the front of his doublet studded with gems, with a jacket of raised gold and a necklace of rubies. He was 'much more handsome than any other sovereign in Christendom' and 'most invincible', with such qualities that the Venetian ambassador considered him to 'excel all who ever wore a crown', making the country 'blessed and happy' in 'having as its lord so worthy and eminent a sovereign'.[11] Hall's praise was fulsome despite stating that the king's charms needed no description:

> The features of his body, his goodly personage, his amiable visage, his princely countenance, with the noble qualities of his royall estate, to every men needeth no rehearsal... I cannot express the giftes of grace and of nature, that God hath endowed him withal.[12]

After him, Catherine was drawn in a litter by two white palfreys trapped in cloth of gold, and wore a dress of white embroidered satin, with a 'rich mantle of cloth of tissue'. Her long red-gold hair hung loose 'hanging downe to her backe, of a very great length, bewtefull and goodly to behold' and a coronet set on her head, made from 'rich orient stones'.[13]

The following day was Midsummer, the longest day of the year, and the feast of St John the Baptist, when the English would traditionally decorate their homes with green branches and keep bonfires alight all night. Dressed in crimson robes, Henry and Catherine processed from the Palace to Westminster Abbey, along a striped - 'ray' - cloth strewn with flowers. Henry swore his coronation oath first, and was anointed by the Archbishop of Canterbury, William Warham, before the crown of Edward the Confessor was lowered onto his head. Catherine's ceremony was shorter, and her crown was lighter, being a golden coronet set with rubies, pearls and sapphires. A contemporary woodcut depicts them seated side by side, looking into each other's eyes and smiling as the crowns were lowered onto their heads, a poignant image of the moment, suggestive of a couple in love, as equals, embarking on a journey together. Above Henry's head was a huge Tudor rose, while Catherine's image was topped by her chosen device of the pomegranate, symbolic of the expectations of all Tudor wives and queens: fertility and childbirth. In Christian iconography, it was also an image of resurrection, featuring in Renaissance paintings of the baby Jesus by Botticelli and da Vinci.

In the first few years of his reign, Henry was the only young player on the international stage. France, Spain and the Empire were ruled by old men, and he was keen to make his mark as the embodiment of a new era. In November 1511, he joined the Pope's Holy League against France and two years later personally led an English army across the Channel. Dressed from head to foot in gold, and with gold bells hanging from his horse, Henry met Emperor Maximilian in a tent of cloth of gold, and it was with the help of an additional 2,000 Imperial soldiers that he won a victory at the Battle of the Spurs that August.

The European dynamic changed in 1515-16, when the deaths of Louis of France and Ferdinand of Aragon allowed for the successions of younger men. At twenty-seven, Henry suddenly found himself the elder statesman of Europe. It was a role he was keen to fill, using displays of wealth to dazzle and influence, and drawing upon European influences, which would culminate at Guisnes. In July 1517, he held a banquet at Greenwich in honour of the new King of Spain, Charles I, and the ageing Emperor Maximilian, his relatives by marriage to Catherine. The occasion was recorded by Spanish delegate Francesco Chieregato, who commented that they 'were accompanied by so noble a train of men and horses, that had the king of Spain himself come in person, he could not have been more honourably attended.'[14] Henry dispatched a guard of 400 to meet his guests and conduct them to Greenwich, where they found the king 'dressed in stiff brocade in the Hungarian fashion, having a collar of inestimable value around his neck', while Catherine appeared 'in cloth of gold, with chains around (her) neck, everything glittered with gold.' The rest of the court 'glittered with jewels and gold and silver, the pomp being unprecedented'.[15]

In a forerunner of the Field of the Cloth of Gold, a joust was held to impress the Spanish, for which Henry wore 'white damask, in the Turkish fashion... embroidered with roses made of rubies and diamonds, in accordance with his emblems, a most costly costume' and he carried a scimitar 'embroidered with pearls and precious jewels'.[16] His armour was covered by a surcoat of cloth of silver, 'wrought through with emblematic letters', each ending in a costly pearl. The gentlemen jousters were also dressed in white, embroidered with the letters 'H' and 'K', which must have 'cost the king a mint of money as during the last four months all the London goldsmiths have wrought nothing but these trappings'. Henry held a buffet for the ambassadors, the table being thirty feet long and twenty feet high, set with dishes, bowls, goblets and basins of pure gold, all for show, whilst the guests ate from smaller plates. They remained at table for seven hours, watching as each course was brought out to the king 'by an elephant, or by lions, or panthers, or other animals, marvellously designed; and fresh representations were made constantly with music and instruments

26

of divers sorts.'[17] Chieregato's detailed account presents a vivid tableau of Henry and Catherine's court:

> The removal and replacing of dishes the whole time was incessant, the hall in every direction being full of fresh viands on their way to table. Every imaginable sort of meat known in the kingdom was served, and fish in like manner, even down to prawn pasties; but the jellies, of some 20 sorts perhaps, surpassed everything; they were made in the shape of castles and of animals of various descriptions, as beautiful and as admirable as can be imagined.
>
> In short, the wealth and civilization of the world are here; and those who call the English barbarians appear to me to render themselves such. I here perceive very elegant manners, extreme decorum, and very great politeness; and amongst other things there is this most invincible King, whose acquirements and qualities are so many and excellent that I consider him to excel all who ever wore a crown; and blessed and happy may this country call itself in having as its lord so worthy and eminent a sovereign, whose sway is more bland and gentle than the greatest liberty under any other.[18]

The occasion was marked by the king's chaplain, Dionysius Memo, whose 'instrumental music' lasted four hours, 'to the extreme delight of all the audience and especially of the king'. He noted that at the feast Henry sat between Catherine and his sister Mary, with a sumptuous repast and dancing until two in the morning.[19] In terms of extravagance and renaissance taste, the visit demonstrated just what an ambitious prince might achieve in order to impress; but even Henry would go on to outdo himself.

The following year, Henry's chief minister, Cardinal Thomas Wolsey, orchestrated an international triumph which established his king as a major player on the European stage. In response to a policy of aggressive expansion of the Ottoman Empire by Sultan Selim I, Wolsey rallied other western leaders to put aside their differences and stand together against the threat of 'heathen' invasion. This resulted in the Treaty of Universal Peace, or Treaty of London, being signed on 2 October 1518. The terms were proclaimed at St Paul's Cathedral, after which Henry hosted entertainments at Durham House, including twenty-four masked mummers, who were led in their dance by Henry and his sister Mary, followed by 'countless dishes of confections and other delicacies', gambling with ducats and dice.[20] The papal ambassador, Sebastian Giustinian, witnessed this 'most sumptuous supper', the like of which he was certain had never been given 'either by Cleopatra or Caligula', in a banqueting hall decorated with huge vases of gold and silver, which he likened to that of King Croesus.[21]

Henry also sought a betrothal as part of the treaty. His daughter, Mary, was two in 1518, and the new Valois king, Francis I, had just fathered a son, so the alliance was formalised two days after the Universal Peace, in the Queen's Great Chamber at Greenwich. The little Princess was dressed in cloth of gold, with a cap of black velvet and covered in jewels, as she stood in front of her mother. Seigneur de Bonnivet, Admiral of France, took her hand and espoused her in the name of the Dauphin, giving her a small ring set with a large diamond. A joust followed, another banquet, and a pageant featuring a dolphin, to pun on Mary's fiancé's title, and the mythical horse Pegasus. Henry also made generous gifts to the French, impressing Francis with a suit of horse harnesses decorated with gold filigree and rich embroidery, and offering the rich robe he was wearing, of 'cloth of gold, lined with cloth of silver', to Bonnivet, after the Admiral had admired it.[22]

Shortly before the Field of the Cloth of Gold, Henry's chief minister, Thomas Wolsey encouraged him to purge his court of bad influences. The minions, the young men in Henry's close circle, had become increasingly boisterous, encouraging the king to reckless behaviour and causing concern among his advisors. John Skelton's *Magnificence*, a political satire and morality play, dealing with the fall of a King from grace into poverty, was probably written during this period as a warning about their excesses.

Skelton was well-placed to comment, having been the King's tutor in his youth and the author of at least one previous work aimed at his personal improvement, the now lost *The Mirror for Princes*. Skelton's work depicted the King as the embodiment of magnificence, or generosity, combined with grandeur and wisdom. The central eponymous character is tempted by Crafty Conveyance, Courtly Abusion and others, but is brought back to the enlightened path by the figures of Measure and Perseverance. The minions, a sort of private boys' club including William Compton and Edward Neville, Francis Bryan, Nicholas Carew and Henry Courtenay, had caused trouble at home and abroad, being 'all French in eating, drinking and apparel, yea, and in French vices and brags', tapping into a latent national francophobia. The last straw came when they made a visit to Paris and rampaged through the streets throwing eggs and insults. The influence of these rowdy young men upon the king was not as strong as that of Henry's old guard, Wolsey, Thomas Boleyn and the Duke of Norfolk, who moved against them in May 1519 and expelled many from the King's intimate service. They crept back into favour gradually, and many were part of the expedition in 1520, but they never quite held the same position at court again. As Henry matured, he was keen to set aside such antics and seek a new identity in the European context.

A unique opportunity arose in 1519, which fuelled Henry's international ambitions further. In January, Emperor Maximilian died, leaving vacant a vast swathe of territories across northern Europe, including Germany, Italy, Bohemia and Burgundy, and a title which rivalled that of the Pope, a title of first among equals of all the Catholic monarchs. To Henry, this was the jewel in the European crown he coveted, but it was equally desired by Francis and Charles. As Maximilian's grandson, the Hapsburg prince Charles was the frontrunner, but he was young, and currently occupied in Spain, while Francis was geographically closer at hand to influence the German Electors, and willing to offer them large bribes. Initially it seemed that the role might go to the French king, but to see his rival promoted in such a way was intolerable to Henry. When Francis asked for English backing for his campaign, Henry professed himself willing in theory, but refused to lend him money and secretly launched his own bid for the title.

That February, Henry's ambassador in France, Thomas Boleyn, was at the Valois court in Paris. When Francis emerged from the chamber where he had heard mass, he drew Boleyn aside into an alcove, and told him he hoped that England and France would 'act in perfect unity... prudently and harmoniously'. Boleyn played along, offering that he believed several of the Electors have 'expressed themselves favourable' to Francis, 'because of the greater service he might do against the infidels', and expressed 'the great desire Henry had for the increase of his honour, and the service he intended to do in advancing him to the preferment of his imperial dignity'. Francis removed his bonnet and made his 'hearty' thanks.[23] However, Henry was playing a duplicitous game, dispatching secretary Richard Pace to visit the Electors in Germany, bearing a letter full of supportive sentiments:

A great responsibility has fallen upon them by the death of Maximilian. They will have to elect an emperor favourable to universal peace, and competent to protect Christendom. Germany has always been a bulwark against those who were covetous of power. Hopes, therefore, they will proceed unanimously and with a view to the public weal. Offers to aid them in maintaining their rights with all the resources of his kingdom.[24]

Henry's secret instructions for Richard Pace, newly arrived ambassador to the Netherlands, were vastly different to those expressed in the letter. His real mission was to sow division. He was charged to 'disappoint the election of the French king and the king of Castile', and to find means, 'by provident and circumspect drifts', to influence the Electors to favour Henry. In a list which resonates with Machiavellian scheming, Henry instructed Pace to use 'the most politic drifts... and enquire which of the electors lean and incline' to favour Francis and which Charles. When he had grasped their allegiances, Pace was to speak to Francis' supporters of Henry's allegiance to France, but when he spoke to supporters of the Spanish, he was to say that Henry supported Charles,

> ...upon knowledge whereof, he may in such wise order the declaration of the same, that when he speaketh with the favourers of the Frenche kyng he may employ words to show the Kyng's inclination to that partie... and in semblable manner, to use hymself to such of the electors as inclined to the kyng of Castile's part, so that the Kyng's highness be not noted to favour or advance the one partie more than the other, but to use pleasant words founded upon indifference to the friends of both (and)... before he enter communication with any such as pretend themselves to be friends to either the Frensche kyng or kyng of Castile, he may be well assured that they be no dissemblers, nor such as by crafty means would search the secrecy of his mind and declare the same to the contrary part, whereunto the King's said ambassador must take special regard.[25]

Believing himself to have fooled his rival, Henry was unaware that Bonnivet had been positioned behind a curtain and overheard Boleyn speaking on the matter, but Francis pretended not to know, and continued to play the diplomatic game, just as he would do in 1520.

Henry and Francis were both disappointed when Charles I was appointed Emperor that June, although they sent their congratulations with a good grace. Sebastian Guistinian wrote that 'it was more necessary than ever to keep the king of England in friendship with France,' but that he 'was not sure of him, because of the hostility of the English towards the French, the Queen's being a Spaniard, and the discord incessantly sown by lady Margaret,' Charles' aunt.[26] Both Henry and Francis, entering into negotiations for a meeting at the Field of the Cloth of Gold, were still smarting from the imperial defeat.

3

CATHERINE

Catherine of Aragon had been destined to become Queen of England since the age of three. In March 1489, English ambassadors arrived at the court of Ferdinand and Isabella to negotiate a marriage between their youngest daughter and Prince Arthur, eldest son of Henry VII. Arriving after dark, they were ushered through the streets of central Spain's Medina del Campo, and over the palace drawbridge, down an avenue of blazing torches. Inside, they knelt before the dazzling spectacle of the Spanish king and queen dressed from head to foot in gold, framed by a canopy bearing their coat of arms. The queen's golden dress was covered in jewels, her red satin cloak slashed with gold, her gold necklace was enameled with red and white roses and her hair was trapped under gold netting, the entire ensemble costing around 200,000 crowns. At her side, Ferdinand matched Isabella's opulence in a long golden gown trimmed with fur. After the bullfighting and jousting, tilting and feasting that followed, the ambassadors met the royal children, dressed to match their parents, reporting back to Henry VII that 'it was beautiful to see how the Queen held up her youngest daughter, the Infanta Dona Catherine, Princess of Wales.'[1] It was pure diplomatic theatre at its best. From childhood, Catherine understood how to project majesty.

Catherine arrived in England at the age of fifteen, in October 1501. She had received a broad and forward-looking education, among the humanist scholars, artists and explorers of her parents' court. In comparison with the hugely influential Spanish territories, which included half of the New World, England was a little backwater of an island. Yet, it was a backwater that was determined to stage a welcome proclaiming itself as a new international power and rivalling anything Catherine may have experienced at home. On the outskirts of London, she was met by the ten-year-old Henry, enthusiastic about his role in the day's proceedings, to accompany her into the city. Tall, sturdy and confident, he would have appeared every inch the young Prince, whose precocious abilities and easy grace had already been noted in the schoolroom at Eltham.

England had a long, rich history of civic pageantry, from welcoming returning kings and foreign brides to celebrating weddings, and the dominant theme of the celebrations planned for Catherine was 'honour'. As she approached London Bridge from the south, the first pageant came into view, a structure with two storeys, painted blue and gold, decorated with the symbols of Tudor heritage: red English lions, Beaufort portcullises for Arthur's grandmother, ostrich feathers of the Prince of Wales and the Lancastrian rose of his father. The qualities of Virtue and Nobleness sat alongside Job and Boethius, Catherine's ancestor Alphonse and the Archangel Raphael, patron of marriage and procreation. Together, they combined to offer the princess lessons on 'policy' or how to rule, as without their help, 'all they that think to reign, or long to prosper, labour all in vain.'[2] Further along the route, a castle decorated with the red roses of Lancaster and the portcullises of the Beaufort family was hung with blue and red cloth of tissue. Before it stood two great posts, painted with the arms of England and gilded, along with gold and azure decoration, and figures representing Catherine and Arthur enthroned as future monarchs.

The entire route of Catherine's journey through the city was marked by spectacle, each more imposing and colourful than the next.

Across the sky in Cheapside blazed a chariot bearing an actor playing God himself. Arthur was associated with Arcturus, the brightest star in the northern sky and Catherine with Hesperus, the evening star, or planet Venus, the 'bright sterre of Spain,' a play on the old Roman word for Spain, Hispania or Hesperia. Above it was a recreation of the heavens, the stars, astrological signs and information about the waning and waxing of the moon, all covered over by a cloth painted in Tudor white and green checks.[3] Later, Arthur was presented as the Sun King, whose brightness illuminated the earth and who dispensed wisdom and justice from a tall construction with pillars supporting Welsh dragons and English lions, against a backdrop painted with stars, angels and clouds. The complex interplay of colour and heraldic devices, fictional and mythical figures, astrology and ancestry, was a coded, visual projection of the power of the Tudor dynasty. The ten-year-old Henry would absorb this lesson.

Catherine rode through the London streets with 'her hair hanging down about her shoulders, which is faire auburne, and in manner of a coife betwene her head and her hat of a carnacioun colour, and that was fastenyd from the midst of her head upwards so as men might well see all her here from the myddle part of her head downwards'.[4] Watching her pass, the young lawyer Thomas More observed that Catherine had 'thrilled the hearts of everyone', and that she possessed 'all those qualities that make for beauty in a very charming young girl. Everywhere she receives the highest of praises, but even that is inadequate. I do hope this highly publicised union will prove a happy omen for England.'[5]

The wedding took place on Sunday 14 November. Inside St Paul's Cathedral, a wooden platform had been erected along the entire 350 feet from the choir door to the west door, standing four feet high and covered in red cloth. Catherine and Arthur were literally to be centre stage, elevated over the heads of Londoners, in something like the culminating pageant of the recent days, only in the flesh, instead of in representation. After they were formally pronounced man and wife, the pair turned to acknowledge the crowd 'so the present multitude of people might see and behold their persons'[6] and walked along the length of the platform, hand in hand. One observer described them as a 'lusty and amorous couple'. They were blessed, the Mass was read, and they retired into the Bishop's Palace, where the wedding feast was served to over a hundred guests. The theme for the feast was 'all the delicacies, dainties and curious meats that might be purveyed or got within the whole realm of England,'[7] which were served up in three courses, of twelve, fifteen, then eighteen dishes.

Catherine's first marriage did not last long. Arthur died after five months, leaving his young widow alone in a foreign country, uncertain of her future. The years of waiting passed in pious devotion, and often ill-health and penury, while Henry VII toyed with the idea of her remarriage. In April 1509, his death released her, and she finally became England's queen, in a second magnificent coronation parade and service, similarly as colourful as her first. Catherine conceived very quickly, around the time of her wedding, and prepared to welcome her first child in early 1510. However, her experience of motherhood was to be one of heartbreak and disappointment. Out of six pregnancies, only a single daughter, Mary, would survive to adulthood. The majority of her babies were stillborn or miscarried, although the prince she bore in January 1511 survived for seven weeks before dying of an unknown complaint. Catherine turned to her faith for comfort, embarking on pilgrimages, making offerings and promises, and prostrating herself in prayer. By the arrival of 1520, two years had elapsed since her last pregnancy, and although she was unaware of it at the time, she would bear no more children.

The daughter of Ferdinand of Aragon was not just England's queen but an important figure on the international stage. From her succession, she acted as an informal ambassador for her father, advising Henry and advocating Anglo-Spanish unity in the Italian wars. Ferdinand, justifying Machiavelli's admiration of him, urged his daughter to impress upon Henry the need to write all his letters in code, as 'secrecy is necessary in great enterprises and that nothing should be written except in cipher.' He suggested to Catherine that 'the king likewise enter secret negotiations with the Pope and the King of the Romans' and that he might approach Margaret of Savoy, Maximilian's daughter, as 'a fit person to negotiate the alliance'. Henry did not need much persuading to send English troops to back Ferdinand's attack upon Aquitaine in 1512, but the enterprise failed expensively and the following year Henry chose to lead his own forces in person. Catherine's influence behind the scenes is evident from Ferdinand's comment that he was 'very glad to hear that the opinions of the King of England exactly coincide with what he had written to England, before he knew the wishes of the king.'[8]

Catherine was appointed Regent upon Henry's departure for France in the summer of 1513. Almost as soon as he left, it became clear that the Scots were about to honour their old alliance and invade England in support of Louis XII. A pregnant Catherine wrote to Wolsey that she was 'very glad to be busy with the Scots... my heart is very good to it... and I am horribly busy with making [of] standards, banners, and badges.'[9] She requested the Great Wardrobe to release certain banners and standards, including those bearing the arms of England and Spain, the lion, the cross imperial and the cross of St George, and met with the Council to discuss their strategy. Once the Scots had crossed the border, Catherine travelled north from Richmond to Buckinghamshire and it is likely that this was where she addressed assembled troops, 'making a splendid oration to the English captains', reminding them that 'the Lord smiled upon those who stood in defence of their own' and that 'English courage excelled that of all other nations.' Catherine certainly intended to look the part, as the royal goldsmith was paid for 'garnishing a head piece with a golden crown,'[10] the precious metal reminiscent of her mother's martial style. Both queens understood that when under attack, the first recourse was to reach for their gold.

The invading Scots were defeated by Catherine's army on 9 September 1513, and James IV was killed. Catherine wrote to Henry, vaunting her trophies of war:

> My Lord Howard hath sent me a letter, open, to your Grace, within one of mine, by the which ye shall see at length the great victory that our Lord hath sent your subjects in your absence. Thinks the victory the greatest honour that could be. The King will not forget to thank God for it. Could not, for haste, send by Rouge Cross 'the piece of the King of Scots coat which John Glyn now bringeth. In this your Grace shall see how I can keep my promyse, sending you for your banners a King's coat. I thought to send himself unto you, but our Englishmen's hearts would not suffer it.[11]

Catherine relished her ambassadorial role. She remained England's hostess, and an important cultural focus at court and beyond, in the years leading up to the Field of the Cloth of Gold. In 1515, she took the Venetian ambassador, Sebastian Giustinian, riding, and one of his party 'addressed her in Spanish, knowing it would please her', to which Catherine replied in her native tongue, speaking about her mother.[12] Ambassador Nicholas Sagudino also witnessed the splendour of the English court at this time, with Henry and Catherine dining on gold and silver plate of great worth, addressing the ambassadors in French, Latin and Italian. On May Day, Catherine was 'richly attired' and accompanied by twenty-five ladies on white palfreys, 'their dresses slashed with gold lama', as she rode into the woods. There, as if by happy accident, she was met by 'the king and his guard in green liveries, with bows in their hands, and in the woods were bowers filled with singing birds'. Afterwards they dined al fresco, played music and jousted. Henry reputedly 'looked like St. George on horseback' and Nicolo Sagudino had never seen 'such a beautiful sight', but he also commented rather uncharitably that Catherine was 'rather ugly than otherwise, and supposed to be pregnant;

but the damsels of her court are handsome, and make a sumptuous appearance.'[13] Similar bucolic imagery was used to describe a visit to Shooter's Hill around the same time, where Henry and Catherine were welcomed by an actor dressed as Robin Hood, a popular theme of their pre-Reformation revels. Again, there were arbours with sweet herbs and flowers and the ladies were dared to enter the woods, where they found the 'outlaws' breakfasting on venison.[14] It would be hard to overstate the centrality of theatre, disguise and play at the heart of the Tudor court, in the decade leading up to 1520. These events were rehearsals for the ultimate fairy tale enactment of knights and fair ladies, chivalry and revels that would come to fruition at the Field of the Cloth of Gold.

Catherine took the role of merciful queen following the May Day riots in 1517. True to the nature of English xenophobia, resentment had been building against foreign merchants, who were not subject to the same strict trading rules that governed the city. Edward Hall captured some of the feeling in London, claiming that the Genovese, French and 'other strangers... boasted themselves to be in such favour with the kyng and his council, that they set naughte by the rules of the citie: and the multitude of strangers was so great about London, that the poor English artificers could scarce get any living. And most of all the strangers were so proude that they disdained, mocked and oppressed the Englishmenne, which was the beginning of the grudge.'[15]

The rioting was incited when an inflammatory speech delivered at St Paul's Cross called upon 'all Englishmen to cherish and defend themselves, and to hurt and grieve aliens for the common weal'.[16] Sebastian Giustinian wrote to the Doge of Venice with the claim of the discontented that foreigners were not only depriving them 'of their industry... but disgraced their dwellings, taking their wives and daughters', so that the intention was to 'cut them to pieces and sack their houses'.[17] The Mayor called an emergency meeting at the Guildhall, but that night, anarchy was loosed upon the streets. Giustinian put the number of troublemakers at around two thousand, bracketing them together as apprentices and bandits, although a number of London citizens also joined the fray. Henry was woken from his sleep at Richmond to be informed of the event and dispatched men to quell the insurrection. Order was restored at three in the morning after a number of rioters were arrested.

It must have been difficult, as a Spaniard, for Catherine to hear of the attacks upon foreigners. Now she chose to act as an advocate for the rioters, soothing the difficult mood in the city by ensuring that they had to thank a foreigner for the restoration of their freedom. Henry made an example of the ringleaders, so that around a dozen were hanged at the city gates and their body parts distributed throughout the city. After that, around four hundred men and eleven women were summoned to Westminster Hall with halters around their necks, crying in the belief that they were about to be hanged. The hall was designed to intimidate the rebels, hung with expensive tapestries and peopled with the king's council and lords of the realm. This was an effective piece of theatre staged by Henry and Catherine, to employ their different roles and strengths. With tears in her eyes, the Queen knelt to ask the king to pardon the offenders, for the sakes of their wives and children. Henry allowed himself to be visibly moved and ordered the prisoners' release, upon which 'they took the halters from their necks and danced and sang.' Word soon spread around the capital and Catherine's popularity soared, being described by the papal nuncio as 'our serene and compassionate queen'.[18]

Catherine was initially not keen to attend the Field of the Cloth of Gold. Her loyalties lay with her nephew Charles, rather than with the traditional enemy of France, and she had worked hard promoting good Anglo-Spanish relations for years. In April 1520, she anticipated a number of problems arising from the proposed visit, and voiced them to her council, as the Emperor's secretary, Jean de la Sauche, reported:

Some days ago the Queen assembled her council to confer about this interview, and while she was holding it the King arrived. On his asking what was going on, the Queen told him why she had called them, and finally they said that she had made such representations, and shown such reasons against the voyage, as one would not have supposed she would have dared to do, or even to imagine. On this account she is held in greater esteem by the King and his council than ever she was. Has not been able to find out, however, what answer the King made to her. There is no doubt that the voyage is against the will of the Queen and all the nobles, though some may already have drunk of the bottle. The whole people say they are leaving their old friends for their old enemies, and that there is no help for it unless the Emperor come, in which case they hope the interview will be broken off.[19]

By 1520, the year when Catherine turned thirty-five, she had accomplished much as a queen. Her influence upon her husband had been constant, both in domestic and international affairs, and her roles as hostess, ambassador and Regent made her a significant figure in her own right, not merely as an appendage of her husband. Her Spanish birth predisposed her towards alliances with Charles, but as England's queen, she agreed to put her adoptive country first, and headed into preparations for the Field of the Cloth of Gold intent upon making a suitably regal and majestic impression.

4

THE ENGLISH PARTY

In April 1515, Nicolo Sagudino, secretary to the Venetian ambassador, Sebastian Giustinian, related his arrival at the English court, and his glimpses of its operation. It was defined by protocol, ritual and magnificence, and peopled by a huge number, all suitably dressed for the occasion. Sagudino's sensitivity and attention to detail makes his account worth reading in full:

> The ambassadors immediately sought audience of the King, which was appointed for St. George's day, when the same two lords who met them on their arrival came to them with a numerous retinue, and escorted the three ambassadors in a large barge, followed by many others containing the merchants and the rest of the Venetians, to a palace on the Thames called Richmond. Landed with about 200 persons. On entering the palace, a collation, consisting only of bread and wine, was served to them, according to custom; which ended, they passed through some other chambers, where they saw part of the King's guard, consisting of 300 men, all very handsome and in excellent array;—never saw finer fellows.
>
> At length they entered a room where the King was leaning against a chair covered with cloth of gold brocade, with a cushion of the same material and a large gilt sword, under a canopy of cloth of gold with a raised pile. The King was dressed

as a Knight of the Garter, of which order he is the superior, and wore a very costly doublet, over which was a mantle of violet velvet, with a very long train lined with white satin. On his head was a richly jewelled cap of crimson velvet of immense value, and round his neck he wore a collar studded with many precious stones, of which he (Sagudino) never saw the like.

Immediately on perceiving the ambassadors the King approached them, and after allowing his hard to be kissed, embraced them with the greatest possible demonstration of good will to the Signory. Then silence was proclaimed, and Giustinian pronounced an elegant Latin oration, which was listened to with attention by all, especially by the King, who understands Latin very well. This address lasted a full hour, and the King caused a reply to be made by a doctor of laws, thanking the Signory, and asserting that the King had ever been the State's friend and protector This ceremony ended, the King invited the ambassadors and all their retinue to hear mass and dine with him; so they went to church, and after a grand procession had been made, high mass was sung by the King's choristers, whose voices are more divine than human; and as to the counter bass voices, they probably have not their equals in the world. The Queen was present.

After mass the King and the nobles with the ambassadors and their followers returned to the palace, into a hall, where a table had been prepared for his Majesty, and another for the knights of the Garter, the ambassadors and the merchants. After witnessing a display of gold plate of immense value, they sat down to table and dined. After dinner the King sent for the ambassadors, and addressed them partly in French and partly in Latin, and also in Italian, showing himself very affable. Then they took leave and departed.

The personal beauty of the King is very great...he is also courageous, an excellent musician, plays well on the harpsichord, is learned for his age and station, and has many other endowments and good parts. Two such courts and two such Kings as those of France and England have not been witnessed by any Venetian ambassador for these 50 years.[1]

When Henry crossed the Channel on the last day of May 1520, he took his court with him. The corridors of Richmond and Greenwich fell silent, the great halls and courtyards were still, the chambers were deserted and kitchen fires turned cold. His own ship, with its golden sails, was accompanied by a flotilla transporting thousands of men, women and horses, and cartloads of clothing, provisions and equipment. In a huge feat of organisation and protocol, almost the entire English court was transported to Calais, in strict hierarchy, from the most important of the royal companions and advisors all the way down through the ranks to those charged with mucking out the stables.

The guest list for the Field of the Cloth of Gold is an exercise in the distinctions between ranks. Surviving sources name by rank those who formed Henry's retinue, including two Dukes, one Marquis, ten Earls, four Bishops, twenty-one Barons, three Knights of the Garter, ninety-seven Knights, ten Chaplains, twelve Serjeant at Arms, sixteen Heralds, 200 Yeomen of the Guard, seventy of the King's Chamberers, 266 Officers of the Household, 205 people in the stable and armoury, musicians and others amounting to 935. However, each attendee was entitled to bring their own staff of personal servants, many of whom had additional assistants. Wolsey alone took 300 servants, of whom twelve were chaplains, and fifty were gentlemen, with fifty horses. The Archbishop of Canterbury contributed another seventy servants and thirty horses, while Richard Foxe, Bishop of Winchester had fifty-six men and twenty-six horses.[2] A Duke was allowed fifty people, ten of whom could be gentlemen, two chaplains and thirty horses; the allowance for an earl was thirty people, including six gentlemen, two chaplains and twenty horses, and barons might take sixteen people, a chaplain and eight horses. A knight could be equipped with ten people and four horses, but a humble squire was only allotted four people and two horses. The list puts the final amount at 4,544 crossing the water in the king's service.[3]

Henry's entourage included some well-known names. It was led by Henry's Chancellor and chief minister, Cardinal Thomas Wolsey, along with the Archbishop of Canterbury, William Warham, who had married the king and Catherine in 1509, and Henry's brother-in-law Charles Brandon, Duke of Suffolk. Also in attendance were Henry's highest ranking male relatives with a claim to the throne, Edward Stafford, Duke of Buckingham, after which came the king's cousin on his mother's side Thomas Grey, Marquis of Dorset; as well as Thomas Ruthall, Bishop of Durham, the Bishops of Ely, Chester and Exeter, and John Kite, Archbishop of Armagh. Henry's ten Earls included some of his leading courtiers: his Lord Steward George Talbot of Shrewsbury; his distant Yorkist relative and privy councillor Henry Bourchier of Essex, who would carry Henry's sword at his meeting with Francis; his maternal cousin Richard Grey of Kent; Henry Percy of Northumberland; and another first cousin and close friend, Henry Courtenay of Devon. There was also Privy Councillor Henry Stafford of Wiltshire; the descendant of his great grandmother's family Ralph Neville of Westmorland; Henry's Chamberlain Charles Somerset of Worcester; the volatile John de Vere of Oxford who was to come of age that August, and Edward Stafford again, as Earl Stafford, as well as Duke of Buckingham. Henry's Barons were the Lords St. John, Roos, Maltravers, Fitzwater, Bergavenny, Montague, Hastings, Ferrers, Berners, Darcy, Delaware, Brooke, Lumley, Herbert, John, Leonard and Richard Grey, Curzon, Daubeney, Edmund Howard and the Earl of Kildare, who although being a mere Earl was 'representing a baron'. The king's Knights of the Garter were warden of the Cinque Ports Sir Edward Poynings, Treasurer of Calais Sir William Sandys and Captain of the Guard Sir Henry Marney.

The thirty knights who accompanied the king were there to joust and guard, feast and dance, and present the best image of English majesty to the French, in the best clothes they could muster. Some were Henry's illegitimate family members, including his uncle Sir Arthur Plantagenet, a future Lord Deputy of Calais, and great-uncle Sir David Owen, then in his sixties, as well as a Henry Owen, who may have been his son. There were members of the extended Grey, Neville and Brandon families, related to the king by marriage, and several of Henry's closest friends from the band of 'minions' expelled from court by Wolsey the previous year, particularly the flamboyant Sir Francis Bryan, later nicknamed 'the Vicar of Hell' for his rakish ways. Bryan's brother-in-law, Sir Nicholas Carew and Sir William Compton, who helped arrange the king's amorous liaisons, were also present. Two famous literary names appear in this section; that of the young lawyer Thomas More, a Privy Councillor and Henry's Master of Requests, as well as William Paston, of the famous Norfolk letter-writing family. The Master of the Chapel Royal, William Cornish the younger, was in charge of the choir boys, whom he trained in singing and acting, and was the composer of masques, pageants and plays. A total of thirty-five other men were attached to the royal chapel, including the king's musicians. Three of Henry's future fathers-in-law were also present: Thomas Boleyn, John Seymour and Edmund Howard. To record his endeavours, Henry took his French secretary, Jean Mewtis or Meautis, and his Master of the Posts, Bryan Tuke, two clerks of the signet and two clerks of the privy seal.

The momentous task of organising the event had largely been entrusted to three men, the ambassadors to France, Sir Richard Wingfield and Sir Thomas Boleyn, and Henry's capable chancellor, Cardinal Thomas Wolsey. Richard Wingfield was the elder statesman of the three, having been born in 1469. The Suffolk-based Wingfield family was linked by marriage to their local Duke, Charles Brandon, and had benefited from Brandon's influence and patronage. Richard's father was a privy councillor to Edward IV, while his uncle was comptroller of Edward's household, and his brothers served the first Tudor king, accompanying him to France and helping defend his realm against usurpers.

Richard had an additional personal connection to Henry VIII, having been briefly married to his great-aunt Catherine Woodville in the 1490s. Two decades later, Richard's diplomatic career was going from strength to strength. In 1511, he was appointed marshal, and later, Lord Deputy, of Calais, as well as being a negotiator for the Holy League, present in the Netherlands in January 1513 from where he helped organise Henry's invasion of France. He fulfilled other diplomatic missions, working on treaties with France and the Netherlands before resigning his position in Calais in 1519 and returning to England to serve as a privy councillor. When the plans for the Field of the Cloth of Gold were advancing in early 1520, he was sent out to replace Sir Thomas Boleyn as ambassador in France, liaising with Wolsey about practical and diplomatic arrangements, and attended the event with his second wife, Bridget. Richard Wingfield was well respected by his peers, who praised his wisdom, expertise and kindness. Francis I and Charles V were both impressed by his understanding of international affairs and Henry VIII considered him a close friend.[4]

The man who Wingfield replaced as ambassador to France was later to become Henry VIII's father-in-law. Sir Thomas Boleyn was a rising star of the Tudor court, the grandson of a Lord Mayor of London, from a family who had made their money in commerce. He married well, into the Howard family and had fought the Cornish rebels of 1497 and accompanied Princess Margaret Tudor to her marriage in Scotland in 1503. Knighted upon the succession of Henry VIII, Boleyn was an early favourite of the king, featuring in court revels and jousts before his linguistic skill brought him his first diplomatic mission to the Netherlands, alongside Wingfield, in 1513. Five years later, he was ambassador in France at the inception of the Field of the Cloth of Gold, negotiating Princess Mary's match with the Dauphin and relating news and gossip about the French King back to Henry. He seems to have developed particularly strong working relationships with the influential women behind younger men in power; Charles' aunt Margaret, and Francis' mother, Louise of Savoy. Thomas Boleyn attended the Field of the Cloth of Gold as part of the English entourage, bringing his wife Elizabeth, his teenaged son George, and his newly married daughter Mary, with her husband William Carey. The absent family member, Anne, future Queen of England, would meet them across the Channel, in the retinue of the French.

For all Wingfield and Boleyn's diplomacy, the real mastermind behind the logistics of 1520 was Thomas Wolsey. The son of a butcher from Ipswich, Wolsey epitomised the new renaissance meritocracy of Henry VIII's court, rising swiftly as a result of his ability to outstrip those of noble birth. From Oxford, he entered the clergy, became chaplain to the Archbishop of Canterbury, then served the treasurer of Calais and undertook ambassadorial missions to the Netherlands and Scotland. Wolsey was appointed royal almoner upon Henry VIII's succession, gathering titles, entering the privy council and swiftly becoming indispensable due to his hard work. In 1515 he was elected a cardinal, the only one in England, as well as being Archbishop of York, Bishop of Bath and Wells, and other positions that brought him an annual revenue amounting to that of the highest subject in the land.

Wolsey was behind the practical arrangements for Henry's French engagements in 1512 and 1513 and maintained a correspondence with Queen Catherine during the king's absence. The following year, he did the same for Princess Mary's marriage to Louis XII, and then mediated her return to England. Playing a central role in all Henry's foreign dealings, the 1518 Treaty of Universal Peace was a personal triumph for the Cardinal, culminating in his delivery of an acclaimed speech advocating peace. By 1519, it was from Wolsey that Francis I sought support for his bid to become Emperor, having been informed that he dictated all Henry's policy. The complicated diplomatic events, hospitality and practical requirements of The Field of the Cloth of Gold would reveal the organisational genius of Thomas Wolsey at its zenith. Polydore Vergil, author of the immense *Anglica Historia*, attributes the motives of ambition and pride to Wolsey, who 'thought it would be splendid for him to be seen showing off his worldly vanity' to the French, but Wolsey's achievement as the main architect of the event cannot be denied.

Wolsey was assisted by his secretary, Richard Pace. He entered Wolsey's service after the death of his former master, the Archbishop of York, in 1514, and was immediately dispatched by Wolsey to Switzerland to negotiate with Emperor Maximilian and encourage Imperial forces to attack France. Using English money to pay for a number of mercenaries, Pace was present in the Emperor's party at the Battle of Marignano, where he was captured and imprisoned by the victorious French. He was sent back to Germany in 1519 at the time of the elections for a new Emperor and, from there, liaised with Wolsey over arrangements for the meetings Henry wished to undertake, separately, with Francis and Charles. He was also made Dean of St Paul's in 1519.

When it came to preparations for the Field of the Cloth of Gold, specific roles were allocated by instructions issued in March 1520. Three older statesmen were charged to assist Richard Wingfield with the job of liaising with the officials of Francis I: the veteran Henry Bourchier, Earl of Essex, a privy councillor and nephew of Henry's grandmother; George Neville, Baron Bergavenny, who had been second cousin to Queen Anne, wife of Richard III, and was now Henry's Chief Larderer, and Sir Edward Poynings, formerly a governor of Calais, deputy viceroy of Ireland, and now warden of the Cinque Ports, who had been among the party conducting Catherine of Aragon to England. All three had participated in Henry's 1513 campaign, being present at the captures of Therouanne and Tournai, and could bring their experience to bear when it came to the terrain and the French court.

The commission to relay the king's orders to the English gentlemen in France was given to four of Henry's trusted servants. Sir Edward Belknapp was a privy councillor, Sir John Peche of Lullingstone was a Marshal of Calais and Henry's champion jouster, Sir Maurice Berkeley of Thornbury had been made Knight of the Bath in 1509, and Sir Nicholas Vaux had grown up in the household of Henry's grandmother, Margaret Beaufort, and also contributed to the planning in 1520. Six other gentlemen, Edward Ferrers, John Marney, Robert Constable, Weston Brown, Thomas Lucy and Ralph Egerton, were given the task of instructing the king's foot soldiers. When it came to the most important meeting of all, the first handshake between Henry and Francis, thirty-nine of the most influential English men were delegated to accompany the king: Thomas Wolsey and William Warham, Archbishop of Canterbury; the king's closest male relatives, Edward Stafford, Duke of Buckingham, his brother-in-law Charles Brandon, Duke of Suffolk, and Thomas Grey, Marquis of Dorset; along with seven bishops, ten earls and seventeen barons.

Another important figure in the practical organisation of the event was Charles Somerset, Earl of Worcester, Henry VIII's Chamberlain, whose role gave him the overview of the *domus magnificentiae*, or royal chamber. Then aged sixty, Somerset was the illegitimate son of Henry Beaufort, a cousin of Henry's paternal grandmother, and his role made him the most senior official of the royal household, responsible for ceremonial occasions, including travel and overseeing the king's daily needs. With the aid of his assistants, Worcester was charged with deciding the time and place that Henry and Francis would first meet, to designate a location for the jousts and oversee the erection of lists and galleries. He was to appoint trusted staff for the king's chamber and 'make a book' of them. After this was complete, and a minimum of forty days ahead of Henry's departure, the Earl was to 'cross the sea' to ensure everything was ready, taking with him 'Arras tapestry and other necessaries for the decoration of the king's house'.

Other key organisational roles were delegated according to expertise. Nicholas Vaux, William Sandys and Edward Belknapp were to travel ahead and inspect the condition and suitability of Guisnes Castle. George Talbot, Earl of Shrewsbury, was also important as Henry's Lord Steward, watching over the court's daily expenditure, and Sir Henry Guildford as Master of the Horse, charged with arrangements for the stables. John Shurley, Henry's Cofferer controlled the purse strings, with John Micklowe and Thomas Byrks working in the Counting House and Sir John Heron as Treasurer of the Chamber. Sir Edward Poynings was tasked to provide sufficient ships, while Miles Gerard and Thomas Partridge were to assign the nobility to the different vessels. Edward Higgins, Clerk of the Closet, was to select ten chaplains to accompany the king and provide the closet with the best hangings, jewels, altar cloths and other trappings. The Dean of Westminster was to similarly equip the royal chapel. 200 of the king's guard, the 'tallest and most elect' persons were chosen to accompany him, equipped with scarlet embroidered coats by the Vice-Chamberlain, Sir Henry Marney. Sir John Peche, George Neville, Nicholas Carew and two others were appointed to allocate lodgings at Calais, while Neville and William Parr as undermarshals were to keep order and punish malefactors. Sir Henry Wyatt, father of the poet Thomas, was charged to import sufficient gold and silver plate to cater for the banquets, while Sir William Skevington, Master of the Ordinance, was to bring the guns it was deemed necessary to take.

Another crucial figure who played a central role in the summer of 1520 was Richard Gibson. Starting out as a young man in the king's wardrobe in 1501, Gibson became yeoman of the king's tents in 1513, accompanying Henry on his expedition to France where he was responsible for housing the men and making essential repairs. The following year, he supervised repairs made to the royal tents in Calais, but his biggest responsibility came at the Field of the Cloth of Gold, as co-ordinator of the vast village of tents pitched around Guisnes and in the valley where the kings met, from the simplest of accommodation for servants to the most magnificent gilded and painted structures used by royalty.

A vast number of servants was required to ensure that the Field of the Cloth of Gold ran smoothly. All the departments of the king's domus *providentiae*, or below stairs household, were replicated in France, including names no longer as familiar today as Henry's courtiers and councillors. Valentine Harrison was in charge of seven men in the bakehouse, Griffith Gwyn presided over thirteen in the pantry, Roger Mynors over fourteen in the cellar, and Nicholas Middleton over three in the spicery. Richard Babham ruled over three in the confectionary, while Robert Lee and Robert Lister shared the tasks in the waffery. Stephen Coope organised six workers in the poultry, and more were assigned to their stations in the ewery (ewers, table linen and towels), scalding house, pitcher house, boiling house, laundry and other departments. A number of children were employed in the scullery and pastry house. Finally, there was the clerk of the stable, plus surveyors, stirrup makers, farriers, grooms, armourers and joiners.[5] These figures give some idea of the vast scale of the operation, as well as the minimum numbers thought necessary to maintain the King's dignity on such an occasion. It must have made a splendid sight, this long train of people, horses and wagons, progressing slowly through the French countryside, glittering with jewels.

As befitted her queenship, Catherine took a large retinue with her to France: one Earl, three Bishops, four Barons, thirty-one Knights, six Chaplains, one Duchess, seven Countesses, sixteen Baronesses, eighteen wives of Knights, twenty-five Gentlewomen, three Chamberers, fifty Yeomen, fifty attendants upon the Queen's chamber, sixty in her stable, all attended by fifty-four Chaplains, thirty-two Gentlemen and 909 servants, giving Catherine a total retinue of 1,260. Added to Henry's total, this made 5,804 people in attendance upon the king and queen. The king and his company also had 2,406 horses while the queen had 817, making 3,223 horses in all.[6]

The queen's party was headed by Thomas Stanley, Earl of Derby, step-grandson of Henry's grandmother, Margaret Beaufort, who had led the English to victory at Flodden in 1513. As his personal allowance, Derby had six gentlemen, three chaplains, twenty-four servants and twenty horses: his wife Anne also attended among the Queen's party of ladies, with a retinue of her own. Catherine had three bishops in her company: John Fisher, Bishop of Rochester, Charles Booth, Bishop of Hereford and George de Athequa, a Spaniard who had come with her to England in 1501, who was now Bishop of Llandaff. Each of them had four chaplains, six gentlemen, thirty-four servants and twenty horses. She had four barons in attendance, William Blount, Baron Mountjoy and William Willoughby, Baron Willoughby d'Eresby, who had married two of her Spanish ladies, Thomas Burgh, Baron Cobham, and Henry Parker, Baron Morley, future father-in-law of George Boleyn. Each had a retinue of their own of chaplains, gentlemen and servants, as did Catherine's thirty-one knights.[7]

The most senior of Catherine's Ladies accompanying her to France was the Duchess of Buckingham, Lady Eleanor Percy, followed in precedence by seven countesses, of Stafford, Westmorland, Shrewsbury, Devonshire, Derby and Oxford, as well as the Dowager Countess of Oxford, each of whom had seven servants. Among her sixteen Baronesses were the sisters of the Duke of Buckingham, Elizabeth, Lady Fitzwalter, and Anne, Lady Hastings, also Elizabeth, wife of Sir Arthur Plantagenet, Henry's uncle, and there were eighteen knights' wives. Elizabeth Boleyn, mother of Mary and Anne, was present, as was the widowed Maud Parr, mother of Catherine. The Queen had three chamberers, Mistress Kemp, Mistress Margaret and Mistress Margery, who were each entitled to take a servant, fifty yeomen of the chamber, with twenty servants between them, and sixty people to take care of her horses. Perhaps the most significant of Catherine's servants on this occasion was Ellis Hilton, who held the Office of the Robes, and the three men in the Office of her Beds, responsible for transporting and reconstructing her bed, and Richard Dynes, her messenger of the chamber. She also had Richard Dycons as her secretary, and a physician, cupbearer, carver and various servers, an apothecary called Master John, clerk of the signet Griffith Richard, ushers, yeomen, grooms, pages and Henry Cheney, her groom of the leash. Sir Adrian Fortescue was charged with the task of waiting upon the queen on 1 May 1520, to accompany her across the Channel.[8]

In addition to the King's wife, the King's mistress also attended the Field of the Cloth of Gold. Thomas Boleyn's elder daughter, Mary, is likely to have been Henry's lover already, with their affair in its early stages by the summer of 1520. Born in around 1499, she had been part of the entourage of Mary Tudor upon her marriage to Louis XII in 1514, returning home early the following year. Rumours of a possible affair Mary Boleyn had with Francis during this time cannot be supported with evidence, and may have been attempts to blacken her character, although Francis later rudely dismissed her as 'a very great whore, the most infamous of all' and as 'the English mare', and 'my hackney'.⁹ Henry had attended Mary's marriage to William Carey, a privy councillor and distant cousin of the king, in the Chapel at Greenwich, on 4 February 1520, making an offering of 6s 8d. The details of Mary's affair with Henry are unknown. It only became knowledge in later years because the king was forced to admit it when he wished to marry Anne. Victorian historians rejected the idea entirely and suggested this was merely a ruse to blacken the Boleyn name further. It has been suggested that Mary's two children, born in 1524 and 1526 were fathered by the king, but this was never confirmed, and Henry notoriously kept his love affairs secret, in stark contrast to his French counterpart. Mary attended the Field of the Cloth of Gold in Catherine's retinue along with her husband, and was one of the lead dancers in masques and entertainments. Her brief previous experience in France may also have equipped her to act as a translator in 1520, and many of Francis' circle would have been known to her.

Henry VIII's retinue in 1520 included the controversial and colourful Edward Stafford, Duke of Buckingham. One of Henry's closest relatives due to his Plantagenet blood, and possessing a significant claim to the throne, Buckingham was ambitious and indiscreet, a familiar and flamboyant figure in court, and in the lists, where he sought to rival Henry's performance and costumes. In the wedding jousts of 1501, Buckingham had drawn attention to his royal blood, riding a horse with blue velvet trappings that depicted the castle motif of Castile and sporting the Prince of Wales' ostrich feathers in his helmet. His pavilion alone was a breathtaking construction of towers and turrets, covered with silk in the Tudor colours of white and green, set with red roses, his servants in his own black and red livery, riding horses which sparkled with gold spangles. At the wedding feast, he had worn an embroidered gown set upon cloth tissue furred with sable worth £15,000. Eight years later, he had ridden in procession between Henry and Catherine at their coronation, dressed in a coat of gold and silver thread sparkling with diamonds. By 1520, his pride and conspicuous arrogance were grating on Henry, although the Duke complained about the expense of being forced to attend the king in France. Vergil relates that Buckingham was a 'high spirited man' who spoke for much of the nobility in complaining about the unnecessary expense, and that he found it 'intolerable to obey such a sordid, importune fellow' as Wolsey, who then began to conspire against him.

The other royal member of the party was Henry's younger sister, Mary, former Queen of France. Born in 1496, the legendary beauty had been raised in the expectation of marriage to Charles V, newly elected Holy Roman Emperor, who was four years her junior. Their wedding had been planned for May 1514, as soon as Charles came of age, and elaborate jousts and celebrations were being planned in Calais as late as 21 March that year.[10] But May arrived, then June, and no wedding took place. Instead, in a fit of pique against Ferdinand of Aragon, Henry threw away an excellent alliance for his sister and for England. Breaking with Spain and allying himself instead with France, he chose the ageing Louis XII, a newly widowed fifty-two-year-old, as his sister's bridegroom. Mary had no choice but to obey, but before she sailed from Calais she extracted a promise from Henry that, after her marriage to Louis, she might choose her second husband for herself. It was an extraordinary bargain, in which Mary drew on her personal relationship with Henry to allow for her own romantic inclination.

The wedding took place in Abbeville on 9 October 1514, a day when the whole of France was en fête in celebration of their patron saint, St Denis. After dressing from head to foot in gold, Mary was led by twenty-six knights, heralds and musicians to her husband, who had also worn gold to echo the choice of his bride. The service was conducted by Cardinal René de Prie, Bishop of Bayeux, including communion and the exchange of promises, before the royal pair kissed in front of the assembled crowd. Later, a ball was held, during which Louis remained attentively at Mary's side, before leading her off to bed at around eight o'clock. In the morning, in a show of sexual prowess, he reported that 'thrice did he cross the river last night, and would have done more, had he chosen.'[11]

Mary was crowned at the Cathedral of St Denis on 5 November, and made her state entrance into Paris dressed in cloth of gold and riding in a gold carriage through streets hung with tapestries, lilies and roses. Seven pageants marked her route to Nôtre Dame, where she heard Mass, before a formal welcome from the Archbishop of Paris. That evening, a state banquet was held in the Grande Salle of the Palais Royale, where Mary sat at a marble table flanked by the women of her new family. She met her stepdaughter Claude, married since May to Francis, and his mother and sister, Louise of Savoy and Marguerite of Angoulême. In 1520, at the Field of the Cloth of Gold, Mary was reunited with her former French in-laws.

Mary's brief spell as Queen of France did not start auspiciously. Days after the wedding, she was distressed when almost all her ladies were sent back to England, writing to implore her brother and Thomas Wolsey for help, but to no avail. To soften the blow, Louis showered his young wife with gifts, huge rubies, diamonds and pearls, and preparations were made for her imminent coronation. From Abbeville, they moved towards Paris, travelling slowly to accommodate Louis' attack of gout. On the way, they were intercepted by Sir Charles Brandon, one of Henry VIII's oldest and closest friends, whom he had dispatched to try and convince Louis to unite with England in an attack upon Spain. He was admitted to the chamber where Louis was lying in bed, with Mary sitting at the side.

Mary had known Brandon all her life. Twelve years her senior, he was the son of Sir William Brandon, her father's standard bearer, who had been killed at Bosworth. Attractive and athletic, he had been raised at the Tudor court, a keen jouster and conspirator in the high-spirited escapades of Henry's early reign. He had been married once before, fathering two daughters, although he had deserted his pregnant fiancée for financial gain, creating a scandal by marrying her wealthy aunt. Although he had enemies at court who resented his rise, he remained a great favourite of the king, who appointed him as Master of the Horse, Viscount Lisle by virtue of his betrothal to his ward, and Duke of Suffolk. The contrast between him and her new, infirm husband, must have been painfully apparent to Mary. Whether she had already favoured him, or these feelings developed subsequently, it was Brandon on whom Mary began to lean.

In the tiltyard at Abbeville, Charles Brandon came into his own. He was equipped with an allowance of £1,000 from Henry, to dress himself, his horses and entourage suitably to lead the jousting, along with Thomas Grey, Marquis of Dorset. Considered to be the best athlete in the field, Brandon easily unseated his opponents, and ran an impressive number of courses, before the French pitted him against a German giant. The pair jousted, fought with spears and blunt swords, before Brandon emerged as the victor again, so that the event was awarded to the English. He rode into Paris ahead of Mary on 24 November, when she made her first formal appearance as Queen of France, before the court moved on to St. Germain-en-Laye. Brandon remained in attendance until mid-December, whereupon he returned to England, reaching Henry's side in time for the Christmas festivities.

Soon after the merrymaking came to an end, news arrived at court of the death of Louis of France on January 1. Just four days earlier, the king had written to Henry that 'his satisfaction with the queen his wife was such that Henry might be sure of his treating her to her own and to his satisfaction.'[12] As a beautiful widow of eighteen, and a queen of France, Mary was potentially prey to the advances of potential suitors, including the new king, Francis, but she turned instead to Brandon, mindful of the promise Henry had made her before her departure. They married in secret, and returned in disgrace, although Henry eventually forgave them after levying a huge fine for their misconduct. By 1520, Mary had borne Brandon three children, who they left behind when they travelled to the Field of the Cloth of Gold.

Mary was unwell in the months before the event. On 16 March 1520, Brandon wrote to Wolsey, upon hearing that he was required to submit a list of names of those who would accompany them to France. He explained he had not attended the council lately, as Mary 'has had several physicians for the disease in her side, and cannot yet perfectly recover her health'. Brandon had attempted to go to London twice 'but both times she sent for him, so that he was obliged to return instantly.' Nevertheless, he added 'she is now so much better' that Brandon hoped to visit Wolsey in person soon.[13] Mary's health had recovered sufficiently to allow her to resume her favourite pastime of dancing to impress the French, and she is named as playing a key role in several entertainments. The numbers for her entourage in 1520 do not survive, but Brandon took with him ten gentlemen, fifty-five servants, five chaplains, thirty horses, his own armour, jousting equipment and garments made from cloth of gold.[14] Husband and wife were key players at the Field of the Cloth of Gold, paralleling Henry and Catherine in excelling in the jousting lists and on the dance floor.

THE FRENCH

Francis I at the Battle of Marignano. Francis' success in warfare far outshone Henry's.

5

FRANCIS I, THE 'MOST CHRISTIAN KING'

Francis of Valois-Angoulême had succeeded to the throne of France in 1515, at the age of twenty. He was described by the chronicler Brantôme as 'a goodly prince stately of countenance, merry of cheer, brown coloured, great eyes, high nosed, big-lipped, fair breasted and shoulders, small legs and long feet'.[1] Over six feet tall, Francis had brown hair and a thick neck, a short beard and cleft chin, 'his eyes hazel and bloodshot, and his complexion the colour of watery milk... an agreeable voice and, in conversation, an animated expression'.[2] He loved fine clothes and was eloquent and charming in manner although, paradoxically, sometimes shy. Energetic and active, he loved to ride, hunt or perform in court entertainments, but was also a man of learning and letters, well read and a composer of poetry. Francis was well known for his licentiousness, with commentators saying of his court that 'both maids and wives do oft-times trip, indeed do so customarily' and describing him in thinly veiled sexual metaphors as 'drinking' from many fountains and 'clothed' in women.[3] Although Henry was far more discreet about his amours than Francis, the parallels between the two kings were obvious, and served to attract and repel each to the other.

Francis had been born in 1494, the only son of Louise of Savoy and Charles d'Angoulême, a great-grandson of Charles V. After her husband's death, two years later the widowed Louise, still in her teens, moved from their native Cognac and raised Francis and his sister Marguerite at the Chateau d'Amboise, an imposing site overlooking the Loire, recently renovated in the Italian renaissance style. The king appointed his cousin, Louis d'Orleans, as the boy's guardian, whose kindness was welcome, and the Maréchal de Gié as his governor, who immediately clashed with Louise after trying to distance her from her son. When Charles VII died in an accident in 1498, he left no surviving children, so the crown passed to Louis, who promptly remarried and fathered two daughters. As Salic Law prevented their inheritance, Louis recognised Francis as his heir, and married him to his elder daughter, Claude, in May 1514. However, the unexpected marriage Louis made to Mary Tudor potentially jeopardised Francis' chances to succeed, and he attended the ceremony, and Mary's lavish coronation, uncertain of his future. The autumn and winter months passed in a state of suspense, as Louis' gout worsened, and Francis feared to hear that the new bride had conceived. However, the king's death on 1 January 1515, propelled the young man onto the throne.

The country that Francis inherited was smaller in territory than France is today. It was still organised into provinces or Duchies, some of which were autonomous, or changed ownership, such as Burgundy, Picardy and Provence, which fell to the throne by default in the 1470s and 80s. However, in 1515, it was still the largest of all the European kingdoms, covering approximately 459,000 square kilometres and had the largest population of around 15,000,000.[4] The largest city was the ever-expanding Paris, with just under 400,000 souls, and was described by Charles V as 'not a city but a world'. It was followed in size by Lyon and Rouen, but over eighty per cent of Francis' subjects lived in the countryside and worked on the land. And that countryside, stretching from the vast fields of the north, through the rich valleys and vineyards of the Loire down to the citrus-growing warm south, was among the most fertile land in Europe. France's long coastline boasted the important ports of La Rochelle on the Atlantic, Marseille, and Toulon on the Mediterranean; and in 1517, Francis founded Le Havre, to increase trade. Since the first French explorers reached the New World, beans, maize and other new crops complemented France's exports of wine, woad and oil, linen, silk and wool. By 1520, after the balance of power in Europe had shifted, the succession of Francis' rival Charles to the throne of Spain and the Holy Roman Empire, created a vast new Hapsburg territory that encircled France, making Francis keener to try and gain ascendancy.

There was little national French unity in 1520, beyond a shared monarch and the rituals of Catholicism. People were identified more by geographical region, government was decentralised and a range of dialects was spoken. One of Francis' most influential acts was to standardise a common language and legal system and, initially, to take a tolerant approach to the religious divisions infiltrating all corners of Europe. Power was vested in the Parliaments, based in Paris, Aix, Bordeaux, Dijon, Grenoble, Rouen and Toulouse, who could approve papal bulls and pass their own decrees. The wars with Italy introduced a lighter, renaissance style of architecture into France's dark medieval palaces, as well as new cultural references and figures. Poetry was being composed in the *grands rhétorique* tradition, with Jean Molinet's translation of the *Roman de la Rose*, and Jean Lemaire de Belges drawing on classical history and witty conceits in his love poems. By 1520, France was experiencing greater prosperity, population growth and a rise of the nouveaux riches at court.

Francis' coronation took place on 25 January 1515, at the traditional location of Notre-Dame Cathedral in Reims. He spent the night before at the nearby Palace of Tau, residence of the Archbishop, next to the Cathedral, which had recently undergone renovations in the Gothic style. In the morning, after the monks' chanting had marked the canonical hour of Prime, the first hour of daylight, Francis processed into the church. The clergy assisted him to place the deep blue coronation robes over his white clothing, and don the red boots and golden spurs, before he was led to the altar, swore his oath to Archbishop Robert de Lenoncourt and was anointed with oil from the Sainte Ampoule. Then the golden crown of Charlemagne, topped with the fleur-de-lys of France and studded with rubies, sapphires and emeralds, was placed upon his head and he accepted the sword of Charlemagne and the gold sceptre. Prayers, blessings and Mass followed. Afterwards, the king returned to the Palace, where the coronation feast was held.

The coronation ceremony, with its rites and apparatus, was typical of pre-Reformation high Catholicism, which continued in the ensuing days. After Reims, Francis travelled north to the priory of Corbeny, where the shrine of St.Marcoul was located, which was associated with the royal power of healing scrofula. Francis was given the saint's skull to hold, after which he cured a handful of sufferers by touch, as part of his semi-divine status. From there, he visited the shrine of the Black Virgin at Liesse, then Compiègne, and underwent a second coronation at St Denis, before making his triumphant entrance into Paris. He was met by the mayor and aldermen on the outskirts, and conducted in a huge procession of liveried supporters, wearing his badge of the salamander. The Grand Master of France and Marshals went ahead, dressed in cloth of silver and gold, the royal seal was carried on horseback in a blue velvet coffer, then musicians preceded Francis' new household. The king himself wore a suit of silver and a white hat covered in jewels, and dispensed handfuls of gold and silver pieces to the crowd, followed by his guard and archers. The route culminated at Nôtre-Dame Cathedral, Paris, where Francis gave thanks, followed by days of feasting, entertainments and jousting.

Just as keen as Henry VIII to chase military glory, Francis resumed the Italian Wars by attacking the Swiss-held Italian village of Marignano. In 1513, the Swiss had taken Milan from the French and handed it back to the Sforza family, at what had been Francis' first military engagement. The new king left his mother, Louise of Savoy, as regent and travelled south with the intent of redressing the balance. He received a hero's welcome in Lyon, where the city gates were decorated with the symbols of his salamander device, and a Tree of Jesse. Pageants lined his route, with one depicting Francis as Hercules and another where he defended peace against his enemies. A mechanical lion devised by da Vinci performed for him by opening its chest to reveal a bunch of lilies, and women stood on pillars, holding the letters of his name. From there, Francis marched south. Having taken a daring new route across the Alps, dragging their cannon, the French captured the Papal commander, prompting a treaty of peace, which was immediately followed by a surprise attack from the Swiss. The fighting continued after nightfall, on until midnight, with confusion arising from Francis' surprise tactics, and into the following morning. With the arrival of the Venetian cavalry in support of the French, the victory fell in favour of Francis.

Since Francis' succession, he had been the subject of curiosity from his English counterpart. Henry was proud of his own international reputation, his French campaign of 1513 and the warm reception he had enjoyed in the Netherlands. On hearing of his rival's plans, Henry had sent a messenger to Francis at Lyon, asking him not to disturb the peace of Christendom, and had privately declared 'If I choose he will cross the Alps, and if I choose, he will not cross.' Francis paid little heed to Henry's wishes, and crossed regardless, prompting the English king to complain he had been kept in the dark about the invasion of Milan. At first, he did not want to hear of Francis' victory at Marignano, but could not avoid it when a messenger brought him two letters written by the French king himself. Monsieur Baupame, charged with delivering the news into Henry's hands, wrote that 'it seemed tears would flow from his eyes, so red were they with the pain he suffered on hearing of the King's good tidings.'[5] Ambassador Guicciardini surmised that he was 'moved by rivalry and envy of Francis' glory, which he felt would greatly increase if he should achieve victory over the state of Milan.'[6] Henry also demanded to know more about Francis, asking whether they were a comparable height and size, and wanting to know who had the better shaped legs.[7] A medal was struck honouring Francis, bearing two globes, one terrestrial and one celestial, of earth and heaven, with the legend 'one world does not suffice.'[8] He was lauded as a new Constantine, 'God's elected king', and a second Caesar. Henry was not impressed.

As a result of Marignano, Pope Leo X changed his policy of keeping the French out of Italy, and invited Francis to visit him in Bologna. The city was decorated to welcome him, with its streets hung with tapestries and garlands, and peopled by the violet-dressed papal officials. Francis entered at 7pm, on 11 December 1515, dressed in black velvet embroidered with silver, accompanied by two cardinals and 300 archers. The observing Bishop of Worcester described the French king as 'tall in stature, broad-shouldered, oval and handsome face, very slender in the legs, much inclined to corpulence'.[9] Later that evening, Francis changed into a suit of gold to meet the Pope, approached and knelt to kiss his foot, whereupon Leo rose and kissed him upon both cheeks. The following day they attended Mass together, with Francis receiving communion from the Pope's hands, then spent the next few days talking and hunting. Leo presented his guest with a diamond reliquary containing a fragment of the true cross and offered him the Empire of the East if he could drive the Turks out of Constantinople. Francis left Milan on 8 January and headed for Provence, where he was reunited with his family, and set off on a long pilgrimage and progress, giving thanks at shrines along the route back to Paris. The Pope wrote to Henry in person, lauding the success of the meeting and asking the English king to 'lay aside his animosity'.[10]

Francis was keen to be a new, renaissance ruler, but like Henry, he embraced a more authoritarian style, driven by personality. As with More in England and Machiavelli in Italy, French writers were exploring the nature of politics and governance. Claude de Seyssel, a lawyer, councillor and Bishop of Marseille started work on his *La Monarchie du France* at the instigation of the king, in 1515. He was in favour of an hereditary rule, although did not consider it perfect, but stressed the importance of parliament, religion, and laws to act as regulatory bodies.

De Seyssel divided France into three social classes, the nobility, the merchants or bureaucrats and the producers or selling class, and promoted the links between warfare, state and social order. Guillaume Budé, a scholar of Greek and leading humanist, presented his *L'Instruction du Prince* to Francis, a collection of ancient wisdom given to rulers. In 1517, the French mathematician Oronce Finé, creator of heart-shaped maps of the world, depicted Francis in an unusual image. It featured in an early travel book by Nicolas le Huen, *Le Grant Voyages de Jherusalem* (sic), which projected the contemporary expectation that Francis had the skills to bring peace to Europe in a way his fellow kings lacked. Finé's illustration showed Francis accepting the standard of the crusade from Pope Leo, while the other European rulers, including Henry and Charles, look on. It fitted Francis' intention to become the central defender of the faith in Europe, commensurate with his title of the Most Catholic King.

After having impressed Francis with his work in Milan, Leonardo da Vinci was appointed 'the King's first painter, engineer and architect'. Arriving at Amboise late in 1516, the sexagenarian brought his favourite students and three paintings, the *Mona Lisa*, *Saint Jean Baptiste* and *Sainte Anne*. He had regular access to the French court through an underground tunnel that linked Amboise to the house Francis granted him, Le Clos Luce, in the chateau grounds. Da Vinci also had ideas for a new chateau to replace the existing one at Romorantin, drawing up plans featuring a series of canals and gardens with fountains, and although this was never built, some features were incorporated into the later redesigning of Amboise and Blois. One surviving sketch he made of the king's home in 1517 shows the array of little roofs and walls in faded sepia, and he helped plan the celebrations for the wedding of Lorenzo de Medici in 1518 at Amboise. Da Vinci died at Clos Luce in May 1519, so the designs for the Field of the Cloth of Gold did not benefit from his extraordinary genius.

When he was not winning real battles, Francis liked little more than jousting and tournaments, news of which was carried across the Channel to his equally martially minded rival. On some occasions, his antics were reckless, dangerous, even proving fatal in the name of sport, but he would not be dissuaded. In June 1515, his mother and wife had to beg him not to fight a duel with a wild boar. Three years later, he planned an entertainment in the grounds at Amboise to celebrate the wedding of Lorenzo de Medici, Duke of Urbino, who would father a future queen of France, Catherine de Medici. It involved Francis leading 600 men in the defence of a model town against an army of the same size, who tried to break through their defences, moat and gun battery. As the chronicler Florange glibly noted, though, it may have been 'the finest battle ever seen and the nearest to real warfare' but it 'did not please everyone, for some were killed and others frightened'.[11] The following year, Francis was almost blinded when he rode into a branch whilst hunting at Blois, and in April 1520 English ambassador Sir Richard Wingfield described to Henry how Francis had dispatched a boar. He would be almost killed in another mock siege at Romorantin in 1521, when heavy loads fell upon him from above whilst he was leaning out of a window.

If Francis had not already incurred Henry's jealousy through his military actions, on the field of battle, and at play, in February 1518 he managed to achieve the one thing the English king most desired. After four years of marriage, and two daughters, he became the father of a son, whom he named Francis. Bonfires were lit across the country and there was national rejoicing, especially after the throne had been passed through cousins, rather than the direct father-to-son line, in recent years. Then, to rub salt into England's wounds, a second son was born to Francis in March 1519, whom he named Henry. The English king sent a gift and £10 in reward to the midwife, and instructed Sir Thomas Boleyn to stand in for him as godfather at the christening. Three months later, Henry also became the father of a son, but little Henry Fitzroy was illegitimate and therefore unable to succeed to the throne. In almost every aspect, by 1520, it seemed that Francis had outshone Henry, fuelling intense rivalry between the two men that lurked behind the veneer of international diplomacy.

When it came to religious reform, Francis was far more open to debate than Henry. It was early in 1519 that the ideas of the German monk Martin Luther were recorded as first having an impact in France. The reformer had nailed his ninety-five theses to the door of All Saints' Church in Wittenberg on 31 October 1517, and his criticisms of Catholic doctrine and practices were spreading on the continent. The Basle printer, John Froben, wrote to Luther in February 1519, that he had sent 600 fresh copies of his works to Spain and France: 'They are sold in Paris and are being read even at the Sorbonne... they meet with everyone's approval.'[12] A Swiss student in Paris, named Pierre Tschudi, described them as being received with 'open arms,' especially the criticism of papal indulgences, which were pardons that could be purchased to exonerate a sinner from punishment.[13] That September, the text of a debate Luther had at Leipzig with the German theologian Johann, or John, Eck, was being debated at the Sorbonne, and Francis' own sister, Marguerite, was disposed towards the evolving Protestant view. Henry, on the other hand, was still devoutly and unquestioningly Catholic. Another seven years would pass before he would ask the Pope to annul his marriage to Catherine, twelve years before he would break with Rome and fourteen before he set himself up as Supreme Head of the Church of England. In 1519 Henry had read Luther's attack upon indulgences and written the first draft of a response. This book, which he first showed to Wolsey in June that year, and later developed with the help of Thomas More, became the *Defence of the Seven Sacraments* and earned Henry the title of 'Defender of the Faith' in 1521 from Pope Leo.

Francis headed into the elections for Holy Roman Emperor with determination, trying to raise loans from Lyons and Genoa, even asking Henry VIII for 100,000 gold crowns. Given Henry's own interest in the title, though, wrote Admiral of France, the Seigneur de Bonnivet, 'even if it rained gold in England, the French would not get so much as a piece to set upon a bonnet.'[14] This did not prove strictly true, as London's Italian bankers offered Francis a loan of 360,000 crowns, which he sent into Germany to try and influence the Electors. However, the German hostility towards France in 1519 was such that Admiral Bonnivet had to enter Frankfurt in disguise, under the name of 'Captain Jacob', and military pressure was brought to bear upon the voters, who were warned no Frenchmen would enter the country 'except on the points of spears and swords'.[15] When even his ally Pope Leo was pressured to back Charles' campaign, Francis saw the wisdom of withdrawing from the race. Disappointed, he retreated to hunt at Fontainebleau, telling Sir Thomas Boleyn that he had been spared 'all the trouble that he would have incurred by becoming emperor'. However, he sent a secret envoy to the Pope, who shared his concerns about the influence of Charles in Europe, and the pair signed a treaty of mutual support in October 1519. Francis was right to be concerned; just five years later, his conflict with the new Emperor would result in crushing defeat at Pavia, which would break the French king and his two young sons. In the meantime, his disappointment with the Electorship made him look towards England for an ally.

6

CLAUDE

Born in 1499, Queen Claude was five years younger than her
extrovert husband, and quite his opposite in appearance and
character. The elder of two daughters born to Louis XII and his
second wife, Anne of Brittany, she suffered from scoliosis, with
the distinctive curved spine that gave her a hunched appearance
and contributed to the regular pain she experienced in her legs.
Claude was also very small and the strabismus in her eyes meant
her vision did not align well, but she exuded a quiet dignity and
had a sweetness of face and disposition that outshone what were
perceived to be any physical imperfections by her contemporaries.
In a *Commémoration* book dedicated to her in 1514, she is
pictured as a tiny figure seated in a large throne, with her feet
resting on a cushion of black and gold. A posthumous illustration
in the Book of Hours of her daughter-in-law, Catherine de Medici,
shows Claude with a devout expression, her dark hair pulled back
under a plain white hood, hands together in prayer, surrounded by
her female relatives.

Claude's survival was little less than miraculous. Her mother,
Anne, Duchess of Brittany, had formerly been the wife of Louis'
cousin, the previous king Charles VIII, making Anne Queen
of France twice over. Yet Anne had not been fortunate in her
childbearing record, losing all seven of her children by Charles

in miscarriage, stillbirth, or in infancy. As Louis' wife, she fell pregnant at least another nine times, but only Claude and another daughter, Renée, survived. The chronicler Brantôme wrote that Claude 'was very good and very charitable, and very sweet to everyone and never showed displeasure to anybody in her court or of her domains. She was deeply loved by the King Louis and the Queen Anne, her father and mother, and she was always a good daughter to them.'[1]

Although Claude was heiress to the Duchy of Brittany, Salic Law in France prevented her from inheriting, but her rights could be claimed by any husband she took. In 1501, she was betrothed to the infant Charles, future Emperor, and three years later, at the Treaty of Blois, was given a large dowry including Burgundy, Blois, Asti, Genoa and the controversial Milan. Europe in 1520 would have looked considerably different had this marriage gone ahead. A French copy of Petrarch's *Remedies for Fortune Fair and Foul* depicts a four-year-old Claude sitting on her mother's lap, surrounded by women of the court, a quasi-Madonna image. However, in 1505, when Louis was ill and despaired of fathering a son, he cancelled the betrothal and promised Claude instead to Francis, his ward. Anne of Brittany and Francis' mother, Louise of Savoy, had never been friends, and Anne actively opposed this new match. However, once Anne died in January 1514, Claude became Duchess of Brittany and, three months later, married Francis, to whom she signed over her Breton inheritance.

Concerns were expressed about Claude's ability to bear children, given her youth and numerous health complications. After six months of marriage, she became pregnant, soon after her fifteenth birthday. Just two months later, with the death of Louis XII at the end of 1514, she succeeded as Queen of France, despite the rumours circulating that Francis intended to put her aside in favour of the widowed Mary Tudor. Mary's rapid remarriage to Charles Brandon belied the rumours and Claude went on to bear her first child, a daughter named Louise, in August 1515. Two months later, after she had been churched, Claude accompanied her mother-in-law south to Lyons and Marseille, to welcome the triumphant Francis returning from victory after the Battle of Marignano. Whilst there, the women paid a visit to the basilica of Saint-Maximin-la-Sainte-Baume, the reputed tomb of St Mary Magdalene, over which a fourteenth-century church had been constructed. Soon after Christmas, she was pregnant again, bearing Princess Charlotte the following October.

While Francis was mostly based at his childhood home of Amboise, Claude's main residence of Blois was twenty miles along the Loire to the north-east. It was a fairy-tale castle, where the wall carvings featured Claude's devices of the ermine, knotted rope, full moon and the swan pierced by an arrow. The Italian Renaissance had reached the interior of Blois too. In the exquisite Queen's chamber on the first floor, and the richly painted gallery nearby, under the archways of the hall and the red brick gothic entrance, woven and painted images presented the anatomical, realistic and balanced ideal of the Renaissance, with their dark backgrounds, often set inside with glimpses of outdoors through open doors and windows. Yet Claude's was a specific, female, maternal, representation of the Renaissance. One such typical image was Sebastiano del Piombo's 'Visitation' depicting St Elizabeth and Mary with child. Painted in 1518, it hung in Claude's chamber, but it is not a romantic image. The weary set of Mary's features bear a realism that would have been familiar to Claude through her personal experiences, while the comfort offered by St Elizabeth combined the queen's spiritual purpose with the maternal figure she missed. Also in 1518, Pope Leo X commissioned Raphael to paint *The Holy Family of Francis I*, depicting Joseph, Mary, the infant Jesus, St Elizabeth, John the Baptist as a child, and two angels. This may have been to mark the safe arrival of the couple's first son, Francis. The walls at Blois were also hung with tapestries depicting scenes from Christine de Pisan's famous sixteenth-century City of Ladies, based on the century-old book celebrating 200 admirable women. Other tapestry versions of this story were owned by Margaret of Savoy, and later, by Anne Boleyn.

Claude's piety was legendary. In 1517, she commissioned a tiny prayer book, full of dazzling miniatures, so small it could be held in the palm of the hand, and a companion volume, a book of hours. Less than three inches tall and two and a half inches wide, the prayer book's diminutive size was a mark of its value, its jewel-like colours depicting the Passion of Christ, the story of St Christopher, and those of St Nicholas and St René, who were responsible for restoring dead children to life. Of particular interest to Claude was the prayer to the Virgin Mary, phrased in Latin in the first person, allowing for a direct, personal connection between queen and saint, at a time when such methods of devotion were just starting to be advocated. In addition, the illustration of Mary and the infant Jesus contains the image of a kneeling young John the Baptist, whose position and gestures echo those found in the 'Madonna of the Rocks,' a work by Da Vinci, then in the collection of Francis I. An interesting reference to Claude's position in the royal family might be inferred from the illustration of the Holy Trinity, which is encircled by a loosely knotted girdle, a symbol of the house of Savoy, a tacit acknowledgement that Claude played something of a marginalised role, and that the real 'trinity' of power was Francis, Louise and Marguerite.

In May 1517, over two years since Claude had become queen, she was finally given a full coronation. The delay had been to accommodate her pregnancies, but the occasion was most certainly not an after-thought, as Francis organised an ostentatious display in her honour. The day before, Claude prayed in memory of her parents at the Church of St Denis, 'in great devotion and contemplation over the tomb and statue of her father and mother, and not without tears and lamentations'.[2] Her ladies helped her into her overgarment and bodice trimmed with the Breton symbol of the ermine from her coat of arms, as a reminder that she was simultaneously queen and duchess. Before her death, Claude's mother had given her a cape to wear for the occasion, 'sewn with little leaves of gold onto silver cloth, filled with beautifully fashioned ermines in the form of raised animals, all completely covered with raised pearls,' with a huge ruby set into the clasp.[3]

Seven sites of pageantry had been created in Paris, along Claude's route. Francis had hired Pierre Gringore, the most famous Parisian poet, actor and playwright of his day, who had recently composed a mystery play about Louis XII but was also known for his satires on the papacy.[4] The first display was staged at the Châtelet, the Parisian seat of justice, featuring the genealogy of Brittany, as designed and related by Gringore: 'The aforementioned lady arrived at the Châtelet of Paris, where she found a tree with many branches, like a Tree of Jesse, on a large scaffolding. In the upper branches were a crowned king and queen... and on each side of these branches were several princes, princesses, kings and dukes of Brittany, demonstrating the line and genealogy from which the aforementioned lady arose.'[5] At St. Denis, an actor playing the queen stood surrounded by six Biblical women, each symbolising one of the desirable qualities of a French queen: fertility (Leah), modesty (Esther), loyalty (Sarah), prudence (Rebecca), amiability (Rachel) and education (Deborah). At the site of Saint Innocents, three large open hearts contained female figures representing Divine Love, Conjugal Love and Natural Love.

Claude was carried into Notre Dame Cathedral on a litter draped in cloth of silver, head to toe in jewels. With Francis observing from behind the customary grille so as not to upstage her, the Duke of Alençon held the heavy crown of Charlemagne above her head, the Constable of Bourbon knelt to hold her train, the Comte de Guise held the hand of justice and the Prince de la Roche-sur-Yon held the sceptre. Under Nôtre Dame's gothic vaulting and great rose window, Claude was anointed and made her promises. She was crowned by Cardinal Philippe de Luxembourg, then an old man of seventy-two, who had ruled on her father's divorce from his first wife in 1498.

At the banquet held afterwards in her honour at the Palais du Justice, food was served on gold and silver plates, set on cloth of gold, covering marble tables. The following day a tournament was held, at which the Knights of the Day, dressed in white and led by Francis, competed against the Comte de St Pol and his black-clad Knights of the Night. Following the Parisian festivities, the French royal family set off on progress. They followed the route of the Seine through Picardy, almost ninety miles to Rouen, where Francis made an official entry into the city on 2 August, dressed in cloth of gold atop a horse decked out in the same material. The following day Claude made her entry, second to her husband according to protocol, but ensuring that she received the limelight in her own right. Conceiving another child around the time of her coronation, the years leading up to the Field of the Cloth of Gold would be dominated by pregnancies and lying-in for Claude.

In February 1518, Claude gave birth to her first son, Francis. The celebrations at court reflected the royal family's relief following years of infant mortality and female births. Claude reputedly instructed a messenger to 'tell the king that he is even more beautiful than himself.'[6] For the christening at Amboise on 25 April, the inner walls of the chateau courtyard were hung with tapestries depicting classical stories and filled with pavilions, which were lit by a thousand candles and were impervious to the heavy rain. Da Vinci had designed the bridge that was erected from the nursery to the chapel, with a roof decorated by dolphins and wax torches burning on gold plates, hung with more carpets. As the procession approached, it was announced by drums. The baby was carried wrapped in cloth of silver lined with ermine. Three cardinals awaited the prince in the chapel, which was hung with cloth of gold and silver, where the font was draped in gold and covered over by a canopy held up by four gold trees. Fanfares announced his anointing, followed by banquets, dancing and masquerades.

Four months after the birth of Dauphin Francis, Claude conceived again. She was due to give birth during the initial negotiations for the Field of the Cloth of Gold, in March 1519, but experienced a state of ill-health. Ambassador Thomas Boleyn explained to Wolsey:

The Queen and my Lady left Paris the same day (11 March) for St. Germain, where the former was to be confined, but was taken ill by the way, and was obliged to rest at the village of La Porte de Neuilly, and that night she was in great danger. False reports were spread, first of her death, afterwards of her delivery; which kept Boleyn away from court on Saturday, when he had appointed to meet the Great Master. He was sent for, however, yesterday, and saw the lodgings of the King and Queen, my Lady the king's mother, the duchess of Alençon... If the Queen is strong enough, she is to be conveyed by water to St. Germain's in 'close barges with chambers made in them;' if not, she must remain.[7]

On 25 March, Claude had reached Saint-Germain, where the child was expected imminently, and 'looketh her time every hour'.[8] Two days later Boleyn saw her 'accompanied with fourteen or fifteen lords and gentlewomen, in a nightgown, and nothing [upon her] head but only a kerchief, looking always her hour when she shall be brought in bed'.[9] It was not until the last day of the month that Queen Claude safely delivered a son, the future Henri II. Francis had arrived at Saint Germain by 5 April at the latest, to greet his new child, who was named after his English godfather.[10] Boleyn described the solemn procession of thanks that was held after the birth, attended by Francis and his mother, 'in honour of the holy cord with which our Lord was bound to the pillar'. Considered to have healing powers, this and other relics had been sent to Claude for her delivery from the Abbey of the Holy Cross at Poitiers. The papal legate and eleven bishops went to Claude's chamber, carrying out the relics on little cushions and then placing them on the high altar.[11] Francis attended the procession all the time, 'bareheaded, with one usher only before him, then came the queen mother an old gentleman bearing her train; a little behind her the duchesse, her sister, having her train like[wise]'.[12]

The christening of Prince Henri was delayed 'because the child hath a disease in his eyes, as he saith all his children have shortly after they be born'.[13] When it finally went ahead in April, Thomas Boleyn took the important role of deputising for Henry as godfather, and more gifts were sent from England, including a gold cup and salt cellar and £100 in gold coins, to be distributed between the nurse, four rockers and gentlewomen of the Queen's chamber.[14] It was on this occasion that in the order of ceremony Francis placed a young woman named Francoise de Foix near the royal princesses, signalling to all that she was his lover. Claude was still closeted away in formal lying-in, so she did not witness this, but the action enraged Francis' mother Louise, who loathed the de Foix family.

In December 1519, Claude conceived a fifth time, at the age of twenty. She was heavily pregnant by the time she rode out to Ardres with the French court the following summer, with pains in her legs, a wandering eye and a twisted spine, but with her piety, sweetness and quiet dignity, she was unquestionably the matriarch of France.

7

THE FRENCH PARTY

The Valois court was a vibrant, colourful and cultured place in 1520. The accession of Francis had propelled his circle of close friends into power, transitioning into roles previously held by the older figures who had guided him during his childhood. In particular, the group of boys who had shared his early years at Amboise, hunting, riding, learning and growing together, and who had fought at Marignano, now set the tone at court, much in the way of Henry VIII's minions. They took leading roles in negotiating and planning the spectacle of the Field of the Cloth of Gold, keen to show off their magnificence and superior jousting skills at the expense of the English.

Chief among the organisers from the Ambroise years was Guillaume Gouffier, Seigneur de Bonnivet, appointed Admiral of France. Born in 1488, he was six years older than Francis, and the much younger brother of the young king's tutor, Artus Gouffier, seigneur de Boisy. Bonnivet had been appointed upon the king's succession, fought with him in 1515 and been in charge of the 1519 campaign for Emperorship. Described as similar in character to Francis, he was a keen jouster and womaniser, reputedly attempting to seduce the king's own sister; their relationship suggests parallels with that of Henry VIII and his older childhood companion, Charles Brandon. A sketch of Bonnivet by Jean Clouet, the French Holbein, depicts a young man with long nose, pale, hooded eyes and thin lips. Bonnivet appears in the correspondence of the English ambassadors, especially Wingfield and Brandon, from the start of Francis' reign, and in 1520, was the main negotiator with Wolsey regarding the location and timing of the event. In late March, Richard Wingfield reported that the Admiral was lying sick of a fever at Vertewell, but that he had recovered by the time Wingfield called upon him at Blois on April 5.[1] Another Gouffier brother, Adrian de Boissy, a Cardinal, Grand Almoner and papal Legate to France since 1519, was also present at the event, riding beside Francis at his first meeting with Henry.

One important job at Francis' court was that of the Grand Master, head of the king's household, which initially belonged to a third Gouffier brother, Artus. According to Thomas Boleyn, Artus was ill that February, confined to his chamber with gout, and he would die on a mission in Italy three months later.[2] He was replaced by René of Savoy, Comte de Villars, 'the bastard of Savoy,' a legitimized illegitimate son, whose half-brother Philibert had briefly been married to Margaret of Austria. He also shared a father with Louise of Savoy, thus making him the king's half-uncle. In 1519-20 he was constructing a grand ship, a carrack, called *Le Grand Maitresse*, which he would launch to protect the Knights Hospitallers against the Turks immediately after the Field of the Cloth of Gold.

Another imposing figure on the French side was Charles III, Duke of Bourbon, born in 1490, who inherited extensive titles and lands in Auvergne. Francis appointed him Constable of France in 1515, an exclusively military title, which entailed supervision of army supplies, commissions and discipline. He had fought extensively in the Italian Wars and commanded the vanguard at Marignano, for which he was granted the Governorship of the newly acquired Duchy of Milan. However, he soon ran up large debts, which Francis refused to honour, and recalled him back to his court. Charles was also very close to the French throne. He had married his cousin in order to unite their two claims to the Bourbon line, and after the death of Charles IV, Duke of Alençon in 1525,

Bourbon would become agnatic heir to the throne in the event of a failure of male heirs. Alleged to be a proud and arrogant figure, there are comparisons to be drawn between Charles' relationship with Francis and that of Henry VIII and Edward Stafford, Duke of Buckingham. Bourbon fell out with the king shortly after the Field of the Cloth of Gold, when Charles' wife left him all her inheritance upon her death, but the king's mother, Louise, claimed it instead.

The Grand Chancellor of France in 1520 was Antoine Duprat, later Archbishop of Sens and first president of the Parlement of Paris, a very powerful and capable man, described by historian Gabriel Hanotaux as second only to Richelieu, for 'the decisive influence he exercised on the destiny of his country'. A staunch Catholic who opposed the Protestant sympathies of Francis' sister Marguerite, Thomas Boleyn found Duprat difficult and unreasonable in his dealings. It prompted the ambassador to draft instructions in May 1519 'in the form of a remonstrance against the demeanour of the chancellor of France',[3] who had been obstructive when asked to compensate English merchants for their losses.

Another key player in Anglo-French arrangements was Anne de Montmorency, first valet of the bedchamber. His father William held office in Francis' household before his succession, and his son Anne (then a unisex name) was just a year older than the new king. He also fought at Marignano and became Captain of the Bastille, before becoming one of the hostages sent to England to pay the French debt when Henry agreed to return Tournai in 1518. It was while Anne was in England that Thomas Boleyn wrote with news that his brother, the Bishop of Limoges, had died at Blois 'of the common sickness', causing Francis and Claude to remove to Amboise. Anne returned to France in 1519 and was present in the king's entourage the following year.

Among the Amboise circle was Robert de la Marck, Seigneur de Florange, born in 1491, who bonded with Francis as children because of his fondness for sport and military feats.

He fought in the Italian wars, and in the Netherlands, was knighted on the field at Marignano and formed part of Francis' Imperial campaign in 1519. He would write one account of the Field of the Cloth of Gold from the French side, including the famous wrestling scene between the two kings. Another old friend and veteran of Marignano was Charles de Lorraine, Duke of Guise, a military general who spent a long time recovering from the wounds he received there. Francis' Treasurer was the renaissance art collector Florimond Robertet, who was born into a family of clerks and worked his way up during the reigns of Charles VIII and Louis XII, so that he was eventually able to buy works by da Vinci and statues by Michelangelo and build imposing chateaus in the Italian style. In 1520, Francis' Grand Butler was Charles de Rohan, Comte de Guise, and his Marshal of France from 1518 was Thomas de Foix-Lescun, both of whom had also fought with Francis in 1515. Additional Marshals of France were Jacques Chabannes, Seigneur de Lapalisse and Gaspard de Coligny, Seigneur de Chatillon. Anthonie Le Viste, Seigneur de Fresnes, sat on Francis' Council and Jean Hurault, Seigneur de Vybraye, was his Master of Requests.

Francis' domestic household, or *Maison du Roi civile*, contained all the necessary offices for the provision of his chamber, table and pleasure. The department of the king's chamber was overseen by the Grand Chamberlain, Oliver de la Vernade, Seigneur de la Bastie, who ruled the king's bedroom, furnishings and clothing. There was also the Bouche de Roi, responsible for provisioning the king, the Grand Bouteiller Adrien de Hangst, who was in charge of the cellars, and the Grand Panetier, in charge of the bread. Numbers of servants, sewers, carvers, napkin-bearers and others waited on the king's table. The Grand Maître de la Garderobe oversaw Francis' clothing and that of his court, his livery men and servants. Francis created a new role of Grand Aumônier, an official in charge of dispensing alms, bestowing it in 1520 either upon Pierre du Chastel, chaplain to Francis I, Bishop of Mâcon or Jean le Veneur, Bishop of Lisieux. The Menus-Plaisirs du Roi was the office who arranged the king's pleasures, or entertainments, and the pageantry at all ceremonial occasions. By contrast, a considerable number of servants also worked within his chapels, as chaplains and confessors.

The role of the Grand Squire, in charge of the king's stables, equerries and horses, equivalent of the English Master of the Horse, was given to Galeazzo di Sanseverino, nephew of the Duke of Milan, friend of Leonardo da Vinci, and cited by Baldassare Castiglione as the perfect courtier in his book of the same name. The Grand Squire worked with the Grand Falconer, who kept the birds of prey, and the Grand Louvetier, who directed the hunts of wolves, boars and bears, of which the king was so fond. The Grand Veneur was the royal hunt master and under Charles VIII in the 1490s he had overseen a department of twenty-seven men and around a hundred dogs. Most of these departments contributed to the Field of the Cloth of Gold, either as direct participants, in an organisational capacity or behind the scenes, necessitating the movement and accommodation, clothing and feeding of vast numbers. When Francis offered his provisional list of attendees in March 1520, it included one other king (Navarre), three Princes (de la Roche, Orange and Tallemont), four dukes, thirteen counts and 'other knights of the Order'. He proposed to take 400 archers of the royal guard, four captains, 100 Swiss, 200 gentlemen in his household and 200 horses.

Four French women played prominent roles at the Field of the Cloth of Gold. After Queen Claude, Francis' contemporaries referred to as the 'holy trinity' of the king, his mother Louise and sister Marguerite, who acted as diplomatic hostesses, but there was also Francoise de Foix, the king's mistress, whose role had been publicly acknowledged since April 1519.

Louise of Savoy, Francis' formidable mother, had been made Duchess of Angoulême after his succession, and served as regent in 1515 while he campaigned against Italy. Louise was forty at the time, and the main rival to Claude's mother, Anne of Brittany, who opposed Francis' marriage to Claude. Widowed at nineteen, Louise was passionately interested in the southern Renaissance, in the Italian influence upon politics, the arts and sciences, giving her two children a humanist education, commissioning books for them and teaching Francis Spanish and Italian herself. Proud, intelligent and fiercely protective of her son, Louise's long years of waiting and passionate motherhood are reminiscent of the role that Henry VII's mother, Margaret Beaufort, played through years of uncertainty before her son reached the throne, and her active participation in his reign.

Louise took an active role in her son's business. She is frequently mentioned in the correspondence of English ambassadors in France, such as Richard Wingfield's account of visiting her at Blois in April 1520, when he found the ambassadors of Spain and Venice waiting in her outer chamber, and managed to gain admittance to see Madame between them. Louise spoke to him about the French plans for travelling to Paris and north, to meet Henry, but was displeased when other ambassadors questioned Francis further, saying they 'meddled with a prince of faith and promise'. She welcomed the English support she had recently received regarding the departure of the Scottish regent, the Duke of Albany, from France, and hoped it would mark a closer Anglo-French friendship:

> Wingfield said he considered this as the first act of their sincerity, and hoped this friendship would continue. She said she hoped the same, and thought things could not have come in so good a train unless God had put his hand thereto, and that when the two princes met they would conclude upon some act which should be to the weal of Christendom and their perpetual loving.[4]

Louise also asked Wingfield what Catherine of Aragon thought of the proposed meeting. No doubt aware of the queen's Spanish loyalties, Wingfield tactfully replied that there 'could not be a more virtuous or wise Princess anywhere' who had 'none other joy or comfort in this world but to do and follow all that she may to stand with the king's pleasure'. Louise wished to know whether Catherine was pregnant at the time, to which Wingfield replied he 'had no such knowledge' but trusted that God would 'send her fruit in time convenient'. Louise suggested that if Francis had another son, he 'could be right well content to send over the dauphin into England... to be there nourished and brought up after such manner as should stand best with the king's highness' pleasure'. She hoped to show him Dauphin Francis, then aged two, but the boy was asleep.[5]

Francis' elder sister, Marguerite d'Alençon, later Queen of Navarre, would also participate in the Field of the Cloth of Gold. Older than her brother by two years, she is now most famous as the author of the *Heptameron*, a collection of stories about illicit love, but has been described as the outstanding female figure of the Renaissance. According to historian Will Durant, 'every free spirit looked upon her as protectoress and ideal.... Marguerite was the embodiment of charity. She would walk unescorted in the streets of Navarre, allowing anyone to approach her and would listen at first hand to the sorrows of the people... calling herself "The Prime Minister of the Poor."'[6] In 1509, Marguerite had been married to Charles d'Alençon, second in line to the throne and the last line of his house, and another veteran of Marignano. Although she and her husband repeatedly prayed and undertook pilgrimages in the hopes of conceiving a child, they remained childless, although by her second marriage Marguerite would become the grandmother of the future Henri IV. Among Marguerite's entourage at the Field of the Cloth of Gold was the poet Clement Marot, a valet de chambre who had presented works to Francis and Claude and would record the events of 1520 in verse.

Taking a less formal, but perhaps no less obvious role, was Francis' first official mistress, Francoise de Foix, Comtesse de Chateaubriant, Louise of Savoy objected to the entire Foix family, perhaps because they were related to Anne of Brittany, and raised at Anne's court, but she disliked Francoise in particular, because of the attention she received from the king. Francoise had an illegitimate daughter, born the year before her marriage when she was still in her teens, and lived at Chateaubriant with her husband until they were summoned to court in 1516. Francis already had a reputation as a womaniser, but Francoise became his first official mistress, around 1518, and he did not attempt to conceal her, placing her in the line of precedence among the princesses. She had initially resisted his advances but the rewards he bestowed upon her family parallel those given by Henry to the Boleyns, for the sake of Mary in 1520, and later to please Anne. Francoise was appointed as a Lady in Waiting to Claude in December 1519 and remained the king's official mistress for a decade.

In terms of precedence, the most significant French female at the Field of the Cloth of Gold was Queen Claude. Being between six and seven months pregnant in June 1520, she required a considerable entourage, not only to care for her person but to accommodate her guests. The household of the French Queen had been expanded considerably by the regent, Anne of France, acting for her younger brother, Charles VIII. In 1490, It contained 109 members, divided into different departments: nine dames and fourteen demoiselles waited on the regent, forty-seven traders supplied her house, from bakers and fruitmongers to the stable and dog handlers, another twenty-five worked in her chamber, in practical and financial jobs, or in running her chapel, with an additional fifteen in various roles.[7] Anne of Brittany was the first queen to benefit from these changes, but welcomed more young women to her court than ever before, creating a more balanced counterpart to that of the king. By 1523, shortly after the Field of the Cloth of Gold, Claude's household stood at 285 in comparison with 540 attendants upon Francis.[8]

Few individual names exist for the women in Claude's household. Her sister Renée, then aged ten, may have accompanied her to

Ardres, along with twelve ladies in waiting. Claude also employed the writer Anne Malet de Graville, depicted presenting the queen with one of her works, in a miniature in Roman de Palamon and Arcita in 1516. There was also Diane de Poitiers, a noblewoman from Drôme in the south-east of France, who was almost an exact contemporary of Claude. Diane had just been married early, to Louis de Brézé, Seigneur d'Anêt, who was almost forty years her senior, but was a grandson of Charles VII. An intelligent and beautiful woman, Diane had been given an education along humanist lines, could read Latin and Greek, speak contemporary languages, dance, play music, converse and hunt, making her the personification of the perfect female courtier of the time. Diane would bear her husband two children, in 1518 and 1521, but would become famous for adopting a lifetime of black and white of mourning upon her widowhood in 1531, and becoming the much older mistress of Claude and Francis' second son, Henri II. It was rumoured that she may also have been one of Francis's many mistresses.

A future queen of England went unnoticed among the French retinue in 1520, too. Dark-haired, elegant and well educated, Anne Boleyn had been placed in the household of Margaret of Savoy at Malines at the age of twelve, thanks to the influence of her father. The change in England's alliances had seen her move to France in late 1514 or early 1515 and remain in Claude's household after the departure of Mary Tudor. By 1520, she had served Claude for five years and knew the French court, its king, and the castles of Blois and Amboise well. She would be reunited with her father, mother and sister when the two sides met at the Field of the Cloth of Gold.

THE PLANNING

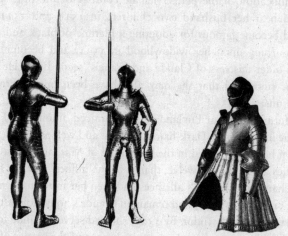

Henry VIII's armour for fighting on foot (left) and armour sent as a gift to Henry by Maximilian I (right).

8

NEGOTIATIONS

The idea of a meeting between Henry and Francis was first suggested soon after the French king's succession in 1515. On his way to the Tudor court in February, the Venetian ambassador, Sebastian Giustinian, wrote that 'the King of England would maintain a perfect understanding with the King of France, who was negotiating an interview with him through the Duke of Suffolk,' and that it 'was settled that the interview should take place at Calais'. This was at the time when Henry was arranging the return of his sister Mary, recently widowed, and he was deeply wary of the unknown nature of the new king. As it transpired, Mary returned home as Suffolk's wife, and the kings did not meet. Another three years would pass before the idea was raised again as part of an official treaty, conceived and nurtured by the most able statesman of Henry's early reign.

In the sumptuous surroundings of Greenwich Palace, in October 1518, Thomas Wolsey achieved his greatest diplomatic triumph so far. After three years as a Cardinal and Lord Chancellor, he was the most powerful man at court, his palace on the Thames at Hampton was rising from the ground, and he was reaching for ever greater glory. At Wolsey's invitation, signatories from France, Burgundy, Spain, the Netherlands, the Papacy and England, agreed to a policy of friendship, whereby they were bound not to assist, not attack each other, and to launch a joint force against the threat posed by the Turks. By the terms of the Treaty of London, Henry was to hand back Tournai to the French, and his two-year-old daughter Mary was betrothed to the Dauphin Francis. It was also proposed that Henry and Francis would meet in person. Over the next twenty months, letters and ambassadors sailed back and forth over the channel, negotiations were made for when, where and how it would become a reality.

In January 1519, Henry formally surrendered Tournai in a letter to Francis. This was a positive first step towards meeting, but as goodwill gestures went, it was costly for the French, setting Francis back 23,000 gold francs. In Tournai, Charles, Earl of Worcester, Nicholas Vaux and Edward Belknapp, ceded the city into the hands of Gaspard de Coligny, Seigneur de Chatillon, and Margaret of Savoy's steward, Philippe de Haneton. Chatillon entered with 500 foot soldiers and 1,200 horse, received the keys from Sir Richard Jerningham, the English deputy of the city, and made an inspection of the walls to ensure all Henry's defensive guns had been removed. Tournai's brief allegiance to England, of which Henry had been so proud in 1513, was ended. Worcester wrote to Wolsey that they would leave the city the following morning 'with no other condition except that the writing under the seal... shall be delivered,' for which Haneton had 'taken great pains'. France also agreed to offer hostages as a guarantor of the surrender and the substantial sum Francis was to pay. Sir William Sandys, Treasurer of Calais, reported that the selected gentlemen, including Francis' own friend, Anne de Montmorency, had arrived in Calais late in January ready to cross the Channel and would reach Greenwich at the end of February.

The French hostages were hostages in name only. They were not deprived, imprisoned or confined, but enjoyed Henry's hospitality as important guests, 'daily resorting to the court, (they) had great cheer... (and) were well entertained.'[1] They arrived in time to witness the revels, or latest renaissance-inspired 'maskalyne' dance, which was held at Greenwich on 8 March. The various influences, details and choices made for the maskalyne, or masque, presaged costumes and dances that would follow at Guisnes, with Italian-style music and dresses ornamented with Spanish work. The royal wardrobe prepared costumes for 46 people, from cloth of gold, velvet, taffeta and sarcenet in various colours, as well as hats, bonnets and masking hoods, followed by the King's saddle and other apparatus for tilting. Two needlewomen, Christiana Warren and Elizabeth Phillip, assisted in the making of thirteen ostrich feathers beaten with fine gold, and wired, pasteboard hoops for the ladies' clothes, which totalled £60 7s 3d, as signed off by John Heron, Treasurer of Henry's Chamber.[2] Such costumes, entertainments and costs foreshadowed the style in which the English king would attempt to outdo his French counterpart the following summer, as well as the swift preparation and skill of Henry's behind-the-scenes workers.

Once the idea of a meeting had been proposed, certain practical arrangements needed to be settled. In mid-March, 1519, resident ambassador Thomas Boleyn wrote home from France acknowledging receipt of letters from Henry to Francis, which included a whole quire of instructions with recommendations about their meeting, and a list of the entourage Henry intended to bring. When Boleyn presented these at court, Francis replied that he was 'determined to see your grace, (even) though he should come by himself, his page and his lackey.' However, as Boleyn advised, the location might prove a difficulty. Francis had an aversion to entering Calais, which was still part of English territory, but Boleyn was sure he might be persuaded 'after both kings have spoken together'. Louise of Savoy tried to dissuade Henry from holding the meeting in Calais, adding that it would be more 'triumphant to be lodged in summer in the field in tents and pavilions than it should be in any town'.[3]

The degree of distrust that needed to be overcome on both sides was considerable. Boleyn mentioned the French king's efforts at friendship, saying he had 'great confidence in Wolsey' and held him in 'great esteem, trust and reputation'. However, even the Francophile Cardinal had a less high opinion of Francis at the time, because this coincided with the French king launching his campaign to be elected Emperor. Some of the Cardinal's private letters reveal the true sentiments lurking behind the mask of diplomatic amity. He wrote to Worcester that 'the French king is straining every nerve, by art or cunning, to obtain the election and succeed in his unbridled desires' and that 'every obstacle should be thrown in his way.' Wolsey made clear, though, that Charles' candidacy was not preferable, 'from whose overgrown power, were he successful, as much danger might ensure hereafter and perilous dissensions in Christendom.' He admitted that Charles was 'the less(er) evil' of the two but advised others to dissimulate 'and to qualify such commendations by trusty and secret messengers... as Henry himself intends to do.' Henry's duplicity was suspected, though, when Boleyn was challenged by Louise of Savoy over a friendly letter he had sent to Charles, a copy of which had come into French hands. Boleyn protested that it was actually 'a plot to sow discord between the two princes', to which Louise replied that she 'had so much trust in England that she gave it no credence, and her son did but laugh at it... and much desires the interview between her son and the king of England.'[4]

Initially, Francis wanted to meet in the summer of 1519. He gushed to Wolsey about his intention to 'bring to the proposed meeting his harness for jousts' and to 'have the fairest ladies there that he can get'. He had already chosen his best horses for the tournament and tilt, 'and some high bounding and stirring horses, which he will give at that time'[5] to Henry. But in June, Henry met this enthusiasm with delay. Replying that he was 'no less desirous' to meet, he regretted it was 'almost impossible it could take place this summer'. although he was keen that arrangements could begin for the following year.'[6] Undeterred, Francis suggested that a meeting might take place at the end of May 1520 at some convenient location between Calais and Boulogne, an offer which was accepted on the English side. Boleyn tried to reassure the French king that although Henry 'had made a peace with the Emperor, yet in consideration of the marriage of the Dauphin with the Princess (Mary) preference would be in all things given to France.' At this point, Francis made the admission that he, too, had made an alliance with the Emperor, and 'though England was an island, assured from all enemies, and he open to attack on all sides, he was not afraid.' Francis expressed his 'great affection to England, and his desire for a firm union', considering Wolsey 'not as his servant, but as his special friend'.[7]

In July 1519, with the proposed date of May 1520 taking the pressure off, Henry made a rather extravagant sartorial promise. As proof of his desire to meet Francis, 'he had resolved to wear his beard till the said meeting.' Hearing about 'this token of affection', Francis 'laid his hand on his beard, and said surely he would never put it off till he had seen him.'[8] And thus, on both sides of the Channel, long beards were grown and the gentlemen of the courts followed suit. However, it was not a popular move with everyone: Catherine of Aragon notoriously disliked facial hair on her husband and complained bitterly.

By November, the continuing existence of Henry's beard was being questioned by the French. Boleyn was with the royal family at Blois, where Antoine des Lettes-Despres, Seiur de Montpezat, arrived from a recent visit to England, bringing rumours that 'the king... had put off his beard, and asked me if I knew not of it,' as he reported by letter to Henry. Caught off guard, Boleyn replied that if it was true, he supposed 'it hath been by the Queen's desire, for... (he had) afore time known when the king's grace hath worn long his beard that the Queen hath daily made him great instance and desired him to put it off for her sake.' He feared Louise may have 'taken some offence' because of Henry's promise. Then, perhaps in a subtle attempt to question Henry's loyalty, the king's mother asked if Catherine 'was not aunt to the king of Spain', to which Boleyn replied that she was, but that 'the king of England had greater affection for her son than any king living.' This appeared to please Louise, the ambassador reported, and she replied that 'their love is not in their beards but in their hearts.'[9]

At the opening of 1520, the negotiations became more specific. Francis wrote to Wolsey, empowering him to act on his behalf to negotiate with Henry and bring the plans forward. He stipulated that the meeting take place between Guisnes (modern Guines) and Ardres, two towns just over five miles apart either side of the border, where the English-controlled Pale of Calais came to an end. Henry was to pitch his pavilions at Guisnes, and Francis at Ardres, providing a base where each could retire at night. When it came to the location of the tents, Francis thought it best that this be determined in April, when it would be right to 'advise upon what is proper for their safety and commodity' before the meeting in May. He proposed that the meeting would take place 'at a fixed day and hour, and on the spot to be fixed by deputies, who would decide the days for the jousts.'[10] Finally, he requested that the number of attendants be regulated by the provisional lists they had drafted last year.

With Francis being so keen to fix the arrangements, some distrust of Henry's enthusiasm lingered that spring. Admiral Bonnivet wrote to Wolsey that there was 'no dissimulation or difficulty here, and the matter depends upon you.' A Monsieur Guyot de Heulle, ambassador to the Netherlands, informed the Chancellor that on his way from London, he had 'heard many complaints against the king passing the sea to visit Francis' and wished him to 'be upon his guard against misrepresentations'. Then, from Malines, de Heulle wrote again to Wolsey that 'there is a rumour here that Henry and the King of France intend to meet each other,' and he doubted no 'great good will come of it' and 'they take it in different ways.'[11] An anonymous letter written from the French court on 20 February reported that 'the king and the king of England are to meet... the pageant to be greater than ever was,' but warned that 'one must beware of the English, lest the same thing happen as at the meeting of Philip Auguste and Henry of England, from which no good peace ensued. The House of Flanders (Hapsburgs) has long tried to break the alliance of England and France; both the English and

Flemings will repent it.'[12] The correspondent was recalling the occasion when Charles' father was driven by a storm to land on the English coast in 1506, kept a virtual prisoner by Henry VII, and forced to sign the treaty *Malus Intercursus*, the 'evil treaty' from his perspective, which favoured English trade rights at the expense of Burgundy.

Towards the end of February, Francis was growing concerned that Henry had not committed to the specific suggestions he had made about the location of the event. Bonnivet approached Wolsey again, intimating that Henry's responses were too general, and that the French king 'retains his great anxiety for the interview'. Wolsey also heard from Francis in person, who was 'heartily desiring the interview, which he trusts will lead to an indissoluble amity,' and he 'begged Wolsey to be as diligent as possible, as the time until May is short, and he must bring the Queen, who was with child.'[13] With Claude due to give birth that summer, correctly timing her comfort was essential on the French side. Francis asked again that 'the day and place must be fixed, so that nothing may remain to be done.' He wrote to his Grand Chamberlain, Oliver de la Vernade, Seigneur de la Bastie, who was then in England, about the 'inconvenience of lodging at Ardres, where, since it was burnt, there have been few houses rebuilt' and he proposed 'to take thither a large number of tents'. He asked de la Bastie to 'confer with the Cardinal about it, that no inconvenience may arise, and to write touching the form of the field, lists etc.'[14]

As Francis was awaiting a reply, Richard Wingfield departed for France, to replace Boleyn as ambassador. Wingfield had detailed instructions from Henry, particularly to 'remember the peace and amity' between England and France, and to explain that Henry 'could not be satisfied without sending one of his trusty and near familiars,' to 'declare his love and affection.' Henry sent specific words for his ambassador to repeat to Francis, that 'although their friendship is established with as many collateral securities as possible, the affection they bear to each other in their hearts was the chief means to knit the assured knot of perseverant amity betwixt them.'[15] Wingfield was also charged to flatter the French king, and reinforce the two kings' similarity:

> For, remembering the noble and excellent gifts, as well of nature, touching their goodly statures and activeness, and of grace, concerning their wondrous wisdoms and other princely virtues, as also of fortune, depending upon their substances and puissaunce given unto them by Almighty God, and wherein more conformity is betwixt them than in or amongst all other Christian princes... though this agreeable consonance of semblable properties and affections do vehemently excite and stir them both, not only to love and tenderly favour each other, but also personally to visit, see and speak together, whereby that thing... shall be brought to the very light, face to face, if it proceed; and finally make such impression of entire love in their hearts that the same shall be always permanent, and never be dissolved, to the pleasure of God, their both comforts, and the weal of all Christendom.[16]

Francis had been right to question the English commitment. Henry had been reluctant to reply, and he now provided Wingfield with an explanation of sorts; that he had initially not pressed for the meeting, 'because he was afraid of hindering Francis in the business he had in hand concerning the Empire' and 'thought it better to postpone it'. Henry tried to allay French fears that he had been put off the meeting 'at the insistence of the now Emperor elect' but though it would be more convenient for Francis to defer because 'most of his nobles were absent.'[17] In response, Wingfield was to thank Francis for his willingness to meet, and his instructions to Wolsey, and 'assure him that Henry is no less desirous of it than he, and no impediment shall be found on his part.' He was to ask for more 'ample instructions' regarding the 'time, place, number and company, with their apparel' that he might 'content' Henry and 'answer those who cast dangers and find difficulties in the same.'[18] It may have been genuine concern for the French king which had caused Henry to prevaricate through the spring, or perhaps he was waiting to see how his talks with Charles would progress, or had his own, personal reservations about the meeting at this stage.

Richard Wingfield's other charge was to present Francis with a sword as a gift from Henry. This sword was something of a puzzle, almost a trick or challenge, as Francis took it and thought it so heavy that it was 'not maniable'. He called upon Bonnivet to feel its weight, who said he had seen Henry wield a similar sword deftly, but that 'for such promise as he had made your highness (Henry), he might not disclose the manner how,' but that 'it was by means of a gauntlet.' Intrigued, Francis was keen to unlock the secrets of the sword, and asked Wingfield if Henry could send him such a gauntlet, offering in exchange, 'to make him a pair of cuirasses, such as he had not seen'.[19] Wingfield offered a number of suggestions about the practical arrangements for meeting, which Francis edited slightly, before they were sent back to England for approval and publication. By this means, the plans would become official, and the kings took a step closer to meeting.

Francis was not the only one to appreciate the firmer commitment. Queen Claude wrote to Henry offering her 'great affection', as did Louise of Savoy, who thanked him 'for his friendship and his wish for a continuance of the alliance'.[20] Admiral Bonnivet told Wolsey that he had 'received your letter by Wingfield, and am glad that he has been sent here, because we are old friends, and he is an honourable man.' He added that Boleyn was now returning home, 'having fulfilled his charge' and would communicate the 'good disposition' of Francis to Henry in person. 'Nothing,' he added, 'can be better than this for the peace and union of Christendom and the honour of the two kings.'[21]

Finally, the English committed to something substantial. On March 12, with just about ten weeks to go before the proposed meeting, Wolsey published the articles 'accepted and approved by the two kings'. The defining concerns appear to be trust and protocol:

1. The king of England shall come personally with the Queen and his sister Mary to the castle of Guisnes before the end of May; the French king, with the Queen and his mother, to the castle of Ardres, within four days after... The king of England to advance half a mile beyond the castle of Guisnes towards France, and to be met by the French king. The two kings to be on horseback, and meet in an open place, not dressed with any pavilions.

2. Next day the king of England to visit the queen of France, and dine with her privately. The king of France to visit the queen of England, and do the same.

3. Both princes to do some fair feat of arms between Guisnes and Ardres; the place to be apparelled, ditched and kept by an equal number of French and English. The kings and queens to visit each other familiarly.

4. When the king of England enters the territory of the French king he is to have the pre-eminence; and *vice versa*.

5. No person to be at the interview with a larger number of retainers than shall be written in letters of licence.

6. To promote the familiar intercourse of the two kings, two gentlemen with sufficient company of equal number to keep the ways and watches, to examine all suspected places, and drive away all suspected persons.[22]

By the end of March, Marshal of France, Gaspard de Coligny, Seigneur de Chatillon, was in Ardres, beginning the practical arrangements, and Wingfield wrote to Henry that 'a great search is made to bring to the meeting the fairest ladies that may be found.' He hoped that Catherine would select 'such in her band that the visage of England, which hath always been the prize', would not be lost.[23] In April, Henry asked for a further delay until the end of June, hoping to buy a little more time to accommodate the meeting he also hoped to hold with Charles. Wingfield confided to Wolsey his belief that a new ambassador was chosen by Margaret of Austria to go to England 'on purpose to prevent the meeting' but the ambassador was ill and had not yet departed. Francis replied that he could not comply, as 'the Queen's state of health will not allow of delay.'[24] He wrote, in hope, that he would be at Boulogne on 4 June, and would wait for Henry to arrive at Calais, after which they might meet for around 8-10 days. At this point, there were less than two months to go in which to complete all the necessary arrangements. Until almost the last minute, the Anglo-French meeting was a tenuous, fragile thing, a potentially beautiful dream of magnificence and unity, and European peace, but it was constantly undermined by practical and personal concerns, particularly by Henry, so that its fruition seemed uncertain.

9

PREPARATIONS

As the winter months crept towards spring, workmen began to arrive on the borders of the Calais Pale. By the end of March 1520, a team of English commissioners led by Charles, Earl of Worcester, were in Guisnes, checking the state of the castle, surveying the land and measuring out the dimensions of the structures that were to be erected. What they found was less than promising. The 1545 painting of the Field of the Cloth of Gold in the Royal Collection shows the town of Guisnes in the background on the left half of the canvas, with houses and a square, gates and the moated castle, out of which ordnance is being fired in welcome. A Portuguese plan of the town and castle made just four years before shows a similar layout, with the castle to the right, surrounded by huge walls, and the town to the left, oriented around a square and church. Six miles south of Calais, and surrounded by marshes, the town was depicted in the painting as being in sight of the sea, but in fact, it was more inland, at the edge of English territory, making the transportation of materials difficult. Much of the castle's structure in 1520 was then three hundred years old and in a considerable state of dilapidation. Henry's investigators quickly discovered that it was unfit for purpose, with the keep being so 'ruinous' that not even 200 masons could fix it all in time, so set about repairing parts, and establishing the location of a temporary palace in the vicinity.

With just two months to go, Henry's designers were ambitious in their planning. The building would go up on the green before the castle gate, in which the king, the queen and Wolsey were each to have three large chambers. Henry's were to be a great chamber 124 feet long, 42 feet wide and 30 feet high, which was 'longer and wider than the White Hall' in the Palace of Westminster; the second was a dining chamber of 80 feet long, by 34 wide and 27 high, which was 'larger than the greatest chamber in Bridewell', and the third was his bedchamber, measuring 60 by 34 by 27. The queen's three chambers were to be just as large, and there was to be a gallery linking hers to the king's lodgings, a waiting space, a chapel and two closets, but Wolsey was not to have such opulence, being lodged 'surely but not pleasantly'. No timber was available in Guisnes, though, so a man had been dispatched into Holland to source some, but the commissioners requested the dispatch of 250 carpenters, 100 joiners, thirty paired sawyers, forty plasterers and 1,000 'of wainscot, for here is none to buy,' and that Vertue, the king's master mason 'may also be sent with diligence with 150 bricklayers'.[1]

As the great pavilion at Guisnes began to rise from the ground, preparations were underway for the events it would host. A 'solemn banquet' was to be held in the great chamber for the entire French court, which task was charged to the officers of Henry's household, with the arrangement and furnishing of the palace overseen by Vaux, Sandys and Belknapp. A mummery was to be prepared by William Cornish for the entertainment, comprising fifty noblemen and women in five groups, with costumes provided by the royal wardrobe. The banquet would be served upon gold and silver plate supplied from the treasury by Wyatt, and any ordnance brought by Skevington. Part of the 'dilapidated' castle was transformed to allow Henry to sleep there, in 'secret lodgings' connected to the pavilion by a corridor.[2]

Chatillon was making parallel preparations in Ardres, whilst also keeping an eye on the English work. He offered to assist Worcester with workmen and timber, but by mid-April he feared that the scaffolding for the jousts would not all be complete by the appointed day. He would ensure that the Queen and her ladies took priority, he wrote to Wolsey, and the rest could be finished on the evening of the first meeting, if necessary. He was erecting pavilions on the jousting field, which would be 'small houses of wainscot, such as are used in princes' camps in time of war,' and promised that the English would not lack for horses or men, and that he had ordered 'wine, flesh and horsemeat' to be available.[3]

Chatillon may have been able to assist with supplies near Guisnes, but in English-held Calais, provisioning proved more difficult. A king had the right to demand that any producers or suppliers in the vicinity yield up whatever they were able to spare, from labour and materials, to corn and ale, fruit or livestock, although those deprived were often compensated at less than market value. This proved an initial problem for Sir John Peche, Marshal of Calais, who reported the situation to Wolsey on 18 April. The area had been 'sore destitute many years past', owing to a disease among the cattle, and what was good had been claimed already by the king's 'takers' in the area.[4] Thus, the Calais butchers had not had beef or mutton for three weeks, nor was there enough fuel to last a week. Provisioning the area was a serious large-scale operation, and Peche asked that the usual restrictions upon Calais shipping be lifted for the moment to remedy the deficiencies.

Lodgings were also required at Calais, the first stop after Henry and his entourage arrived safely across the Channel, and the last stop before their return home. Peche was charged to appoint them, placing Henry and Catherine at the Exchequer, the king's house in Calais usually known as the Chequer, but an additional large hall of 'slight timber' and two new chambers needed to be constructed, in which the king's attendants and the queen's ladies could rest and dance. For his chapel, it was planned that Henry would use Calais' St Nicholas' Church, and instructions were sent that all interior seats be removed and a gallery constructed between it and the king's lodgings. However, on his return to Calais at the end of the event, it appears that Henry favoured Our Lady of St Peter's. The Dean of St Paul's and ministers were to provide books, jewels, copes, hangings, altar cloths and vestments that the king owned. In the event of French royalty visiting Henry at Calais, Francis and Claude were to be lodged at the Staple House, which was to be prepared by Somerset with necessary furnishings, wine, provisions and servants.

Houses, businesses and other properties in the area were 'pressed' or requisitioned for the use of the royal party for the duration of the event, with the owners being recompensed later. Guisnes was a small village, and the locals had to endure the arrival of thousands of additional people, animals and baggage, suspending their daily lives, work and activities. Where existing facilities such as hearths, shelter and accommodation could be adapted for royal use, it saved on creating whole new buildings. The wool house of Mr Yerford was commandeered to serve as a pantry, and other wool houses became wet and dry larders, while the home of Cornelius Baker and Mary Thomas was taken for a bakehouse. Rooms in a house occupied by Nicholas Mychell, William Rice and William Mumbre became the offices of John Shurley the cofferer, John Micklowe and Thomas Byrks in the countinghouse. The properties of Margaret Goldsmith and Mychell Bynde were adapted for use as butcheries, and John van Standley opened his doors to the clerk of the kitchen.[5] In reality, these residents had little choice when it came to the king's command; just as he could appropriate their buildings and possessions at will, so he could with their goods, assets, time and livestock, even their manpower and their persons. This is what it meant to be a subject in the sixteenth century, whose very existence continued only at the king's will, and most gave gladly to their king, seeing it as an honour. Those whose space, time and labour were given during June 1520 were recompensed at the royal rate, although this was sometimes slightly lower, in practice, than the market value.

Warrants were issued to the English nobility whose attendance was required. These commanded them to wait upon the king with 'able and seemly persons, well and conveniently apparelled and horsed', and requested that each guest dress according to rank, 'as to his degree and honour belongeth'. Likewise, the head officers of Henry's household were warned by the council to attend on the King 'in their best manner, apparelled according to their estates and degrees'.[6] In England and France, sumptuary laws dictated the type, colour and nature of clothing that people might wear, according to social class, and to transgress was a serious breach of etiquette. These orders echoed instructions of 1519 that 'no man should wear Prince's apparel, in order that the king's estate might be above all as to his pre-eminence' and 'all nobles were to come apparelled as belonging to their decree.' Those in the king's guard were dressed by the royal wardrobe, each man issued with two coats, the first of scarlet and gold, with goldsmith's work and the King's device, the other to be red, with a rose and crown upon the breast. The men chosen were to be 200 of the 'tallest and most elect persons'.[7] General servants wore the Tudor livery of white and green.

Ships were also being prepared to transport the thousands of men, women, horses, dogs, supplies and chests of necessaries across the Channel. The task fell to Sir Edward Poynings, warden of the Cinque Ports, to provide sufficient vessels, including forty great hoys, small barges used for freight, and several named ships, including the *Mary Rose*, the *Great Barke*, the *Little Barke* and the *Katharine Pleasance*. The expenses for the *Katherine Pleasance* alone indicate what immense organisation and cost this process required.[8] On 22 May, a selection of the payments made for the preparation and provision of a single ship included:

John Tadder of Walberswick, for 17 chalder of coal, at 6s each.

Thomas Matoke and Champneys of Thames Street, £4 of iron at 10s a ton.

William Loveynge of Woolwich, 6 loads of stores at 18d

Robard Pope and Henry Comfort, for timber from 12d to 18d a load.

Richard Wyncham of Lewisham, for carriage of a load to Deptford, 13 miles, 2s.

Nicholas Ford, fishmonger of St Magnus, and Peter Swynbank of Petty Wales, brewer, for fish 26s 8d per 100, herrings, 5s 8d the barrel, pease for porridge, 12s and 15s the bushel, beer 6s 8d the pipe.

Charles Horton, baker of Deptford strand, 5 score dozen bread £5

Lord Bergavenny for timber from Hatfield and Woodham Par, 12d a load.

Carpenters' wages 6d a day.

To the keeper's wife for keeping the gates open at Hatfield, 6d.

John Cox, fellmonger, 36 dry loads of timber at 5s 8d.

John and William Hobard, for carrying 2 carts of timber to the sawpits, for 2 days 4s

Harry King of Beckham, for carrying timer from Chelsam, 2s a load, from Bromley Parish 1s 6d a load.

Wages of 11 carpenters hewing timber in Thundersley Par, paid at 4d and 6d a day, 33s 9d.

Carriage of 31 carts to Benfleet at 4d each.

Wages of 15 carpenters working on the ship, 2d to 8d a day.

William Harper of Harwich, 18 long oars at 18d.

John Austen, prior of Farley, 14 loads of timber at 16.

William Causten, for a piece of wood that was a forefoot and another for a stem piece, 16d the load.

John Royal, for making room to lay the keel, 3 days at 5d.

Thomas Weder of Hereth, for 750 overlapping boards at 4s the 100.

John Whitlock, 2 masts, and the laying of the postwyches to row at 57s 4d.

William Jonson, turner of Eastcheap, 2 dozen platters at 20s, a dozen drinking bowls at 6d, 2 2-gallon tankards 16d, 4 pails at 12d, 2 dozen saucers at 4d, 4 dozen dishes at 12d, 3 tankards at 12d, 2 ladles at 1d.

John Webster, of Peckham Rye, 2,000 tiles at 10s 2, 3 loads of lime at 3s, 3 loads of sand at 15d, 2,000 lath nails and pins, at 16d, for the stable that was broken to launch the ship, 117lb of spikes at 1 1/2d the lb, 1,000 tenpenny nails.

William Cardmaker, 24 st oakum at 6d, 240lb tallow at 9s the cwt, 17 bushels of salt at 6d.

Richard Painter of Barking Creek, for butter and mustard, from Easter to August 1519, 10s.

Goodwife Bingley, for lodging 6 carpenters in 2 beds for 14 weeks, 3d a week for each bed.

John Baker the younger, lodging 15 carpenters in 5 beds for 3 weeks, 3s 9d.

Goat's hair for the boat, 10d.

John Hopton 13s 4d for Spanish nails.

John Twill, for butter and oatmeal for porridge for the workmen, 19s, and 20 oxen £21 10s.

Huge amounts of provisions were required to feed the thousands of travellers. As well as seeking supplies locally, estimates had to be reached concerning the quantities of food and catering items to be shipped. For the consumption of the King and Queen in France those estimates allowed for £420 worth of wheat, £770 of wine, £27 of sweet wine, £560 of beer, £24 for Hippocras wine, £624 for 340 pieces of beef, £33 for four hogs, £6 for mutton, £200 for veal, £300 for salt and freshwater fish, £440 for spices, £1,300 for all kinds of poultry, £300 for table linen and cloths, £200 for wax, over £26 for white lights, £300 for pewter vessels, £200 for braising pans, turning spits and other essentials, £40 for rushes. Twenty cooks were to be hired at the fee of 20d a day, twelve pastillers at the same salary, twelve brewers and twelve bakers, both at a daily rate of 8d again. £130 was allowed for the transportation of necessary items back and forth between Calais and Guisnes 'from time to time'. Wolsey wrote to ask Peche whether flour was as cheap in Calais, or if he should have it packed in barrels and sent over, and asked whether at Mrs Baynam's house, beer was as cheap, good and plentiful as in England, whether wine was available, and as to the supply of mutton, veal, green geese, capons, chickens, rabbits, quails, storks and other dainties, as well as fuel and necessaries for the kitchen. Sir Richard Wingfield predicted that they could provide for an incredible 40,000 people, 'if need were.'[10]

On April 10, Sir Nicholas Vaux reported to Wolsey on the progress of the Pavilion at Guisnes. Henry, Catherine and Mary's lodgings were 'advanced' but they lacked timber and sawyers. Work on the chapel and banqueting house had been temporarily halted, as Richard Gibson, sergeant of the royal tents, who was to cover the canvas with roses, had not yet arrived. 'It is high time his works were in hand,' commented Vaux, with some frustration, 'for it must be painted on the outside' and John Rastell and Clement Urmeston were waiting to garnish it with gilt knots and batons.[11] A week later, he was more hopeful, thinking they would complete the square court by the end of May. Rastell, Urmeston and John Browne, the king's painter, were now working, creating large, stately roses, but required more money, and Vaux begged Wolsey to intervene so that 'the king be not disappointed of his roses'.[12] Charles Brandon's batons had been painted, and various of Henry's arms, and his heraldic beasts had been cast in moulds. He reported that Francis was making 'great preparations' for his 'triumph at Ardres', having taken four houses in the town and part of the Abbey, where he intended 'much of his pastimes shall be showed' according to the master of the works there.[13] Using timber from Rouen, they were setting up the tilt, lists, stages and barriers, similar to those Vaux had previously seen in Paris.

Francis' tents were being assembled in the city of Tours, around 350 miles away in the Loire, under the supervision of the Grand Maître de l'Artillerie, Galiot de Genouillac, a veteran general with a long career serving the French crown. Timber for the masts was sourced in the forests of Auvergne and Forze, and in order to complete the designs, one official travelled to Florence seven times to purchase fleur-de-lys cloth of gold. Once completed, the tents were transported to Ardres by 104 carters and 466 horses, where 200 men had prepared the ground in advance. In total, between 300 and 400 French tents were erected, bearing the arms of their owners, whether royalty, nobility or service tents.[14]

In the first week of May, four weeks before the event was due to begin, Richard Wingfield was taking delivery of horses for Henry. He had sourced seven 'goodly coursers', the 'most esteemed pieces that were in Italy' whose like was 'not to be found on the far side (of) the mountains'. The horses would be ready for the king two days after their arrival at Calais, 'for I never saw or heard horses to be so far led in such plight and courage.' Wingfield was also finalising arrangements for the tiltyard, which was to be limited to six courses, 'considering the number of challengers that may come, and that some will be so vainglorious as to wish to run as long as the day lasts.'[15] He anticipated that there would be over 200 participants on the French side alone, and arranged that challengers should present themselves to their opposing king, with English knights hanging their shields on the French platform and vice versa, in an attempt to make the numbers equal on each side.

Wingfield was in Paris on 7 May, awaiting Francis, whose arrival was expected that day. Claude and her ladies had already been in residence for two days before they joined the king to travel to Abbeville, anticipating reaching Montreuil or Boulogne by 20 May. Wingfield travelled with them and a week later they had reached Crevecoeur-le-Grand, about 100 miles north of Paris, halfway to Boulogne. While confirmation of Henry's departure still had not been received, the ambassador reassured Francis that the English king thought of their meeting every day, and had done so for the past year, 'at which Francis greatly rejoiced'. He replied that his desire to meet was 'no less strong', as Wingfield might see, 'considering the continual travel he caused the Queen here to take, being in the case that she is in', and that Henry 'would have no little compassion if he saw the poor creature with the charge she beareth'.[16] Francis intended to wait at Abbeville until he heard that Wolsey had arrived in Dover, after which he would head for Ardres. Wolsey, though, was unwell. Word reached Wingfield that the Cardinal was suffering from jaundice and colic and he, along with Francis, wrote to implore Wolsey to recover his strength before departing, but that a 'change of air would do him good' and that Francis had 'better physicians than could be found elsewhere'. Wingfield commented that the French king 'spoke with such affection'.[17] It appeared by his countenance and manner that Francis was clearly touched to hear of Wolsey's affliction.

By mid-May 1520, when there were only two weeks to go, preparations across the Channel were advancing, with around 15,000 men dispatched for Ardres in the French king's livery colours of black, white and tawny.[18] Worcester wrote that the ground had been marked out for the tiltyard, but he had discovered it was too far from the Queen's gallery to ensure a good view, and requested Henry's permission to move it closer, although this conflicted with the intention of Wolsey and Chatillon. On May 21, Nicholas Vaux, William Sandys and Edward Belknapp of Tournai, who were inspecting Guisnes Castle, co-authored a letter to Wolsey explaining the large costs resulting from their work so far: 'The expense has been great, owing to the distance the stuff had to be carried, and the shortness of the time, but when finished, Wolsey will think it well bestowed.'[19] The material for the roofs had not yet been sent out, nor had the man to gild them, and they feared the project would not be completed before the king's arrival. With only ten days to go until Henry crossed the Channel, questions were being raised about the number of additional buildings added to the original plans. These included his houses of office, stables, the armoury and the camp, 'which will amount to a great charge'. Chatillon was concerned that the ditch and paling in the tiltyard would not be ready in time. Payments were made for the provision and delivery of lime, to the King's painters, the glaziers, for glass and timber, and for 'canvas for the dragon'. 4,000 feet of glass were bought at St Omer by John Tybott, and a further 1,000 feet from a glazier named Cornelius Maste, with Henry's own glazier, named Galyon, being paid £20 for setting up the glass.[20]

In spite of this state of unreadiness, Henry and Catherine left Greenwich for Dover on 21 May. Four days later, at Montreuil, Francis assembled his court after dinner and announced that he had been informed of Henry's departure, and that he 'trusted the meeting would take place shortly'.[21] While Henry was waiting in Kent to welcome Emperor Charles, whose ships were crossing the Channel, Francis announced that he intended to entertain Henry as 'the prince of the world whom he esteemed, loved and trusted most,' urging his nobility to receive the English 'in a friendly manner and avoid bringing any evil advised persons to the meeting'.[22] The following day, Francis issued a proclamation, which was to be posted at all thoroughfares and public places: all vagabonds were to leave the area within six hours of the posting of the notice, on pain of hanging, no one was to attend without a ticket signed by their master, no gentlemen or officers were to transgress rules of clothing, and the assembly were to pay respect to the English.

The royal wardrobe department in England was in a frenzy of activity through the spring months of 1520, preparing to equip Henry, Catherine, Mary, their court and retinues. Receipts for April and May give an idea of the nature and opulence of the queen's clothing: a Louis Harpsifield was paid almost £150 for providing her with two pieces of white satin more than eighty-six yards long, fifty-eight yards of green velvet, seventy-three yards of green Bruges satin, yellow and russet velvet, black velvet, crimson velvet and green cloth of gold. Barker 'of Chepe' (Cheapside, London) supplied the Queen with more white satin and his neighbour, Barton 'of Chepe' sold her black sarcenet and green and russet velvet. An agent named George Bryggus purchased 14s 4d worth of crimson velvet for her from 'Colier of Chepe', who also received an order for yellow damask from the Lord Chamberlain for the Queen's use. A John Norris in Friday Street supplied linen cloth, Master Smith of Watling Street gave red kersey, and broad grey cloth was bought from an unspecified vendor at Blackwell Hall.[23]

New bedding was also bought for Catherine, as her own bed would have been dismantled and transported to Guisnes. Over seventy-seven yards of blue sarcenet was purchased to make bed curtains, and the mercer William Lock had supplied cloth of silver for scutcheons and arms, red stain and yellow damask, for lining her chairs, and violet satin for lining a gold valance. The Queen's retinue were well catered for, with payments made for their coats and doublets in the Tudor colours of white and green, for an embroiderer named Ebgrave to sew the motif of feathers onto their doublets and for crimson velvet to line their cloaks. Milan bonnets were bought for them from Gerard the capper, at 6s each; the account includes bucklers, swords, shirts and points, as well as orange-coloured boots at 4s 3d a pair, spurs at 6d a pair, coifs of gold for the Queen's ladies at 10s each, while eighteen shirts cost 8s each to be made. The footmen received scarlet cloaks, grooms were to wear green satin from Bruges and the men carrying Catherine's litter were to be dressed in black and yellow, velvet and satin. Sir Andrew Windsor, master of the Great Wardrobe, was paid for 'preparing stuff for the King', £746. 3s. 8d and Robert Amadas, the royal goldsmith received for mending and making 'gold stuff' £414.[24]

The final payments were signed off at Greenwich on 20 May and at Canterbury a week later, while Henry was entertaining the Emperor. The last-minute expenses included £66 13s 4d for the recruitment of a hundred carpenters, fifty glaziers, twenty-four painters, six lead foulders and six of tin, to complete the pavilion at Guisnes, £971 to Pieter Van Halft for Arras tapestries, and £1,475 to Richard Gresham for sables and velvets, while Clement Armeson and Henry Saddler were paid £366 13s 4d for making buttons and other garnishings to decorate the pavilion. John Hopton was paid £100 for rigging ships and Sir William Fitzwilliam was compensated to the tune of £259 for provisioning five ships to transport the king to Calais.[25] All that remained was for Henry and his court to embark from Dover, and for Francis to ride north to meet them. But, before they did, Henry had a detour to make, and another king to meet.

THE EMPEROR

What, potentially, had been at stake. 'Allegory on the Abdication of Emperor Charles V in Brussels' by Frans Francken (II). In 1555 the ailing Emperor would divide his vast empire – represented by the four figures in the right foreground who personify the four continents – between his brother Ferdinand and his son Philip. (Courtesy Rijksmuseum)

10

CHARLES V

The Holy Roman Emperor, Charles V, did not attend the Field of the Cloth of Gold. He was the spectre at the feast, the third man, the other member of the triumvirate of European rulers whose rivalries prompted the event. While the French made their final preparations at the end of May, Charles was meeting Henry and Catherine in Kent, and as the gold tents were being dismantled a month later, the English met the Emperor near Gravelines. Initially it appeared that Henry and Charles colluded to undermine the burgeoning Anglo-French friendship in a complex game of duplicity and national interest, but Henry's intentions may have been more honourable in the pursuit of European peace.

Charles was born in 1500, the eldest son of Philip of Burgundy of the Austrian Hapsburgs, and Joanna of Castile, making him nephew to Catherine of Aragon, Queen of England, who favoured him over the French. After the death of his father in 1506, and the incarceration of his mother Joanna on the grounds of poor mental health, Charles was brought up by his aunt, Margaret of Savoy, at her palace in Malines, (or Mechelen) in the Netherlands. The newly renovated Hof van Savoye, where Charles lived, was a dazzling mix of patterned red brick, tall, narrow stepped gable-ends, long windows and shorter dormer ones topped with gables, archways and steps, sloping roofs, colonnaded walks and flower beds.

Since childhood, Charles' long-standing engagement to Mary Tudor had guaranteed good relations between England and the Hapsburgs, but Henry's abrupt volte face in 1514 had changed the European dynamic. Upon the death of his maternal grandfather in 1516, Charles inherited the throne of Spain, and title of 'the Most Catholic King,' but was forced to respect the French victory in Milan as part of the long conflict of the Italian wars. His election as Emperor three years later brought him greater power and territories, so that Francis now found himself surrounded and the rivalry, and conflict, between them intensified.

Charles' aunt Margaret of Austria, Princess of Asturias and Duchess of Savoy, was one of the most powerful and influential women in Europe. Having been widowed three times, she became Governor of the Netherlands upon the death of her brother, Philip, and guardian of his son, Charles. She hosted the English party in 1513, and after the success of Thomas Boleyn's embassies, offered a place to his daughter Anne at her finishing school. Margaret was independent, powerful and cultured. According to Jean Lamaire, her court historian, she was 'skilled in vocal and instrumental music, ...in painting and in rhetoric' and 'in the French as well as Spanish language'. A contemporary described Margaret's appearance as 'truly imperial and her smile full of charm'[1] while Castiglione referred to her as one of the 'noblest' examples of contemporary womanhood, who governs her state 'with the greatest wisdom and justice'.[2] Jean Molinet, her almoner and librarian, praised her splendour, virtue, honour, goodness and renown, her stoicism after having lost three husbands, and the universal love in which she was held.

No friend of the French, Margaret corresponded with Henry and his ministers throughout 1519 and 1520, on behalf of her nephew. Immediately after the end of the Field of the Cloth of Gold, she accompanied Charles to meet Henry at Gravelines, bringing Charles' younger brother Ferdinand, who was then a youth of seventeen. Despite his age, Ferdinand had recently commanded his brother's fleet and Charles would appoint him to rule Austria from 1521. A portrait of him a decade after the Field of the Cloth of Gold, by Jan Cornelisz Vermeyen, shows Ferdinand to be similar in features to his brother, with large, hooded eyes, aquiline nose, thick lips and prominent chin.

A handful of individuals from the Imperial court are prominent in the ambassadorial letters of 1519-20. William de Croy, Lord of Chièvres, had formerly served Philip the Handsome and following his death became regent and governor to the young Charles. In 1509, he also became the boy's tutor, his Grand Chamberlain in 1515 and closest advisor. Chièvres was an unpopular figure though, gaining too much influence over Charles, leading him to reopen the Italian wars in 1521, the same year Chièvres was murdered by poisoning. He was replaced by Mercurino de Gattinara, a former legal advisor who Margaret considered her chief councillor and chancellor to Charles. Gattinara followed a Christian humanist vision of Empire, along dynastic lines, to establish global rule against the Turks and Lutheranism. The Emperor's chief secretary and ambassador was Jean de la Sauche, was first dispatched to England in July 1517, to request a loan of 100,000 gold florins for Charles. He was clearly influential, as in February 1518, it was the opinion of Sir John Stile that Charles was 'ruled entirely' by Chièvres, Gattinara and de la Sauche. That summer, the secretary was issued with instructions for a new mission to England, which included the belief that 'Francis only wishes to dissolve the friendship between him and England, as he has so often tried to do.' He was also able to claim that he had been in Chièvres' service for thirty years.

Also in Charles' household was his secretary, Philippe Haneton. In the same year as the Field of the Cloth of Gold, he commissioned the Haneton tryptich from Bernard Van Orley, depicting his mother and five sisters. Van Orley had been appointed court painter to Margaret in 1518, and painted Charles' portrait in 1519, with the full, protruding Hapsburg jaw, aquiline nose and thick lips. When instructions were issued in February 1520 for the Emperor's visit to England in May, the commission included Haneton as

Audiencer and Jean de la Sauche as Secretary, as well as Gerard de Plaine, Master of Requests, and Bernard de Mesa, Bishop of Elna, who had first been sent out to by Ferdinand in 1514.

Charles was concerned to hear that his ally and uncle-in-law Henry VIII was planning to meet his great rival Francis. Polydore Vergil believed the Emperor foresaw it would 'work to his great disadvantage' and 'decided that it should by all means be obstructed', although Vergil's account was written retrospectively. Through the influence of letters and ambassadors, Charles sought to influence Henry by drawing on English francophobia. He warned Henry that his subjects would be seeing 'Frenchmen at home' and have to 'converse, eat and drink with men they had always disliked, because nature brings about that we love those who love us and shun those who hate us.' He advised that it was not safe to make an enemy such as Francis a 'partner in his plans' and that the meeting could 'in no way profit him,' and would only 'create suspicion with his most loyal friends'. Vergil says that many English subjects agreed with Charles' view, as Catherine clearly did, but that the meeting was the pet project of the 'boastful beggar' Wolsey, who desired to display his 'peacock's tail'.[3] However, Henry informed Charles that he could not alter plans that had already been made, so the Emperor, who was then in Spain, brought forward his departure to the Netherlands, in order to meet Henry before Francis did.

At the end of March, Margaret of Savoy stepped in to negotiate a meeting between Charles and Henry, making three points, each of which made resentful reference to the Anglo-French arrangement:

1. If the king of the Romans, on returning from Spain, wishes to land in England before the king of England cross to France, be it in May, June, or July, he shall land at Sandwich, or some other place convenient, as shall be agreed upon, where the interview shall take place.

2. If he cannot come before Henry has left, but has passed into Flanders, he will hold the interview in such place and time as shall hereafter be agreed upon.

3. If the king of England insist that after his interview with the French and return to England the king of the Romans shall land in England on his return to Spain, the ambassadors shall demur to it by all fair means, and not agree to it until they know Charles's pleasure.[4]

Until the last minute, it was still uncertain whether arrangements for the Field of the Cloth of Gold would proceed. Charles' renewed friendship with Henry even led him to hope that the whole venture might be cancelled. As late as 7 April 1520 de la Sauche was writing to Chièvres about what he hoped to achieve when he met with Henry. First, he aimed for 'the breaking off of the French interview', which was 'very unpopular with all the nobility and people of England', but he understood it would be very difficult 'seeing how much Wolsey is set upon it'. If it did go ahead, he hoped to influence Henry so that the friendship with France might 'grow cold' and that 'little love should come of it.' For these reasons, he hoped that a meeting between Charles and Henry could be scheduled before the English crossed the Channel, and feared that failure would mean 'to lose everything, and make (Henry) entirely devoted to France, which would be very awkward, considering that they do not know what terms they are on with the Pope.' De la Sauche anticipated that Wolsey might propose a three-way meeting between the powers, and suggested in a Machiavelli-like stroke that they give polite response but commit to nothing: 'When we deal with men, we give good words, and promise wonders, but having attained our object, there is an end of it.'[5]

Four days later, on 11 April 1520, a treaty for the meeting of Henry and Charles was completed between Bernard de Mesa, Gerard de Pleine, Philippe Haneton and Jean de la Sauche, on behalf of the Emperor and Thomas Ruthall, Bishop of Durham, Cuthbert Tunstall, Master of the Rolls, Richard Pace, chief secretary and Sir Thomas More, on behalf of the English king. It was agreed that, in May, 'unless prevented by weather or other reasonable hindrance',[6] Charles would land in Sandwich on the

Kent coast and proceed to Canterbury, where he would meet Henry and Catherine and visit the relics of St Thomas Becket, as that year marked the 350th anniversary of his martyrdom. The day of his arrival was fixed for 15 May. If he was delayed, they could still meet in Calais at the end of July. Catherine was also keen to meet her nephew, and influenced Henry to ensure the meeting took place. On 30 April Charles wrote to thank her 'for what she has done to promote his interview... the arrangements for which (had) given him the greatest satisfaction'. He 'trusted to see her at the time appointed' but if any delays occurred, hoped 'that she will get the king to wait for him, as she had given him hopes that he will do.'[7]

An embarrassing moment arose when Chatillon and Worcester met to discuss progress on the Guisnes and Ardres sites at the end of April. The Earl was taken aside by de la Bastie, who expressed a desire 'for the love he beareth to the king's grace, to tell him one thing, which he feared might be an obstacle to the interview.' De la Bastie swore 'as he was a true gentleman' that he was not commissioned to mention it, but that it was 'noised through all Flanders'[8] that Henry's meeting with Charles was contrary to a promise made to Francis by Wolsey in the king's name. Uncomfortable, Worcester replied that he was unaware of any promise made by Wolsey, but as he reported to Henry, Chastillon called upon him every day, and so he desired to know the king's mind on the matter. A short while later, Vaux commented that the French commissioners were now working better than they had been, but that they 'seemed doubtful of their master's coming'.[9] Henry pressed on regardless, determined to meet both Francis and Charles, and keep hold of the reins of European diplomacy. Whether or not Wolsey had made such a promise, by Henry's command or on his own initiative, is not recorded. It did not impede arrangements, though, which pressed ahead.

Wolsey's agent at the Imperial court was Thomas Spinelly, a Florentine by birth, who had been conducting English business in the Netherlands since at least 1510. On May 3, he wrote to

Wolsey that Charles was ready to sail for England, but the tides were against him, blowing in a North-Easterly direction, in spite of 'the opposition of the moon' and 'to the great displeasure of all the company'. With an awareness of the impending Anglo-French meeting, Spinelly was concerned that their inability to cross the Channel might be misconstrued. They did 'not desire the king to break his promise of meeting with Francis, but to delay it until they come',[10] but this still would have necessitated Henry making a choice, and prioritising the Emperor over the French king. By 4 May, the Imperial secretary, Jean de la Sauche, had imparted news of Henry's readiness and Charles himself wrote to reassure him that he was only waiting for the right tide:

Has been waiting in this port for three weeks, the ships being all ready; but the wind remains contrary, and prevents him either crossing himself, or sending back De la Sauch in the usual bark... to give Henry warning of his departure. Sends this post by land, that Henry may know what detains them, and will come as soon as the wind changes.[11]

When writing similar news to Wolsey, though, Charles was more explicit. He hoped 'the proposed interview may take place, that no advantage be given to those who wish to malign it.'[12] This must have reassured Henry, as on 8 May, he ratified the treaty for a meeting between him and Charles, which had been made in April. It was signed again by the same men as before: Ruthall, Tunstall, Pace and More on the English side, and de Mesa, Haneton, de la Sauche, de Pleine, for Charles.

Henry had requested that notification of his forthcoming meeting with Francis be posted in various locations across Europe, to allow for the attendance of ambassadors, guests and potential jousters at the tournament. He now heard, though, that Margaret of Savoy had not yet carried out his request and suspected her of attempting to frustrate his wishes. Coupled with Charles' excuses about the tides, when de la Sauche had been able to cross the

Channel successfully at some point between 4 and 8 May, English suspicions were fuelled. Word reached Margaret and she wrote to reassure Henry on 12 May:

> Has heard from Norris, king at arms, and from Guillaume des Barres, Charles's secretary, that Henry is displeased at the delay in the publication of the chapters for the jousts at the approaching interview with the king of France, which were brought hither by Norris, and that he is not satisfied with her excuses. Has now, notwithstanding her reasons against the publication, had them published as solemnly and honourably as possible.[13]

The following day, Charles gave instructions to his ambassadors, realising that the proposed meeting date of 15 May was now impossible: 'The king of England means to keep his promise to France and be at Guisnes on the 31 May, but will wait for the Emperor as late as the 26th... so that if the wind be not be propitious within six days, there is no chance of the interview taking place this month.' His messengers, he wrote, 'must be empowered to tell the King (Henry) that the Emperor is quite confident he will not treat with France to his prejudice, but keep himself open to treat with him for the common good.' They were also to try and persuade Wolsey 'not to trust the French but accept the Emperor's offer'.[14] He was also sending letters in Castilian, to Catherine of Aragon, written in his own hand, 'expressing regret at not being able to fulfil his engagement'.[15] Special instructions were issued to de Mesa 'to find out what practices take place between France and England.'[16]

Margaret wrote to Henry and Wolsey again on 16 May, dispatching her Maître d'Hotel, Jean de Hesdin, with letters. Presumably he crossed the Channel by a different route, or on a smaller vessel which was more easily handled, or was prepared to take a greater risk than the full Imperial fleet, which was still in harbour. Again, she asked Henry to postpone his meeting with Francis, because of Charles' 'great desire' to see him, and hoped Henry would 'consider the inestimable advantages which would result from an interview.'[17] She was even more direct in her communication to Wolsey, knowing his pro-French tendencies, openly begging him to wait for Charles.

On 21 May, Henry, Catherine and Mary, Duchess of Suffolk, left Greenwich for Canterbury. The city was prepared in their honour, with the streets cleaned and sanded, the civic officials decked out in new gabardines (cloaks), and the keys to the city's Westgate being tied with a new ribbon, in advance of being presented to Charles. The royal pair were cutting it very fine, with Henry and Catherine due to be in France on the last day of the month, but terrible conditions in the North Sea still kept the imperial ships in harbour on the coast of Flanders. On May 26, the weather finally allowed Charles to sail and his fleet appeared not at Sandwich but near Hythe, from where they were conducted safely around the coast to Dover by England's Vice Admiral, Sir William Fitzwilliam, 'with six of the king's shippes well furnished'.[18] Wolsey was already waiting there to greet Charles, and Henry followed swiftly on the heels of his chancellor, meeting the Emperor on the castle stairs. Charles embraced him 'lovingly' and the pair withdrew gladly into the chamber to talk 'under the cloth of his estate of the black eagle all splayed on rich cloth of gold'.[19]

Catherine's meeting with her nephew had to wait until the next morning. She remained as a guest of William Warham in the Archbishop's Palace at Canterbury, with its fine wooden panelling, marble pillars, gardens and library, of which only an arched doorway remains. On 27 May, Henry and Charles arrived in the city and attended Mass in the Cathedral, to celebrate the feast of Pentecost, before processing along a purple carpet into the Palace, where they were greeted by twenty-five of the 'handsomest and best apparelled' court ladies and twenty of Catherine's pages dressed in 'gold brocade and crimson satin in chequers'. It was Charles' intent 'specially to see queen of England, his aunt', and Catherine was waiting for them at the top of a flight of fifteen marble steps and wept as she greeted her nephew.[20] She would have seen a tall, thin young man, physically awkward with a pronounced lower jaw, his face long and narrow, with an aquiline nose and big lips. In 1520, though, he was only twenty, more like the image painted the year before by Bernard von Orley, Although his jaw and lips are thick, almost to the point of deformity, his face is clear and open, his chin cleft, his blue eyes narrowed in focus, and his brown hair cut in the fashionable bell of the time. He wears a wide brimmed black hat adorned by a gold medallion in a surround of pearls and the chain of the Order of the Golden Fleece hangs across his fur-adorned shoulders. Other contemporary portraits of Charles are less flattering, with one anonymous Flemish picture showing him open mouthed, with a more rounded nose and chin, while another makes his jaw appear almost dislocated.

After their initial greetings, Catherine changed into a dress of cloth of gold lined with violet velvet, a headdress of black and gold, decorated with jewels, and a string of pearls about her neck, in the centre of which hung a large diamond. Charles also had the opportunity to meet Princess Mary, who, but for the quirks of diplomacy six years before, might have been his Empress. The Elizabethan chronicler Raphael Holinshed adds 'peradventure the sight of the Lady Mary troubled him, whome he had sometime loved, and yet through fortunes evill hap might not have her to wife.'[21] Charles would have been aware that the 'evill hap' was more down to Henry than fortune, but their renewed friendship made that a thing of the past.

Vergil, with his open dislike of Wolsey, describes how Charles used all the 'care, effort and counsel he could muster,' leaving 'nothing undone' which might 'separate the English from the French.' He had learned, according to Vergil, that the Cardinal 'could be caught by a preferment like a fish by a baited hook' so he 'bent all his strength to entice, ensnare and capture him by promising honours, by promising rewards, by giving presents for the moment,' and experienced a degree of success, claiming Wolsey's 'corrupt mind' and desire for rewards made him promise to attempt to detach

Henry from Francis. Vergil adds that Wolsey 'asked Charles to do nothing to discredit the conference' as he so burned with desire... to flaunt his loftiness' in France.[22] This interpretation, written in the aftermath of Wolsey's death, appears to assign Charles with far greater influence over the Field of the Cloth of Gold than he really had. The contemporary correspondence reveals that Henry was the prize over which Francis and Charles were fighting, with Francis outwardly optimistic and privately doubtful, and Charles almost pleading with Henry to meet and trying to persuade him to favour the Empire over the French.

A letter from an anonymous individual at the French court attempted to play down the meeting of Henry and Charles, for the consumption of the suspicious Francis. The secretary of the Venetian ambassador, likely to have been Antonio Giustinian, brother of Sebastian Giustinian, ambassador to England, had reputedly 'gone to see England, and chanced to be there at the time of the Emperor's arrival.' This appears to have been deliberately timed, as the secretary had 'ridden from Canterbury to Dover to catch a glimpse of his Imperial Majesty' and reported with the expected bias, that Charles' court was 'very mean and insignificant,' so much so that he 'passed him on the road without recognition, such being the splendour and amount of his retinue!'[23] He reported that Henry was a 'handsome a jovial man,' as was his court, but the star of the show was Wolsey, who was accompanied by 200 gentlemen clad in crimson velvet and wearing massive gold chains, and a body-guard of 200 archers. Dressed from head to foot in crimson satin, on a mule trapped with gold, Wolsey 'was the proudest prelate that ever breathed.'[24]

Mingled with the final costs for the Field of the Cloth of Gold, are the details of Charles' brief stay in Canterbury. Henry and the Emperor made offerings of 20s each at the high altar at Christ Church Abbey upon Charles' arrival, again at High Mass, and upon the three days that followed, between 28 and 30 May. A Mr Knolls was rewarded with £6 11s for building a partition in the hall of the Archbishop's Palace for the banquet, and the heralds were given £100 in largess. Henry also gave large tips to Charles' Chancellor, Chamberlain, Master of the Horse and secretaries. Fresh horses were procured from Sir John Cutt, to take Charles back to his ships, at a cost of £20.[25]

Catherine's travel arrangements are also recorded in detail for the month, with a Roger Brown being paid 20s for taking the stuff of the guard from London to Canterbury, and a man named Parker received 53s 4d for painting the 'close car.' More of her henchmen's 'stuff' travelled by barge to Gravesend at a cost of 5s, then on to Canterbury by road at 2d per mile, for twenty-six miles. Her clothes and linen were likely to have been transported in the five spruce chests with hanging locks which cost 32s 8d and her tailor Thomas Kelevytt made garments for the Queen's use at a price of £28 3s 4d. Some of Catherine's items were washed at Dover before she embarked for France, which cost 16d, and the carrying of the same items from the ship to her lodgings in Calais cost 14d.[26]

After four days of festivities, on May 31, Charles bade farewell to his hosts and departed for Sandwich, from where he sailed to Flanders. That same day, Henry and Catherine headed for Dover, where they boarded ship for Calais, arriving at eleven o'clock that night. A partner painting to the 1545 image of the event itself shows Henry embarking for France in a ship with golden sails, and the castle on the clifftops behind. The fleet, whose vast number is suggested by more craft in the background, is saluted by guns from two towers on the coast as they head for choppy waters. What followed would be magnificence on an unprecedented scale, known to history as The Field of the Cloth of Gold.

THE FIELD OF THE
CLOTH OF GOLD

Henry's arrival.

II

THE ENCAMPMENTS

By the end of May 1520, the area between Guisnes and Ardres had been transformed. It was a colourful, busy simulacra of Tudor majesty, designed to impress, to inspire, even to awe. As the French and English royal parties travelled ever closer, the paint was drying on the golden tents, on roses and dragons, on tiltyard rails and galleries, wood was being chopped, ovens stoked, beds assembled, kitchens stocked, instruments unpacked, horses grazed and plates stacked. Nobody living within a radius of at least twenty miles could have been in any doubt that something very important was about to happen. Locals relinquished their homes and businesses, traders were divested of their goods, the roads were active with carts dragging timber and vast rolls of canvas, and beggars were sent away.

The location of the valley where the kings met has been identified as the village of Balinghem, lying midway between Guisnes and Ardres, around 3km from each, and bisected by the present Rue du Camp du Drap d'Or. The sides of the valley were carefully levelled in 1520, taking protocol to the extreme, to ensure that neither the English or French were elevated above the other. The actual spot where Henry and Francis were to come face to face had been determined by Richard Gibson, with four green and white flags, but reputedly, Chatillon disapproved and removed them.

The subsequent dispute between them had to be mediated by Bonnivet. The site is marked today by a granite block along the modern D231, ten miles south of Calais. Typical of the area, which is one that was also decimated by First World War shelling, the fields stretch away on either side of the road, vast, long and very flat. Five hundred years ago, it was shimmering with colour and activity.

One witness to the preparations made in the area was a foreign resident of the French court, Gioan Joachino, secretary to Octavian Fregoso, Governor of Genoa, who wrote to his master with a number of descriptions. Ardres, he explained, was an 'open village' about the size of Urbino, which the English had burned in their campaign of 1513, while Guisnes was 'larger and stronger'. The lists were to be between them, Joachino explained, within the English Pale, 'where they have selected a large plain, 400 paces in length and 200 paces in breadth', around which a ditch had been dug, and its earth used to form a 'bank or bulwark nine feet high enclosing the Field, as they call it'. There were two entrances, one at each end, and between them, the lists for jousting were 150 paces in length, and stages had been erected on either side. Around 220 men at arms in total were intending to joust, he wrote, and were 'in excellent condition'.[1]

On 1 June, the summer sunlight exposed the extent of the temporary village built at Guisnes, radiant in its gold leaf and bright colours. Standing on the field outside the Castle was Henry's pavilion, 'the most noble and royal lodgings before seen'.[2] The contemporary chronicler Edward Hall, who was then a law student at Gray's Inn, relates that it was a palace comprised of quadrants, the side of each being 328 feet long, and the whole creation 'set on stages by great cunning and sumptuous work'. Its dimensions were huge, with the great chamber alone being 'six score and four (124) foot in length, 42 foot in breadth, and 30 foot high, which is longer and wider than the White Hall (of Westminster); the second chamber to dine in, to be in length four score foot, in wideness 34, and in high 27 foot, which is larger than the greatest chamber in Bridewell; and the third chamber to withdraw his highness in shall be in length 60 foot, in wideness 34, and in height 27 foot.'[3]

The pavilion's foundations were made of stone, the walls built of brick and the rest wood, covered with cloth painted to look like more brick. Huge first floor windows, with many panels, stretched right up to the crenellation that marked the roof line. In the 1545 painting, the dark, rectangular roof of painted oil cloth appears open in the centre above the inner courtyard, set with small casement windows, plain chimneys and heraldic beasts bearing flags. Even the French and Italians enthused about it, with French chronicler Florange describing 'half the house' being made of glass and the Mantuan ambassador, Soardino, saying it had a clarity, as if it were on display' and particularly praised the 'very large diamond-shaped panes of very white glass'.[4] It was likened to a palace in Ariosto's *Orlando Furioso* and one Italian commented that da Vinci could not have done better.[5] Venetian visitor Paulo Camillo Trivulzio described it as 'one of the handsomest and costliest ever and so well adorned... as to appear a miracle, and the French hold it in great account.'[6] A Count Alexandro Donado, who saw the building in person, estimated that it covered four square acres and that the gates outside bore the figures of the God of Love and 'Carita,' perhaps a goddess of hospitality, and Bacchus outside.[7]

On the little green in front of the palace entrance stood two fountains, one a pillar wreathed about in gold, topped by a golden figure of cupid, with his bow and arrows ready to 'strike the young people for love'. The other fountain was covered with gilt and 'fine gold' and decorated with 'antique' works, a popular renaissance nod to the classical world, multi-faceted and crenellated like a little castle, it poured out red and white wine from the open mouths of lions affixed to the sides. Over the top, the message 'faicte bonne chere quy vouldra'[8] (make good cheer whoever wishes) was written in gold. This fountain was recreated in the Base Court of Hampton Court in 2010, based upon Hall's description and the 1545 painting in the Royal Collection, where it still stands, along with some of the recreated figures from the work.

Entrance to the pavilion was through a tall arched gateway, with red pillars on each side, with battlements across the top. Along the roofline, on top of the pillars, were figures depicting men of war, ready to cast down great defensive stones. Above the gate sat ancient princes and warriors such as Hercules, Alexander and others, richly painted in gold and the English colours. The 1545 painting also shows the space above the arch being painted with two Tudor roses, garlands, the English arms and topped with a scallop-shaped decoration. A porter in royal livery stood guard at the lodge within the gate. Passing through, visitors found themselves in a beautiful courtyard filled with glazed windows and clerestories, decorated with gold and resin figures, the outward parts 'illuminating' the eye of the beholder with 'sumptuous works'. Statues in silver armour with 'sore and terrible countenances' guarded the way between the doors to the many palace chambers.[9]

Temporary as it was, and swiftly built, Henry's pavilion had two complete storeys. On the ground floor were offices, a cellar and some of the kitchen departments. A list surviving in the Rutland Papers, a nineteenth-century collection of various documents, includes a privy pantry and hall pantry, privy cellar and hall cellar, privy and hall butteries, pitcher house for plates and pots, a room for silver scullery plates, a spicery, a ewry and confectionary divided by a partition, scullery, saucery, wardrobe for the beds, chandry, jewel house and a room for John Shurley, the cofferer, and clerks of the green cloth.[10] According to Soardino, the cellar contained 'some 3,000 butts of the choicest wines in the world… malmsies and other wines, the best that could be found in Flanders and France', and all visitors were 'compelled both to eat and drink,' and 'never was such abundance witnessed as in this house.'[11] There was also a banqueting hall, or two in some accounts, both containing five or six cupboards, which were used less for storage than display, 'all full of vases and flasks of gold, and sundry other golden vessels, forming the most stupendous sight in the world'.[12] Soardino paints a lively picture of the banqueting hall in use, during one of the visits of the French royal party:

In the long hall were prepared two large cupboards of silver-gilt vases, constantly used by persons drinking; and the Englishwomen never gave those bowls and flasks any rest. Then when the most Christian King banqueted there, the eating and drinking witnessed were incredible, and the odour of the viands very noisome; and on those occasions there was an additional and marvellous display of costly and beautiful plate... As usual in England, the wooden floors of the hall and chambers were strewed with rushes, so that the planks could not be seen.[13]

Count Alexandro Donado noted that the great staircase led to a first floor hall 'as lofty as that of the Pesaro Palace at San Benetto' in Venice but longer, with a ceiling of 'green sarcenet and gold roses, decorated with hangings of silk and gold, woven with figures and horses represented to the life'. The hall occupied one quarter of the building, 'the rest being divided into sundry corridors, chambers and closets, with ceilings of cloths of gold and silk, and the appearance of being in the open air'. These chambers were large and airy, also decorated in silk, with more burnished gold and roses, upon the walls and ceiling, being 'engrailed' and made into baton shapes with cloth of silk, and fret with cuts and braids. Others were hung with tapestry of gold and silver cloth, interlaced with the Tudor colours of white and green silk and the grounds were strewn with rushes. Each was so furnished that 'no living creature might but joy in the beholding thereof.'[14] Crests, royal arms, antique knots and gold bosses decorated the walls, from which hung tapestries from floor to ceiling.

In the ceremonial rooms, gold embroidered cloths of estate hung above chairs covered in gold cloth and set with tapestry cushions. Mary, former Queen of France, had two chambers in the pavilion, which she shared with her husband, Charles Brandon. The first was decorated with tapestries of gold and silk, the second with crimson velvet and gold tissue, where her bed was hung with gold brocade, still embroidered with the porcupine device of Louis XII, and the initials M and L, with gold love knots. Wolsey also had a bedchamber there, sleeping in a very large bedstead with gilt posts and a canopy of gold, gold pillows and a counterpane that reached the ground.[15] Henry and Catherine both had lodgings in the pavilion, although Henry chose not to base himself there. In order to facilitate access between the pavilion and the castle at Guisnes, a winding alley was constructed, covered with greenery, like something 'of the days of the knights errant', so Henry might escape to his secret castle lodgings.[16]

The account of the visiting Genoan secretary, Joachino, gives more details that are usually left out of English accounts of Henry's pavilion, which he calls 'fortress house', and later, a 'stockade'. Joachino told his master that he would be 'surprised to hear of its architecture, but more delighted to behold such a structure, built to last a day, and no longer'. The whole building was a trompe l'oeil, as 'it appears to be that which it is not, and it is that which it does not appear to be.' He describes it as standing 'at a bow's shot' from Guisnes Castle, and being 'well-nigh square', with four connected ranges of buildings, a round tower in each corner and a lofty portal, built of brick. He noted the armed statues on the battlements and the fountains at the front, topped by images of Bacchus, discharging wine into 'very large and handsome basins'. The external walls, Joachino estimated, were around 50 feet high, with a frieze midway up, and a sloping roof, upon which 'a beautiful scale pattern' had been painted on brass.[17]

The Genoan's account then moves inside the pavilion, into what he describes as an 'atrium or vestibule' 100 paces long and 30 paces wide, which leads to a 'handsome covered stair in the Italian fashion' as wide as the atrium itself. There were fifteen steps, according to Joachino, or eighteen, in the Mantuan and Venetian accounts, then the staircase wound around with fifteen more, before 'you arrive at a great door and enter a hall 160 paces in length and 30 wide.'[18] The hall was lined with a gilt cornice, from which hung magnificent tapestries, above it was a line of windows and the floor was alternating checks of white and yellow taffeta intersected by red roses. The hall, and each of the other rooms, had a large lantern in the centre, in the form of a crown, 'with octagonal windows, more for ornament than for light,' which made the walls so 'luminous… it is like being in the open air.'[19] Another Italian account describes the palace as being 'adorned with silk and red roses, and the emblems of the King of England... but marvellous were the tapestries with which the whole palace was hung, all of gold and silk, some representing figures, others foliage, which it would not be possible to paint more beautifully; the figures really seemed alive.'[20]

The palace chapel was furnished with 'golden items' chosen by the Dean of St Paul's, Secretary Richard Pace, and it was intended to impress on a temporal level. The chapel quire was lined with cloth of gold, fretted with silk, and the altar was hung with cloth of golden tissue, decorated with pearls and a canopy of 'marvellous greatness'. Upon the altar sat five pairs of gold candlesticks and twelve gold icons, each about the size of a four-year-old child. The vestments were woven especially, in cloth of tissue of gold, embellished with red roses powdered with fine gold, outshining anything that might be made in the city of Florence, the contemporary centre of material richness. There were three huge, rich crosses, to be carried on ceremonial occasions, and basins, censers and other vessels of gold. The chapel contained two closets, one each for the king and queen. Inside Henry's was a gold chair and cushions, placed before an altar adorned with an embroidered cloth of precious stones, pearls and the work of royal goldsmith Robert Amadas. Upon it stood a gold crucifix, an icon of the Trinity, another of Mary, and twelve others, all made in fine gold with gems and two pairs of gold candlesticks. The walls were hung with little tapestries, with more jewels and pearls, and the roof was gilded and painted with bice (blue) and senaper (crimson.) Catherine's closet was similar, with a richly apparelled altar, gold icons and an abundance of jewels and pearls.[21]

Around the pavilion, a number of other tents had been constructed to serve as offices for the various departments of the royal household, 'that to such an honourable court should appertain'. The Rutland papers count sixteen additional 'halls' and explain the purpose of these, most of which were built to contain large fires, or accommodate cooking, so they were physically distanced for reasons of safety and comfort. There were ten houses, some with hearths, 'to serve for working houses and larders', two houses and two halls for the poultry, a scalding (boiling) house, scullery and mill, two large ovens, six ranges and a working hall for the pastillers and other subtlety makers, three more larders and two halls for the accommodation of kitchen staff, and various other offices.[22] ('Subtlety' – also soteltie, sotelty, suttlety – was used in France until the 17th century. It refers to skilled craft work by the cook or confectioner. Subtleties can be non-edible, partly edible, or totally edible.) Some of these houses are visible on the 1545 painting, from tents by outdoor assembly lines where food is being cooked and prepared, close to a huge round free-standing oven, and tents designed for fine dining. One such dining tent immediately to the right of the pavilion shows high-ranking people sitting on either side of a long table covered with a white cloth, upon which a meal is set. The white tent has green drapes, pulled back to reveal the inside, while its roof is beautifully painted with Tudor roses and geometric designs.

Hall also states that extra lodgings for 820 people were created in the sea of tents around the main camp. These would have varied in size and material depending upon the class of those sleeping within. Visible behind the pavilion in the painting is a swathe of plain white tents, a series of interlinked white and green tents, but also two of the most elaborate kind, bright with gold, one of which is multi-chambered. Designs for some of the most complex tents survive in the collection of the British Library. One of the largest comprises four interlocking rectangular sections in a straight line, like a series of rooms, with five small circular tents attached on each side, all under what appears to be red velvet embroidered with gold and topped with large heraldic beasts and ridgeboards with gold fleur de lys. Others are blue and gold, or green and white, with similar decorative features. Inside, such tents echoed the structure of the Tudor palace, with varying degrees of privacy and withdrawal, and sections divided off by hanging tapestries.

In the top right-hand corner of the 1545 portrait, the completed tiltyard is visible, although it would actually have been around three miles away, situated in the field between the two towns. Initially, its dimensions caused difficulty, as the ladies' gallery was not close enough to the action to afford them a good view, but such questions had been resolved by the end of May. An open, sanded square with a tilting barrier down the centre is featured in the painting, overlooked by a railed roof gallery, inside which the two queens are seated. The crowds are ranged around the other three sides, with visible rows of knights on horseback awaiting their turns, whilst two more clash in the centre. Other sport takes place undercover, as Francis wrestles with Henry inside the second of the golden tents, with its fleur-de-lys curtains considerably drawn aside for the hundreds of onlookers.

Francis had established his camp a little way out of the town of Ardres, the first town across the border from English territory. It had suffered serious devastation in the wars of 1513 and the castle was quite ruined, so that Francis had its ramparts repaired. There were between 300 and 400 tents, halls and pavilions pitched near a river outside the town, although the king also commandeered four houses in Ardres itself and part of the Abbey of St Médard d'Andres, burial place of the Counts of Guisnes. The king's main tent was twelve feet high, held up by two masts lashed together, its canvas covered by gold brocade with three wide strips of blue velvet, powdered with gold fleur-de-lys. On top of the tent stood a statue of St Michael, holding a dart in one hand and a shield in the other, which had been carved from walnut wood by Germain Arnoult and the king's painter Jean Bourdichan had turned it blue and gold.[23]

Joachino thought that the French tents were handsomer than the English ones. He was impressed by Francis' 'magnificent affair' topped by St Michael, with its tall masts tied together 'such that it would certainly suffice for a ship of 400 butts.' He reveals the further details that the saint's statue stood upon a large golden ball, out from which twelve zig-zag rays darted, made from azure-coloured velvet, and the tent's ropes were woven in the black, white and tawny hemp of Francis' personal colours. Four smaller tents linked to the large one were covered in the same gold cloth and twelve others with crimson satin, although when Joachino observed them on 5 June they were not yet complete. Many of the constructions were decorated with golden apples, perhaps executed by the French court painter Jean Clouet, who became a Groom of the Chamber in 1523, or his brother Clouet of Navarre, in the employ of Marguerite d'Alençon. The unfinished banqueting hall was a rotunda, with a circumference of 240 paces, and was intended to be covered with azure cloth painted with golden lilies and hung with tapestries.[24]

Francis had three other tents for his own use, one of which was used as a council chamber, one for his wardrobe and the other was a chapel which also doubled as a secret chamber. In addition, there were fifteen other small tents around them. Francis' chief venue for entertainment was a large tent called the house of solace and sport. It was supported by a single, central mast, the ceiling was painted blue, decorated with stars and gold foil, and the planets were set on a crescent-shaped sundial pointing towards Ardres, hung with branches of yew and box. The entire thing was set upon brick foundations, with walls of board about thirty inches high, painted to resemble brickwork.[25] Unfortunately, the French workers were unable to complete Francis' banqueting house in time, so it was not used. Claude, Louise of Savoy and the nobility had their own tents, which were considered beautiful by observers, one commenting that they surpassed the pyramids of Egypt. Beautiful as they were, though, the French tents were not as strong as the English ones. As Soardino notes, they remained up for only four days, before it 'became necessary to strike them... on account of the wind and rain... to the very great regret' of Francis and all his company, 'as they were the pride of France' and the answer to the English pavilion.[26]

As the sun rose on Friday, 1 June 1520, the six-mile stretch between Ardres and Guisnes bustled with activity. From the brightly coloured buildings and tents, to the liveried servants making final preparations, the thousands of guests dressed in their finery, the smoke and cooking smells arising from the temporary hearths and the flags fluttering in the breeze, the stage was set for the most extravagant piece of theatre of the century. The costly, long-awaited Field of the Cloth of Gold was about to begin. But was it to be the 'mock international chivalric court festival par excellence', as described by Professor Sydney Anglo, or A. F. Pollard's 'most portentous deception on record?'

12

FRIDAY, 1 JUNE – WEDNESDAY, 6 JUNE

The night of 31 May had seen a terrible storm raging in the Channel. As a result, the crossing from Dover to Calais had been turbulent, and mostly took place after dark owing to the late hour of departure. Arriving in the port at eleven at night, it is unlikely that Henry and Catherine were in bed at the Chequer much before midnight on 31 May. The Venetian ambassador, Antonio Surian, was with the Papal ambassador in one ship, which was forced to land at Boulogne due to the violence of the weather, but although he had 'nearly drowned,' they were lucky as many others had been 'wrecked in crossing'.[1] No records survive of any ships, cargoes or lives lost on this occasion, although this does not mean that Surian's comment can be discounted, as damage may still have occurred.

As a result of their ordeal, the English royal party were 'fatigued and unwell', and unable to proceed to Guisnes as planned the following morning. Henry dispatched a messenger to Francis, waiting at Ardres, to explain the situation, but adding that if the French King should be 'dissatisfied with this excuse, he (Henry) would proceed immediately on post horses'.[2] Francis was not inclined to insist. He sent Monsieur de St Marceau back to Calais, insisting that the English should not trouble themselves to move today, 'but he besought (Henry) not to fail being present at the appointed place, on the day named for the interview.'[3] At this late date,

Surian commented, Francis still found it difficult to believe that the meeting would actually happen. Even Henry's presence in Calais did not fully reassure him, given the recent visit of Charles to England, and on 1 June the ambassador was still opining to the Signoria of Venice, that 'King Francis had been doubtful whether his interview with the King of England would take place, by reason of the conference held with the Emperor' and that 'the negotiations... had been very secret, and their purport was not known.'[4]

Yet having accomplished the first phase of his three-part plan, Henry was keen to reassure Francis. Instead, he proposed that Wolsey travel to meet Francis that afternoon at the Ardres camp. The French King sent Bonnivet to Calais to accompany the Cardinal back, and before them rode Wolsey's cross bearer, dressed all in red, carrying two crosses. When they passed the border, the bearer left one cross on the Guisnes side before continuing with the other into French territory. Half a league from Ardres, they were met by Francis' brother-in-law, Charles d'Alençon, and Charles, Duke of Bourbon, both Princes of the Royal blood.[5] Trivulzio related how Wolsey was accompanied by 400 horse, 150 gentlemen wearing massive gold chains, archers and others of his household all dressed in embroidered, crimson velvet doublets, forming a 'gallant company' who were 'highly commended by the French'.[6] Giustinian adds that the Cardinal himself wore crimson satin, a red hat with hanging tassels and rode a 'richly caparisoned' mule, the traditional mount of nobility in the Bible.[7] Joining in the almost universal praise, Surian expressed the view of Wolsey's importance: 'the Cardinal governed the realm of England as quietly and absolutely as his own archiepiscopal see.' The Venetian confirmed, 'the King [of France] is extremely satisfied with Cardinal Wolsey, and says he is a most estimable personage, eloquent and prudent, and worthy to rule England. He (the King) promised himself much from him.'[8] When Wolsey was within three bow shots of the gates of Ardres, Francis rode out of the gate, also on a mule, embracing his guest and exchanging compliments. He escorted the Cardinal to lodgings within the royal tent, in anticipation of a full meeting the following day.

Some of the surviving written accounts conflate the events of the first and second of June. One main source is a printed account by Jehan Lescaille, created for Paris printer Pierre Vidoue, which is preserved in the English State Letters and Papers of Henry's reign, and allocates only one day for Wolsey's visit to Ardres.[9] However, the cavalier, or horseman, Delacroix (Della Croce) records him arriving on the Friday, two hours after dinner, then staying as an overnight guest.[10] Contemporary English chronicler Edward Hall states that Wolsey 'sojourned at Ardres, in the French court, for the space of two days', after which he went to Guisnes Castle to join Henry, which would have been on Saturday 2 June.[11] Although Henry and the English party did not formally travel to Guisnes until Tuesday 5 June, the lack of accounts describing the two days before, might allow for the king to have visited Guisnes, to inspect the progress of the works, where the Cardinal might have met him. It is typical of the eye-witness accounts that they reflect the nature of personal memory, the bias and allegiances of their authors and the somewhat arbitrariness of their recording, often conflating several days into one narrative, or muddling events. It must also be remembered that they served a specific purpose, which was to report back the message ambassadors believe their recipients would wish to hear. Equally, they can only reflect the aspects of the event to which those ambassadors had access, filling in other details with hearsay and the observations of others. While the ambassadors' accounts are of great assistance, they must be compared and contrasted, and handled with care. Likewise the chroniclers, whose accounts were often composed with hindsight and for a particular purpose.

Wolsey's talks with Francis, which may have taken place on the evening of Friday 1 June, or during the Saturday, were conducted with suitable splendour. The route to Ardres was lined with gentlemen and archers, while trumpets, fifes and other instruments 'played most melodiously' and the artillery 'made such a noise you could not hear'. Francis met the Cardinal with 'great signs of affection' and led him to his lodgings, where 'they talked together for a long time, with the other princes and lords, all magnificently dressed,' while all his company were treated to 'good cheer'. Having received much praise, Wolsey was quick to state that 'he would no such power receive without the consent of the king of England, his sovereign lord.'[12] After which, Wolsey made his farewells and departed, either to go to Calais, or to Guisnes, depending upon which source you read. Lescaille relates that it was on Saturday 2 June, that Wolsey 'revisited the King with a small company at Ardres, and remained about seven hours,' and that Bonnivet, the Archbishop of Sens and other French Lords visited Henry at Calais. That evening, his account continues, Francis rode to Marquise, a town situated between Guisnes and Boulogne, which Claude and Louise had reached, no doubt travelling slowly due to the queen's condition.[13]

Trinity Sunday fell the next day, on 3 June, an important day of Catholic devotion that both the English and French would have observed in their separate camps, through attending the mass, prayers and feasting. Henry made offerings totalling 13s and 4d[14] and as Vergil observed, Wolsey 'celebrated the mass again and again in pontifical style'.[15] The Grafton chronicle states that 'great repair of noblemen came to the town of Calais from the French court, to see the king, and to salute him, which were of his grace, princely entertained.'[16] This may refer to Bonnivet and others on 1 June, or also to subsequent visits that took place during these days. Monday 4 June appears to have been a rest day in both camps, probably devoted to organisation ahead of the English relocation to Guisnes.

On Tuesday 5 June, the English party, including Catherine and Mary, departed from Calais and travelled the seven miles south to the town of Guisnes. A Venetian witness sent his account to the royal senator, Pietro Montemerlo, of Henry riding a bay courser, wearing a 'garment of brocade ribbed with crimson satin' and a hat trimmed with black feathers. He was a 'very handsome king', in the Venetian's opinion, 'both in face and figure, with a red beard, and his countenance resembles that of Giovanni Cristoforo Troto,' presumably a contemporary Venetian standard of beauty.[17] Catherine rode beside her husband on a palfrey, followed by her gold litter and her ladies, after which came a wagon covered in gold cloth drawn by six horses, more ladies including Mary, Duchess of Suffolk, and then three more wagons. 200 archers followed, half bowmen, half halberdiers, dressed in green velvet and white satin, embroidered with the king's arms of a rose surmounted by a crown. The Venetian account offers a reminder of just how many material goods required transportation from one location to another, on carts across the English and French countryside, and across the Channel. Almost the entire English nobility were on the move; the church, and all their entourages, the catering departments with the tools of their trade, wardrobe departments, stables and horses, entertainers with all their props, servants in livery and others for all the various aspects of the stay, amounting to a train of thousands crossing the countryside. The journey to Guisnes alone would have taken several hours, as one of the receipts of costs for the transport of men from London to Dover shows that they travelled at a rate of 12 miles a day. Eventually, the king and court had their first sight of the Guisnes village, the pavilion, fountains, and sea of colourful tents, in all their splendour. The night of 5 June was spent settling all the newcomers into their accommodation, unpacking and putting the new circular ovens to the test in catering for them all. On the same day, Claude and Louise of Savoy arrived at Ardres.

On Wednesday, 6 June, the day before he was due to meet Francis in person, Henry rode out from Guisnes to the Golden Valley at Balinghem to inspect the lists appointed for the jousts. Taking a hundred gentlemen and fifty archers, he led six large coursers, trapped with crimson velvet, covered with roses of beaten gold and little bells. One Italian observer recorded it as 'a fine sight'. At the lists, Henry 'made trial of the horses, one after another', and then raced them against each other, 'laughing the whole time, being in truth very merry' for the entire two hours he remained in the lists.[18] During the planning of the event, it had been decided that 6 June was to be the day when a tree would be chosen for the jousts, 'bearing the noble thorn entwined with raspberry', upon which the challengers would hang their shields. It was to bear three coats of arms, black and grey, gold and tawny and the last, silver, below which the knights would hang their names, to ensure an equal division of French and English on both sides.[19] No doubt Henry was keen to inspect that fair play was taking place, and that a suitable tree was in place. A small French party also appeared at Balinghem that day, headed by Monsieur de Chateaubriant, 'to whom the English king gave the best possible greeting.'[20]

Wolsey was busy whilst Henry was in the field, having ridden out again to Ardres. Mindful of the terms of the 1518 Treaty of London, he ratified the marriage arrangements between the four-year-old Princess Mary, left behind in England, and the young Dauphin Francis. The treaty included provision for the sums of money France was to pay England, and an arrangement of friendship with France's traditional ally, Scotland, which was to be settled between Wolsey and the king's mother, Louise of Savoy. Later the same day, it was ratified by Henry at Guisnes, and for a second time on 13 June.[21]

That evening, Admiral Bonnivet, Etienne de Poncher, Archbishop of Sens, and Louis II, Monsieur de la Trimoulle, Count of Guisnes, among others, rode to the English camp dressed in cloth of gold. They were conducted to Guisnes Castle by George Talbot, Earl of Shrewsbury, where Henry received them 'very honourably' amid 'great noise of artillery and music'. Afterward, the English lords feasted them 'in their tents marvellously, from the greatest to the least', as 'if they were their brothers', and a 'great company' saw them home.[22]

The same night, while Henry entertained his gallic guests, Charles V was a hundred miles away, at Ghent in the Netherlands. According to the Venetian Francesco Cornaro, he was 'awaiting the result of the interview between the Kings of France and England', at which he hoped 'Cardinal Wolsey was endeavouring to make peace between the Emperor and France,' and engineer a triple conference.[23] However, Henry had no intention of attending a three-way meeting. It suited him far more to treat with Francis and Charles separately. As he bid his guests goodnight that Wednesday, he was preparing to come face to face with the French king for the first time the next day.

13

THURSDAY 7 JUNE

Thursday 7 June was the feast day of Corpus Christi, when mass was traditionally celebrated to honour the body and blood of Christ. It was also the day when years of competition and rivalry, the diplomatic missions, ambassadorial messages, letters and promises, negotiations and arrangements, hopes and fears, would come to a head. The two kings were about to accomplish that which, until only days before, had still not felt guaranteed. Both understood the nature of majesty and the effects of display: the first impression had to be one of overwhelming magnificence, to surpass each king's rival in terms of numbers and appearance, so Francis and Henry threw all the resources they had into it. Vast quantities of cloth of gold and silver, cloth of tissue, velvets, brightly coloured satin, jewels, plumed hats, leather boots, capes, doublets, saddles, weaponry and adornments from the crown reserves were utilised by both courts. Servants lifted heavy gold chains around their masters' necks, glittering buckles were secured and hands sparkled with rings. Then, on each side, the colourful companies assembled according to protocol, riding horses trapped in gold and satin, hung with bells and attended by servants in livery. Musicians brought their trumpets, horns and fifes, ready to fill the air with their sound. If ever one single day encapsulated the material splendour of the Tudor and Valois courts, it was Thursday, 7 June 1520.

Wolsey went out to Ardres again in the morning, to clarify the final details. He dined with Francis, waited upon by the Lord Steward, Adrien du Boissy, and discussed arrangements for the meeting. The Mantuan ambassador, Soardino, observed that 'after dinner so many difficulties arose that it was feared the conference would not take place; but at length all was arranged.'[1] The Cardinal left at about three, and was accompanied much of the way back by Bonnivet, Châtillon and the French Master of the Horse, Galeazzo di Sanseverino. Returning to Henry at Guisnes, he confirmed that the French were prepared to meet that day, and that artillery would be fired from each camp to signal their departure.

Joachino notes that Francis left Ardres about half past four in the afternoon, behind an entourage of around 1,000, comprising the gentlemen attendants of the king and his circle, 140 gentlemen pensioners, 400 archers of the guard on foot with halberds and battle axes, bearing royal emblems including Francis' salamander. One hundred of the Swiss guard followed, wearing satin doublets and hose in the king's black, white and tawny, with matching feathers in their bonnets. Then came all the French heralds, the trumpeters and fifers, the porters, esquires of the body and the gentlemen of the chamber. Francis himself rode a great bay courser, with half a surcoat of embroidered cloth of gold.[2] According to Trivulzio, the French retinue was the larger of the two, and 'in more costly apparel, namely in gold and silver brocade', and that velvet, satin and other silks were not considered good enough.[3]

The second Venetian ambassador, Giovanni Badoer, had arrived at the site late on the night of 4 June, and hurried to join his partner, Antonio Giustinian, and to meet with Francis. According to his account, three guns were fired in the English camp at 5pm as a signal for the two kings to mount in readiness. He describes Admiral Bonnivet and his horse as being most prominent, and 'covered with jewels, pearls and other ornaments'. The princes of the blood and the ambassadors to France were all wearing gold and silver tissue, as was Badoer himself, who was paired to ride beside Charles de Bourbon, while Giustinian rode behind him, beside Charles' brother, Francis de Bourbon,

Monsieur de St. Pol. Being present in the procession, he was well placed to notice certain details, including the messages being carried between the kings as they drew closer, to clarify the articles agreed between them.[4]

An anonymous account in the Venetian papers describes Francis' horse as a black Spanish horse, 'caparisoned with embroidery and pearls' and the king himself in a 'doublet of very costly cloth of gold and a cloak of the same material'. His jerkin was 'embroidered and slashed' and on his breast and black velvet cap he wore 'sundry rich and beautiful jewels'.[5] Another version describes it set with rubies, diamonds, emeralds and huge pearls.[6] The military trumpeters, fife and horn players went ahead, followed by gentlemen of the chamber and wardrobe, in gold and silver, the Switzers in battle array, the king's macers, then Francis himself. The ambassadors and Princes behind him were dressed to match the king in slashed doublets of gold and similar cloaks. This second account also singles out Bonnivet, confirming Giustinian's comments about his costume of silver and gold, pearls and jewels, adding that he also wore a sailor's gold whistle at his side, signifying his role as France's Admiral.[7]

According to Joachino, Francis wore a black velvet cap with matching black feathers, set with some large jewels, which was estimated to cost 2,000 ducats. He teamed this with a slashed shirt under a doublet embroidered with gold knots, and a cloak of embroidered cloth of gold, with a gold half-mantle over his left shoulder ornamented with jewels, and white boots. Charles, Duke of Bourbon rode before him, in an embroidered cloak of gold cloth, carrying the sword of state, and also with the king rode Bonnivet, Cardinal Adrian Gouffier de Boissy, the Dukes of Alençon, Lorraine and Vendôme, and others, cited by Joachino as 'all the princes, lords, and barons of France, not one of whom was missing' dressed in gold, including all the knights of the order of St Michael, wearing their insignia and gold tabard.[8] There were at least 300 people wearing cloth of gold, in his estimation, and a great number in velvet, as well as the ambassadors from Spain, Venice, Mantua and Ferrara, with their retinues. They were accompanied a short distance out from Ardres by Claude and Louise, riding in a litter, in order to witness 'the pomp of France'.[9] However, the women were not to play a formal role in the day's events, so they set themselves apart as an audience and as Francis passed them by, he left his place and spoke a little while with them, before rejoining the ranks. Soardino tells us that all the French princes, including Lorraine and Vendôme, brought their wives, and that the Princesses of Navarre were also present.[10]

When the kings were about two leagues apart, they sent ahead ambassadors to announce their approach, with Wolsey leading the English party. Lescaille's account describes his huge entourage, which seemed more to advance the Cardinal's glory than that of the king. Fifty gentlemen mounted on good horses and clothed in crimson velvet went first, then fifty ushers carrying gold maces as large as a man's head, then the bearer of his double cross of fine gold, with a 'beautiful crucifix of precious stones,' also in crimson, displaying goldsmith's work. Four lackeys followed in doublets of cloth of gold, carrying bonnets adorned with huge plumes, before two guards leading Wolsey's mule and two 'tall young men' in 'paletots of velvet' embroidered with the Cardinal's arms, each carrying a long, golden baton. Wolsey himself, in robes of velvet upon crimson velvet, figured with a design of ruched fine linen, in his red, fringed Cardinal's hat, rode a mule trapped in crimson velvet with studs, buckles and stirrups of gold. Five or six bishops followed, with Thomas Docwra, the Grand Prior of Jerusalem in England, and 100 of the king's archers.[11]

One Venetian was impressed by Henry's costume of cloth of silver, richly jewelled, with white plumes in his cap, as well as his entourage.[12] The king was flanked by Edward Stafford, Duke of Buckingham, Charles Brandon, Duke of Suffolk, Henry Percy, Earl of Northumberland, George Talbot, Earl of Shrewsbury and John de Vere, Earl of Oxford and Grand Chamberlain, and a select group of others, with archers, wearing hocquetins, or jackets of the king's guard, of white and green velvet. Trivulzio related that Henry had a 'handsome retinue, richly clad', all wearing massive gold chains, superbly dressed. Henry himself wore 'a treasure of pearls, diamonds, rubies and other stones', a costly doublet made from cloth of silver and large gold chains. Unlike his followers, the king wore no gold chain, but a jewelled collar and matching belt of great value. He rode a bay horse 'of the breed of the Duke of Termini, with trappings like those of King Francis, and perhaps more rich in jewels'.[13] As the ambassador particularly attached to Francis' court, it is no surprise that Joachino judged the *pompa*, or display, on the French side 'far exceeded that of the othe..'[14] Grafton praises the English footmen for conducting themselves 'so in order, that from the first to the last, never a person of the footmen broke his place or array, but kept themselves so well, that never servingmen themselves better demeaned'.[15]

The meeting took place in the golden valley at Balinghem, midway between Guisnes and Ardres. The English had pitched a 'handsome tent of brocade without, and tapestried internally with very costly arras, embroidered in gold and silver'.[16] Joachino described it as 'small but elegant', adjoined by two awnings, which acted as separate chambers. Eighty paces away were two other tents, 'well supplied with most excellent wines'.[17] As each company approached, they ranged themselves around the outside, where barriers of pikes driven into the ground had been placed at 100-pace intervals for a mile each way. The English had arrived first, and watched as the French took their places - but even then, suspicion and doubt still lingered.

Meeting in this way, with two vast sides face to face like an army, opened considerable questions of trust. Within firing distance of each other, both kings feared the possibility of an unexpected slight or attack. Many of the attendants were sent back, 'most especially on the French side', as one ambassador observed, 'because so great an amount of persons caused suspicion to King Henry.' As a result, 'certain gentlemen carried messages to and fro,' and the French, also, 'took umbrage at so great an amount of infantry', as Henry himself had between 3,000 and 4,000 in his retinue.[18] According to Soardino, 'Chatillon was sent to number the English troops... and reported that the English had some 1,500 foot men more than their [stipulated] number. His Majesty replied, 'Having come thus far, I will not fail to keep my promise, and gratify my wish, on this account,' and ascended the mound, 'on our side', making himself visible to Francis.[19] Surian observed that 'the French Court sent certain delegates to inspect the number of the King's retinue and guard, amounting to some 4,000 (*sic*) infantry, whether they bore arms or not, and found that, according to the articles, they carried no weapons. The like inspection was made by the English with regard to the French, and with the same result.'[20] Satisfied, they waited on each side, in anticipation, until the signal came to advance. Then, led by their Masters of the Horse, Sir Henry Guildford and Galeazzo di Sanseverino, the two kings slowly descended their respective slopes and made their way towards each other.

The first interaction was musical: 'after a short pause, the English instruments struck up, and the French responded.'[21] Then, once the musicians had fallen silent, the two kings moved forwards on horseback, flanked by two mounted attendants, Wolsey and Thomas Grey, Marquis of Dorset with Henry, and Bonnivet and Charles, Duke of Bourbon, with Francis. As Constables of their respective countries, Dorset and Bourbon bore the swords of state, unsheathed with naked blades, as the parties advanced towards a spear that had been planted in the middle point of the field. When the two kings were some thirty paces from the spear, they both removed their headwear and saluted each other, bareheaded, then rode forward and embraced three times on horseback. Dismounting, they embraced again, so that witnesses on both sides could hardly 'avoid shedding tears of joy or gladness' and 'such were the embraces that,' the Venetian writer did not 'know whether closer could be imagined, and they were upwards of twenty in number.'[22]

The two kings headed for the gold tent, arm in arm, caps in hand, where they had an amicable disagreement about protocol, each insisting that the other enter first. At length, 'King Francis took precedence, without, however, once quitting the arm of King Henry.'[23] Initially, they were accompanied inside by Wolsey and Bonnivet, while Dorset and Bourbon waited outside with symbolic drawn swords. Quite how Gioan Joachino, secretary to the Governor of Genoa, was able to accurately relate what happened inside the tent is unknown, but his account includes a conversation that may have become wider gossip afterwards, judging by its tone and subject. Upon entering the tent, Cardinal Wolsey read to their Majesties 'the articles and conventions stipulated between them' and when he came to the words 'Henry, King of England and France', Henry laughed, 'expunge this title,' and told Francis, 'They are titles given me which are good for nothing.' Francis called him brother, adding 'Now that you are my friend, you are King of France, King of all my possessions, and of me myself,' to which Henry rose and embraced him, saying 'My brother, I swear to our Lord God, although I have been very deeply in love, that I never had so strong a wish and desire to gratify any of my appetites, as that of seeing and embracing you.' He promised Francis that he would never 'love anybody so much as I love you, and should you ever find me fail in this love... I am willing to be accounted the most base and sorry prince and gentleman in the world.'[24]

Another version of the meeting, related by chronicler Edward Hall, puts different words into both king's mouths, which may have been recorded, or be an approximation of what was later reported to have been said. Hall has Francis say, 'My dear brother and cousin, thus far to my pain, I have travailed to see you personally, I think verily that you esteem me as I am. And that I may, to you, be your aid, the realms and signories show the might of my person.' Henry replied, 'Neither your realms nor other places of your powers is the matter of my regard, but the steadfastness and loyal keeping of promise, comprised in charters between you and me, that observed and kept, I never saw Prince of my eyes, that might of my heart be more loved. And for your love I have passed the seas, into the farthest frontier of my realm, to see you presently, the which doing now gladdeth me.'[25]

After a quarter of an hour, the Cardinal and Admiral were dismissed and shortly, wine was brought to the two kings. For three quarters of an hour, Henry and Francis were alone 'and seemed unable to tear themselves away from each other'. Had the sun not already begun to set, 'their loving conference would have lasted longer,' but as darkness approached, they each invited the chief noblemen in their trains to pay their respects. Charles Brandon, Henry's brother-in-law, led forward twenty-two Englishmen while Francis' brother-in-law, Charles d'Alençon, headed a party of forty Frenchmen. Each side was given 'a very gracious reception' and were 'well supplied with barrels of good wine'. drinking together and repeating the toast 'good friends, French and English.'[26]

When they emerged from the tent, the kings embraced again, repeatedly, 'as if they had then met for the first time, addressing each other in such language as to leave it doubtful whether they were more brothers than friends.'[27] This anonymous account describes how the kings then embraced each other's retinue, to the sound of trumpets and other instruments, 'so that it seemed a paradise'. Lords on both sides offered 'profound obeisances down to the ground, whereupon another collation was served' and 'all the gentlemen, especially the French, were served with as much beverage as they pleased.'[28] Another source described how the wine was brought in silver-gilt cups, 'nearly six feet high' and other 'large gilt bowls with feet of such a size that the hand could scarcely hold them,' along with spiced cakes.[29] Hall adds that Hippocras was the main drink on offer, and offers a vision of Francis striding out of the tent, 'stately of countenance, merry of cheer, brown coloured, great eyes, high nosed, big lipped, fair breasted and shouldered, small legs and long feet'.[30] After their refreshments, the two sides parted, and returned to their separate camps, with Francis arriving at Ardres after nightfall. Hall's account concludes with the detail that 'on his return his horse kicked the Admiral (Bonnivet) on the leg and the English ambassador (Wingfield? Boleyn?) also, but they were not seriously injured.'[31] Apart from that, in spite of wind, weather and doubts, the first meeting of the kings passed off smoothly.

14

FRIDAY, 8 JUNE –
SUNDAY, 10 JUNE

In comparison, the following day was much quieter. Upon the signal of three guns being sounded, Henry and Francis proceeded to Balinghem with a small retinue each, where they spent four hours planning the tournaments and jousts for the coming days. Back on 13 May, Henry had ruled at Greenwich that a joust was to be held, necessitating certain preparations by Richard Gibson. The usual centrepiece of a 'tree of noblesse,' to be hung with challengers' shields, was created by Gibson's team; a 'whitethorn' in English, or 'albypene' in French, a hawthorn that produced white, scented flowers in May, which was to be mixed with a 'framboseyr,' or raspberry 'tree'.[1]

The tree was made from 103 yards of green satin, 318 yards of green damask and 108 yards of sarcenet, which were used for the boughs. 262 dozen, or 3,144 hawthorn flowers and buds of silk were made by a Margaret Davy 'and others', at a cost of 6½ d per dozen, plus more in cherry-coloured satin. Elizabeth Philips was paid for sleeved silk and 'whipping wires' to shape the flowers, 14d went to a wiredrawer in Soper Lane, London, and the grocer Richard Miller supplied reams of paper for lying in the glue between the pieces of sarcenet. The tree was mounted upon a railed, twenty-foot-square carriage, decorated with eighty-four yards of green damask, thirty-eight yards of green satin and covered with green leaves made from forty-five yards of sarcenet, stabilised by thirteen spars that were each forty feet long and fifteen smaller ones. Production had moved across the Channel by 24 May, when 60lb of horn glue was purchased in Calais and wagonloads of wood were sourced from Guisnes forest at 3s a load. On 29 May, a painter named Allyn was paid for 8lb of verdigris at 12d a pound and 4d for the hire of a stone upon which to grind it.[2] The tree itself ended up being twenty-two feet long, wrapped in cloth of gold, as were its roots and principal blooms. Thirty-five more workmen were paid 6d or 8d daily for completing it by 3 June, and on Friday 8 June, it cost 9s for a wagon to transport the tree from Calais to Guisnes, ready for the tournament the next day.[3]

On Saturday 9 June, preparations began early to ensure the lists were ready. The Rutland papers have the organisational details, with the first task of 'ordering the field' assigned to the King's Marshal, perhaps John Peche, or George Neville, and six other gentlemen. Sir Wistan Brown, Sir Edward Ferrers, Sir John Marney, Sir Robert Constable and Sir Thomas Lucy, with twenty guards, positioned themselves early in the valley, to keep out hangers on, to ensure that 'no more of the king's train resort to the said camp, but such only as be appointed.'[4] Three more knights, Sir Griffiths Rhys, Sir William Bulmer and Sir Richard Tempest, were to ride about the area with their companies, to 'discover the country for the king's surety (safety)'. It was as late as 8pm, 'at about the 20th hour' when the two kings and their retinues rode out to the lists at Balinghem. On the gates at each side stood a guard of twelve English and twelve French archers, but they did not 'refuse entry to any persons honourably apparelled'.[5] Galleries for the crowds were hung with tapestries and a glazed chamber had been prepared for the queens, although they were not to meet for another two days. The tree of noblesse had been 'planted' at the foot of the lists, along with a triumphal arch and pillar, or 'perron', upon which the kings attached their shields. There was a brief disagreement over who should hang their shield first, and which should occupy the position on the right, over which Bourbon and Dorset were called to adjudicate, before Henry acquiesced and offered Francis the prized place.[6] Trivulzio relates how Henry rode a Neapolitan courser, which he subsequently offered to Francis as a gift, while Francis rode 'Dappled Duke', a Mantuan stud which Henry so admired, that it was given to him in response. The kings accomplished 'several feats' that day, before taking leave of each other.[7]

Only one source gives information for the early morning of Sunday 10 June. In their joint letter to the Signory of Venice, Badoer and Giustinian mention that Francis visited Guisnes Castle early in the morning, with only a small company of ten. Henry 'immediately went to meet him' and after they had embraced, gave his visitor a collar of jewels and pearls, which sounds like a description of the one he was wearing at their first meeting three days earlier. In response, Francis gave Henry his 'gold bracelets studded with jewels of great value', but doubting whether the gifts were equivalent, sent an additional six horses. The French only remained a little while before returning to Ardres, according to the Venetians.[8] However, this sounds very similar to what happened the following Sunday and, as it is not corroborated by any other source, might be a mistake in the dating of events. The Rutland papers contain the beginning of plans made for the kings to meet in the lists on Sunday, but these were not completed, suggesting this idea was abandoned, and has nothing about the two kings meeting.[9]

The seventeenth-century French historian, Bernard de Montfaucon, expands upon the arrangements for the rest of the day. The kings swapped courts for dinner: Henry rode to Ardres to dine with Queen Claude, while Francis was entertained by Catherine at Guisnes. A letter from the scene, written for the royal senator Pietro Montemerlo, describes how an artillery signal prompted both kings to leave their camps, passing each other in the Balinghem field at the halfway point, where they embraced and conversed before continuing. Henry was accompanied by 'his chief Lords, in good array', but, as the French writer asserted, 'not to be compared to ours'.[10] Henry rode the bay charger given to him by Francis the day before, and had Wolsey at his side. They were met near Ardres by Francis' brother-in-law, the Duke d'Alençon, the King of Navarre and Cardinals of Lorraine and Bourbon, splendidly dressed so that 'nothing was visible but gold and silver, and fortunate the tailor who can cut suits better.'[11]

Henry was dressed in a 'double mantle of cloth of gold made like a cloak, embroidered with jewels and goldsmith's work', a beautiful headdress of fine gold cloth and a gold collar made of jewels, three of which were prominent. Trivulzio adds that one of these jewels was 'supposed to be a carbuncle, bigger than a Mocenigo ducat' and there was a ruby in his cap, a belt across his breast, which was a 'treasure of jewels, principally rubies and diamonds' and that the folds of his doublet were 'loaded with precious stones'.[12] Another Venetian source described him as 'a very handsome prince... in manner gentle and gracious, rather fat, and with a red beard, large enough and very becoming'.[13]

Henry was conducted to the King's lodgings, but as one pro-English source commented, 'The decoration of this French palace was very beautiful, but neither so beautiful nor so costly as that of England.' A banqueting tent had been planned, 'all of cloth of gold and tissue, with colours and figures', but it had not yet been completed, so 'the banquet took place within the town of Ardres.'[14] Most sources place Louise of Savoy at the entrance of a hall, where she met Henry, 'and they embraced each other'. Louise was dressed as a widow, in contrast to the cloth of gold frieze worn by Queen Claude, with its gold kirtle and sleeves covered in diamonds and jewels. On her breast, the queen wore a fine diamond known as 'The Point of Brittany' and rich ornaments on her head, set with rubies, emeralds and more diamonds. He also met Claude's ladies in waiting, 'the most beautiful that could be,' among whom, it is likely, was the young Anne Boleyn, having then been in Claude's service for at least five years. Claude rose in her chair of state to meet Henry, who kissed her, with 'one knee on the ground and bonnet in hand', before kissing all the ladies present. Claude then took him by the hand and made him sit beside her, with Louise and Marguerite close by, and the Cardinal de Boissy, in a chamber hung with cloth of gold from top to bottom.[15] One Venetian, however, differed by describing the room as a hall 'covered in pink brocade'.[16]

The king's house stewards were dressed in cloth of gold, and the Grand Master, René of Savoy, held his gold baton symbolically up to his shoulder, while the other maîtres d'hôtel pointed theirs down to the ground. Two dozen trumpeters played to announce each course, which was delivered on vessels of gold, with golden covers, carried by lords and gentlemen, to more 'vocal and instrumental music... the like was never heard before.' There was a great variety of food, 'as many as could be devised.'[17] Entremets, or sweet dessert courses were served up, being something like the traditional English subtleties made from marzipan, in the shape of heraldic beasts; salamanders, leopards and ermines, bearing the arms of the French king and queen. After the tables were removed, Claude led Henry into a 'high room richly adorned with tapestry of cloth of gold and carpeted with crimson velvet', where they 'talked at leisure'. They remained at table 'upwards of four hours'[18] before the dancing began. The guns were fired to mark the agreed departure time of around 5pm, although some sources say it was 'almost night'.[19] Henry embraced and kissed Claude, Louise, Marguerite and the other duchesses, and as he mounted his horse, he 'gave it the spur and made it bound and curvet as valiantly as a man could do.'[20]

In a reciprocal arrangement, Francis rode over to Guisnes, where he dined with Catherine and Mary. In his entourage were the Dukes of Lorraine, Bourbon and Vendôme, Admiral Bonnivet, and many others 'all clad in gold brocade', while the king 'was dressed in royal cloth of silver, all slashed, the slashes being joined by silver bosses' and 'covered in pearls'.[21] The witnesses were impressed by the great fountains outside the pavilion, with silver cups so that anyone might drink the free-flowing wine.

They were received 'in the most courteous manner possible' by Catherine and Mary, who conducted their guest into the pavilion and seated him at the centre of the table opposite Catherine, both under a 'costly canopy'.[22] Mary sat three yards away from the king and another source contradicts the account of Wolsey accompanying Henry to Ardres, to place him at the same table at Guisnes.[23]

Trivulzio relates how the dinner was served entirely by Englishmen with the exception of the cupbearer, who was French, and 'none but Frenchmen were admitted into the banqueting room as spectators; the only English present were those who served.' He also made particular mention of two display cupboards, 'on one of which were many vases of massive gold, and set with beautiful jewels,' from which Francis and Catherine were served. On the other cupboard sat vases 'also of massive gold, but not set with jewels, and these served for the other guests at the royal table,' as well as a number of silver-gilt vases.[24] The Venetians declined to attempt a description of the food, because it was 'more dainty and exquisite than can be told',[25] but probably because they were not present. After the meal, there was dancing, in which Francis performed, and flirted, as 'part of the time he made love to the ladies there.' On the ride back, he passed Henry at the lists. They paused, embraced each other, laughing and asking 'what cheer?' before returning to their relative camps.[26]

15

MONDAY, 11 JUNE – FRIDAY, 15 JUNE

On Monday, 11 June, the jousts began and the two queens met for the first time. The thirty-five-year-old Spanish Catherine, Queen of England for eleven years, regent during the Scottish defeat at Flodden, mother of one surviving daughter, came face to face with the twenty-one-year-old Claude, Queen of France for five years, daughter of Anne of Brittany, frail, and heavily pregnant with her fifth child. Both were 'present with their ladies, richly dressed in jewels' and with 'many chariots, litters and hackneys covered with cloth of gold and silver and emblazoned with their arms.'[1]

Catherine arrived first, in a beautiful litter covered in crimson satin, embroidered in gold, followed by the Mary, Duchess of Suffolk, in a litter of cloth of gold wrought with lilies, embroidered with L and M, and the porcupine motif of her first husband, Louis XII. Three wagons followed, one gold, one crimson and one azure, filled with ladies, the rest of whom followed on palfreys, 'handsome and well-arrayed.' Claude rode in a litter of cloth of silver, covered with gold knots, dressed to match in cloth of silver with her undergarments of gold and a necklace of precious stones. She was accompanied by twelve ladies in brocade and jewels, with three more wagons following, before Louise of Savoy's black velvet litter and ladies in crimson velvet with sleeves lined in gold.[2]

According to Hall, they saluted each other 'right honourably' and entered a glazed gallery prepared for them, 'right curiously hanged' and specially for the Queen of England there was a tapestry made all of pearls called 'Huges Dike', which was 'much looked at for the costliness of the same'. Hall describes it as a wooden platform hung with brocade.[3] Venetian sources have them talking together about the tournament and amusing themselves, 'surrounded by great personages and their favourite ladies', however the language difference meant that they had to rely upon interpreters.[4] Trivulzio continued to favour his French hosts, with the observation that 'the French women were better arrayed and handsomer than the English.'[5] Another witness commented that the ladies were 'all vying with each other in beauty and ornamented apparel' and that they provided the traditional focus of the joust: 'For love of them, each of the jousters endeavoured to display his valour and prowess, in order to find more favour with his sweetheart.'[6]

The Mantuan ambassador, Soardino, was positively rude about the English women. He judged that Catherine's retinue of ladies 'were neither very handsome nor very graceful', being 'ornamented in the English fashion, and were not richly clad'. Both queens had about 40 women with them, all riding upon 'hackneys or hobbies' trapped in gold and velvet, but Claude's entourage were 'richly dressed and with jewels'.[7] Soardino wrote to the Marquis of Mantua that he saw the English women 'ranged in front of the platform' and that 'One of the number took a large flask of wine, and putting it to her lips, drank freely,' before passing it to her companions, 'who did the like and emptied it.' Not content with this, though, 'They drank out of large cups, which, during the joust, circulated more than twenty times amongst the French lords and those English ladies.'[8] A similarly disparaging comment was made by Vergil, who observed that 'The women of England adopted a new manner of dress from the more wanton ladies of France, not very fitting for their modesty,' abandoning 'the very honourable style of their ancestors', and continuing to wear it after their return home.[9]

Hall relates how, at the appointed hour, the two kings arrived. Francis rode a courser covered in purple velvet, broached with gold and embroidered with raven's feathers, in black picked out in gold. The word for 'raven' was 'corbyn', so Francis chose as his device the 'cor' or heart, which was embroidered upon his clothing, and with the English word for feather being 'penne,' he jousted under the symbol of the heart in pain, the 'cor-pen.' Henry's horse was trapped in cloth of gold tissue, 'cut in waves of water work' and each wave 'rawe through and frised with damask gold', laid loose over the top of russet velvet, knit together with gold points that symbolised the narrow waters, perhaps of the Channel. In attendance upon Henry on horseback were Sir Henry Guildford, Master of the Horse, Sir John Peche, Deputy of Calais, Edward Guildford, Master of the King's army, and a Monsieur Moret, of the French court, all apparelled in the king's livery which was 'white on the right side and on the left side, gold and russet, both hose and garment'. On foot, Henry was attended by six knights, twenty squires, a hundred officers and twelve 'persons', of which all the knights and gentlemen had particoloured coats, half silver and half cloth of gold and russet, and the other officers clothed similarly in satin.[10]

With 'honour and noble courage' the two kings and their companies entered the field and presented themselves to the queens, and 'did them reverence'.[11] Then they rode about the tilt and took their places as challengers, awaiting the arrival of answerers. The lists, which had been prepared and checked, on 9 and 10 June, were ready for the jousting to begin, and the kings' shields were hung upon the tree of noblesse, surmounted with crowns. There were also two wooden houses, so that each had somewhere to change attire and don their armour. The first knight to answer the challenge was Charles, Duke d'Alençon, with ten men riding coursers trapped in black and white velvet and tinsel satin, then came Admiral Bonnivet, with a troupe of twelve, in russet satin, broached with gold, white and purple satin, with great plumes. The challengers rode about the lists and paid reverence to the queens and ladies before the first courses were run. The four English judges appointed that day to oversee the proceedings were Henry Percy, Earl of Northumberland, Charles Somerset, Earl of Worcester, the Lord St. John and Sir Edward Poynings. On the French side, there were Dorval, the Governor of Champagne, the Marshal de la Pallice and Daubigny.[12]

First, Francis ran against d'Alençon, with the French king doing 'valiantly' and their spears breaking 'mightily'. Next, Henry ran against a Monsieur Graundeuile, 'with great vigour, so that the spears broke in the king's hand.' On their second clash, Henry gave his opponent such a blow that a part of his headpiece broke, 'although the same was very strong', so that he was forced to withdraw. The Duke de Vendôme took the third run, meeting his counterpart 'right nobly' and breaking spears. He was followed by the Duke of Suffolk, who rode the complete five charges with his opponent, 'right nobly together like good men of arms'. Trivulzio relates that they 'jousted upwards of three hours, and many spears were broken.' The kings acquitted themselves well, he thought, 'especially the King of France, who shivered spears like reeds, and never missed a stroke,' although he admitted there was little to choose between the two sides, as 'in truth, the English behaved well.'[13] Soardino was less impressed, writing that 'few spears were shivered and no notable strokes were made' except for one encounter, when Henry's spear was splintered 'but his hand received no injury.' He thought that the tilting began at 4 or 5pm and lasted until after 7.[14] Royal Senator Montemerle was informed by his correspondent that it began to rain towards evening, so 'all went to disarm, after which the Kings ascended the ladies' stages and amused themselves' while the Comte St Pol and Sanseverino performed feats upon two horses, 'which were always in the air.'[15] Then, the kings embraced and returned to their lodgings.

A set of rules had been agreed in advance between the English and the French, which give some idea of the nature, and dangers, of the joust, and sixteen gentlemen of 'name and blood,' eight on each side, 'for the honour of God and the love of their ladies', were charged to maintain these articles. As a result of 'the numerous accidents to noblemen' in the past, sharp steel was not to be used, 'but only arms for strength, agility and pastime'. The challengers were to face all comers, 'with blunt lances in harness... without any fastening to the saddle, which might prevent mounting or dismounting with ease.' Each was to have middle-sized lances, 'or greater, if any of the comers prefer it' and 'as many strokes to be given as the comers demand.' Single-handed swords were permitted, with blunt points, and the judges would be the arbiters of the number of strokes given. There were also specifications about the style of headwear, with no helm, demi-helm nor bassinet allowed.[16]

The ritual and protocol were also clearly outlined. Those who wished to run in the lists must touch the black and grey shield on the tree, and deliver their shield of arms to the herald, who would record their names and the number of courses they wished to run, and the size of their lances. Those requesting to enter the courses in the field should touch the second shield, and those intending to fight at the barrier, the third shield. If the judges decided that a combatant had been beaten, he must give a gold token to the lady of his opponent, and anyone disarmed was ruled out, and 'must be content with what he has done for that day.' If a horse bolted from the lists, but ran the course, it would still count, and it was fair that the comer should have a fresh start. If a challenger struck or killed his opponent's horse, he should not run again that day without the permission of the ladies, and those striking a saddle would be penalised two lances. All Sundays and feasts of the French and English churches were to be observed, 'by abstinence from running'.[17]

The costs of the jousting at Guisnes also survive in full detail, running to quantities, fabrics, colours, and design. The true story of the event is perhaps revealed not in the lances broken by knights in splendid armour, but in the workers behind the scenes, the commercial transactions and the scores of individuals who never made it across the Channel, but whose work contributed to the name and fame the event inspired. Henry's four horseback attendants, Henry and Edward Guildford, John Peche and Monsieur Moret, required thirteen yards of cloth of gold, received from a Jasper Worley, and six more for the harnesses of their horses. A board with a dragon, lozenged with gold, silver and velvet required almost four yards of cloth, while seventy yards were provided for seven bases for lords challengers. The four men with Henry required 365 yards of cloth of silver of damask for their coats, as well as for the half-coats of the six foot-knights. Decorative boards were embroidered with heraldic devices: a lion, dragon, greyhound, white hart, black bull, falcon and fetterlock. Those specifically for Henry had eglantine roses, a hand, truelove knots and the letters H and K. Also on the list of expenses were Venetian cloth of gold of tissue, and 368 yards of Venice cloth of silver, 108 yards of white velvet, bought from Nicholas Slynge a merchant of St Omer, russet and yellow velvet, 110 yards of russet satin, yellow damask, 150 yards of white damask and sarcenet, eight ells of linen cloth from Holland and fifty-six pieces of black buckram. During the encounters, several bases were lost, as well as pearls and gold from the side of the king's trapper. Later, when the lists were closed at the end of the visit, people pulled the branches off the tree of noblesse and wore them at court.[18]

Other interesting figures emerging from the accounts are Assamus the armourer, who received a coat, Robert the Devil, who was clothed in russet satin, and Mr Crochet, who was surveyor of the stable. There are also the suppliers; George Senesko, who contributed flat gold and silver damask, John Demolens and Thomas Foster, who sold Venentian gold, Elizabeth Phillip the silkwoman, for her cordels, fringe and ribbon, used 'on this side the sea and beyond the sea', red hose for the King's footmen, and white, yellow and 'marble colour' for quarter hose for the armourers. A haberdasher named John Northrop was paid for sixty-two bonnets, at 2s 8d each, and 13b of wool was required from an unnamed tailor at 5d a pound, for stuffing the king's headpieces and mantlets.[19]

On Tuesday, 12 June, the jousting continued, even though the weather was bad. Soardino reported that four challengers ran three courses, two against the English and one against the French, but 'as it was windy, they ran badly.' After a while, they gave up tilting, and watched 'wrestling by Breton and English men', where the latter proved more successful.[20] Catherine and Claude did not attend, but Mary and other English ladies were present, as were Madame de Vendôme and Madame la Grande, wife of Cardinal Boissy, with a small company. An anonymous letter adds that Monsieur de l'Esparre entered the lists 'with a band to attack the King, who, however, were not armed,' and places the Queens at the event[21] in contradiction to Soardino, as does Edward Hall's version. Nor does Hall mention the bad weather, but places the kings in the field, ready to meet challengers, including tilting with ten gentlemen dressed in velvet with silver knots, and eleven knights led by Monsieur de Tremoyell, in yellow and black velvet, who ran and ran, finishing the day valiantly.[22]

A letter from Sir Richard Wingfield to Wolsey, listed in the English State Letters for June 12, exposes some of the diplomatic interactions that were taking place behind the colourful public scenes. Wingfield, then in his fifties, had been suffering from pain in his legs for around three days, which prevented him from travelling. He had been entrusted by Wolsey with a message for Louise of Savoy but, being unable to deliver it himself, had sent for Francis' Treasurer, Florimond Robertet, who came to Wingfield's lodgings to collect it and deliver it to the king's mother. The content of the message is not explained in the record, but when Robertet returned, he told Wingfield that Wolsey had 'promised in a few days to tell her some things which no one else must communicate,' and that Louise 'shows herself like a woman,' being 'very anxious to speak with you' and begged that while the kings were at the camp today, Wolsey might visit her, 'or if not today, tomorrow'.[23] Exactly what Wolsey said, and how Louise replied, are sadly not reported.

Wolsey was already very busy with arrangements and preparations, though. That evening, he hosted a banquet, at which

1. A young Henry VIII had already reigned for eleven years in 1520, a larger-than-life character known for his love of costume, dance and display. Having led his own campaign against France, Henry was now keen to make his mark on the international stage as a peacemaker. Torn between alliances with Francis and Charles, he decided to pursue both, creating an uneasy tension in the summer of 1520. (Rijksmuseum)

2. Catherine of Aragon, as Mary Magdalene. Henry's Spanish queen was initially opposed to a French alliance, preferring that with her nephew, Charles V. Attending the meeting with a large entourage, she entertained Francis I at Guisnes and presided over the jousts at Balinghem. (Detroit Institute of Art)

3. Cardinal Thomas Wolsey, Henry's able minister and architect of the Treaty of London, was pro-French in policy. Liked and trusted by Francis, he smoothed the diplomatic path for the meeting of the two kings and masterminded much of the organisation. (Wellcome Collection)

4. Charles Brandon, Duke of Suffolk, Henry's life-long friend and brother-in-law since his marriage to Mary Tudor. One of the best jousters of Henry's court, he featured prominently during the entertainments and hospitality of the Field of the Cloth of Gold. (Metropolitan Museum of Art)

5. Thomas Boleyn, ambassador to France, one of the main negotiators of the event in 1518-19. Henry's future father-in-law attended with his family, including both his daughters.

6. Francis I, king since 1515, was keen to meet his English counterpart despite being aware of Henry's ongoing negotiations with Charles. Mercurial and charming, Francis rivalled Henry in the beauty of his clothing and his temporary village at Ardres, but a genuine friendship appears to have been sparked between the two men. (Rijksmuseum)

7. Claude, Queen of France, depicted in a manuscript image portraying her coronation in Paris in 1517. Heavily pregnant in the summer of 1520, Claude attended the meeting with the English and entertained Henry at Ardres. She met Catherine in the jousting lists, and the two corresponded after the event.

8. Louise of Savoy, mother of Francis I, who acted as hostess at the Field of the Cloth of Gold, and negotiated particularly with Wolsey. Louise welcomed Henry to Ardres and attended the jousting and other ceremonial occasions, but refused the limelight. (Fondation Bemberg)

9. Below left: Marguerite of Navarre, formerly d'Alençon, sister of Francis I, who was present at the Field of Cloth of Gold with her first husband, Charles d'Alençon.

10. Below right: Guillaume Gouffier, Seigneur de Bonnivet, Admiral of France. A veteran of Marignano, he had run Francis' campaign for election as Emperor in 1519, and was a key figure through the negotiations and events of the Field of the Cloth of Gold.

11. Charles V, elected Holy Roman Emperor in 1519 at the age of 19. Keen to preserve a volatile alliance with England, Charles hurried to meet Henry immediately before the Field of the Cloth of Gold, and again afterwards, although he found Henry more Francophile than he had hoped. In subsequent years, it was Charles who became the more powerful, crushing Francis after the Battle of Pavia. (Rijksmuseum)

12. Margaret of Austria/ Savoy, Regent of the Netherlands, aunt of Charles V and former sister-in-law to Catherine of Aragon. Margaret and Henry met during his French campaign of 1513, and she continued to work hard to influence him in favour of a closer alliance with the Hapsburg Empire. (Metropolitan Museum of Art)

13. Pope Leo X, with whom Francis I established a connection early in his reign. Determined to create a Catholic league in Europe to combat the threat of the Turks, Leo encouraged Henry in his role as peacemaker. (Museums and Heritage Antwerp)

14. William Warham, Archbishop of Canterbury, had married and crowned Catherine and Henry, and hosted Charles V in his Canterbury palace in May 1520. He then participated at the Field of the Cloth of Gold, with ten horsemen and ten footmen in his retinue.

15. John Fisher, Bishop of Rochester, was one of the three bishops in Catherine's company in 1520. Six months after the event, he preached a sermon about the Field of the Cloth of Gold, with the focus upon its temporality in contrast with spiritual riches.

16. Henry Guildford, Master of the Horse to Henry VIII, who rode at the king's side when he met Francis in the golden valley on 7 June 1520. He also took part in the jousting in Henry's company.

17. Nicholas Carew, one of Henry's early friends, the rowdy 'minions'. He was given the job of allocating lodgings for the English party upon their arrival in Calais, jousted and took part in the revelry at Ardres.

18. Thomas More, then a lawyer and privy councillor, was a signatory of the treaty for the meeting between Henry and Charles, and attended the event in 1520.

19. William Fitzwilliam, Earl of Southampton, was Vice Admiral of England, responsible for selecting and equipping the ships that would transport the English party across the Channel. The surviving records indicate just what an immense task this was.

20. A private man, William Parr worked for Sir Nicholas Vaux, before being employed in the household of Henry's illegitimate son, Henry Fitzroy. He attended the Field of the Cloth of Gold with twenty attendants, and his sister-in-law, Maud Parr, mother of Catherine Parr, was in the entourage of Catherine of Aragon. William was given the role of being an undermarshal responsible for keeping law and order in Calais.

21. A Tudor procession from a parliament roll of the 1510s, showing the young Henry VIII amid the strict protocol and majesty of the early Tudor court.

22. Departure at Dover. The huge flotilla of English ships set off late on 31 May, arriving at Calais at 11 p.m. after a turbulent crossing.

23. Balinghem field, photographed in the early twentieth century. The location where Henry and Francis first met was carefully measured to be between Guisnes and Ardres, and flattened in advance, so that neither side should be higher. (Library of Congress)

24. A roll of jousters at the Field of Cloth of Gold, featuring the coats of arms of Henry and Francis. Jousting provided a chivalric 'bonding' framework for the two kings to establish their friendship. Both were celebrated in the lists and brought their challengers, dressed in matching costumes, to clash in what could, sometimes, be a dangerous game. (© North Wind Picture Archives/Alamy)

25 & 26. The earliest dated armour from the Greenwich workshops, set up by Henry VIII in 1515. The design is attributed to Holbein, and the armour includes pieces specifically for tourneying, such as a left-hand gauntlet reinforcement and a lance rest. The suit is believed to have been made for Henry and later gifted by him to a French ambassador in 1527. (Metropolitan Museum of Art)

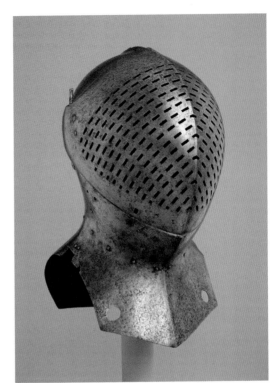

27. A helm belonging to Sir Giles Capel, one of the challengers in Henry's retinue in 1520. There is a good chance this very helm, made for combat on foot, was used in the tournaments of 1520, as it was his 'best helm'. (Metropolitan Museum of Art)

28. A tapestry depicting the wrestling match between Henry and Francis.

29 & 30. A replica of the Guisnes fountain at Hampton Court.

many of the French nobility were present, with 'great decorum, ceremony, pomp and formalities'.[24] This may have been held in his gold-draped lodgings in the pavilion, as one source commented that 'the extreme splendour of his dwelling is incredible.'[25] In the eyes of one Venetian, this was a great sign of peace, as 'both parties kept open house like perfect friends, giving hope of goodwill and union between these two nations, which for many years have been bred in hatred of each other.' The change was 'effected through the wisdom and virtue of both the sovereigns, who are anxious for the peace of Christendom.'[26]

While Wolsey was entertaining, English lords went to Ardres to perform a Meskeller, or maskalyne, the Italian masque style, already popular at Henry's court. Ten revellers including the Earl of Devonshire, Sir Francis Bryan and Sir Nicholas Carew, were dressed in crimson velvet cloaks and doublets, with wide sleeves lined with yellow tinsel satin. Their cloaks and hats were guarded with gold and silver damask, their hose and shoes were cloth of gold, with purses and girdles of seal skin, their horses trapped in white and yellow damask. Next came ten more performers, in blue satin gowns embroidered with gold, hats, tippets, purses and girdles of gold 'of the ancient fashion', then ten more in princely gowns of cloth of gold and black tinsel, tied with white silk cordels and lined with green sarcenet, gold bonnets with tinsel hoods and black tinsel satin on their horses. In the fourth and final phase of performance, three actors wore gowns in purple gold camlet and 29 yards of blue tinsel, with green bonnets and hoods and the same yellow and white horses.[27]

The high winds continued the following day, Wednesday, 13 June. Hall describes Francis' entourage dressed in purple satin, broached with gold and purple velvet, embroidered with little rolls of white satin, upon which was written 'quando', the Italian for 'when' and the letter 'L,' signifying 'elle', or 'she' in French, equating to the message 'when she?' relating to Francis' first device of the heart in pain. The English wore cloth of silver damask featuring lozenges of russet velvet, inside which were gold eglantine roses, conveying the warning that the rose was sweet and pleasant, 'if it be kindly and friendly handled' but if it was 'rudely dealt with, it will prick,' and anyone trying to pull up the tree 'will be hurt'. An eyewitness wrote that 'it blows a terrible gale, and as the Kings were unable to joust, they went to the lists to see some Bretons and Englishmen wrestle.' Whether or not this was the famous occasion when Francis defeated Henry in a wrestling contest, none of the accounts confirm.[28] Florange's version has Henry grabbing Francis by the arm and saying 'brother, let us wrestle,' whereupon Francis 'crooked' the English king's leg and laid him out on the floor. When Henry rose, flushed and angry, the timely announcement of dinner defused the situation, although Florange's editor, Michelet, considers this was the moment when Anglo-French relations began to sour.[29] None of the other sources mention this incident, though, so it may be apocryphal.

Once again, contrary to the other accounts written at the scene, Edward Hall has jousting taking place on Wednesday 13 June. His version of Wednesday has Francis running against a Monsieur Bussy d'Amboise, who was perhaps George d'Amboise, who would die at Pavia in 1525, a relative of Louis de Clermont, seigneur de Bussy, who inspired George Chapman's later play of the same name. He also has Henry running against a 'Monsieur Liskew' or Monsieur de l'Escu, and the Marquis de Salons, breaking spears, 'course after course' and although their counterparts acquitted themselves valiantly, 'the two kings surmounted all the rest in prowess and valiantness.'[30] The discrepancy between accounts may exist because Hall himself, then a recent graduate of King's College, Cambridge, now studying law at Gray's Inn, did not attend the Field of the Cloth of Gold in person. Around this time, he became friends with the son of Robert Fabyan, an earlier chronicler of London, sparking his interest in recorded history, but his famous chronicle was not written until later, and thus the different days may have been conflated by distance. Richard Grafton's chronicle, printed in 1562, avoids this trap by not attempting to recapture the events of the individual days of the joust, but speaks of them collectively.[31] An anonymous letter to Pietro Montemerlo, written on 14 June, may well have been Hall's original source, as it conflates Tuesday 12 June and Wednesday 13 June into one, but refers to the jousting of de l'Escu without attaching it to a particular date. When the writer speaks of events happening 'today', he refers to Thursday 14 June, but, confusingly, places Francis wearing his 'quando' outfit (of Wednesday) upon that day.[32] Soardino adds to the uncertainty, referring to Wednesday as the 12th, when it was in fact the 13th,[33] but setting aside the confusion over exact dates, the letters and chronicles give similar details of what happened, and thus a vivid picture of the jousting.

The two kings and their queens were at the lists by midday on Thursday 14 June, which is Hall's Thursday 13th. Soardino relates how Catherine wore a Spanish headdress, with 'a tress of hair over her shoulders and gown', a dress of cloth of gold and jewels around her neck. She travelled in an open litter, completely covered in gold, embroidered with crimson satin foliage worked with gold, which had little gold columns inside, 'like a triumphal car'. Henry and his entourage wore 'bi-parted garments', half silver and the other half gold, silver and black velvet, and Francis rode the Neapolitan courses given to him by Henry, 'but it did not do him good service,' as it 'carried him very well for 12 courses, and then commenced swerving... and he was obliged to change his horse.'[34]

There were eight challengers that day; Henry, Francis, three French and three English, but the wind was so strong again that three of the five tilting spears were broken or lost. Hall lists Francis Bryan, Henry Norris, Lord Herbert, Leonard Grey, Lord Montague and Arthur Poole as taking part, all richly apparelled, with one side wearing blue velvet embroidered with a lady's hand pouring water upon a man's burning heart, while the others wore white satin embroidered with gold letters. Edmund Howard, the uncle of Anne Boleyn, led a company of eleven dressed in crimson satin sewn with gold flames, and ran five courses against Francis. Henry ran against a 'strong gentleman named Raffe Broke' and shattered his spear 'right nobly'.[35] A similar version states that

Henry and Charles Brandon 'did marvels' and all returned home at about 7.[36]

Emperor Charles, a short distance away at Brussels, was receiving daily updates from his ambassador Bernard de Mesa, Bishop of Elna. He wrote to Henry on the 14th, keen to strengthen their bond and not to be forgotten - perhaps even with a twinge of jealousy. Having been informed of Henry's 'health and disposition, his good cheer and joyous pastimes at the meeting' Charles longed to see Henry again and 'inform him of some good things which have happened since (his) departure'. The Emperor added that he had been in good health and 'occupied in visiting his subjects, hunting and hawking' and as he took 'great pleasure' in hearing news from Henry, hoped the English king would not fail to send more.[37]

On Friday, 15 June, as the Mantuan Ambassador explains, the queens did not attend the lists at Balinghem and although the kings were there, they did not run, amusing themselves instead with the ladies. Again, it 'blew a gale' but some brave souls tilted, including Monsieur la Trimouille and the Marquis of Saluzzo, who broke six lances out of eight, and 'to the present time, no one has broken as many as he.'[38] In contradiction, Hall has both kings dressed in splendour and taking part in the lists that day, with Henry running 'so freshly' that one of his horses dropped dead of exhaustion, or injury, later that night. Hall puts Henry in half gold, half silver, set with pearls and gold ciphers of letters knotted together, spelling out 'God my Friend', 'My Realm' and 'I May', which Francis matched in purple velvet, embroidered with little books of white satin, with blue chains, in which were written 'A Me,' and 'Liber,' making 'Libera Me,' or free me; the meaning was that the English should set Francis free. Henry rode against Robert III de la Marche, or Marck, Monsieur de Floranges, who was dressed in crimson and tawny velvet embroidered with silver shepherds' hooks and led twelve men in similar attire. Hall certainly does confuse his dates, but usually by mixing the calendar date with the next day of the week, and there were no jousts on the

Saturday following, so the conflicting information for Friday is difficult to resolve.[39] The Lescaille account confirms that 'Friday, the 15th, the kings did not run' but that other challengers did.[40] Perhaps Floranges did run, and Hall was mistaken that it was against Henry.

As might be expected from such a large encounter between two former enemy nations, small frustrations and tension arose between the French and English. On Friday, Sir John Peche and five others wrote to Wolsey complaining that they did not like the answer they had received from a Monsieur de Fayette, Captain of Boulogne. The nearby area of Conneswade had formerly been granted by Richard Wingfield to certain gentlemen at arms to farm, but now, presumably for purposes serving the Field of the Cloth of Gold, Peche had requested that the area be evacuated. The French reply to this does not survive, but it does not appear to have been that which the English had hoped for, and serves as a reminder of the continuing small-scale Anglo-French dialogue for precedence that underpinned the diplomatic friendliness.

16

SATURDAY, 16 JUNE – FRIDAY, 22 JUNE

That Saturday was a day of rest in the camps, following the week of jousting and the masques planned for the following evening. Perhaps it was also hoped that delay would give the terrible weather a chance to dispel. It seems, though, that Wolsey was still working behind the scenes, attempting to negotiate a peace between Francis and the Emperor, and a three-way meeting with Henry. As Vergil reminds us, this was the result of pressure put upon him by Charles in Canterbury the previous month, but it also played to Henry's new-found desire to be the peacemaker in Europe. Giustinian, who had been present during the Emperor's visit to England, wrote to inform the Signory that the Cardinal was proposing that Francis would have the Duchy of Burgundy in exchange for returning the Duchy of Milan. Wolsey may have been exceeding his remit here, attempting to pull off a diplomatic coup similar to the 1518 Treaty of London, but Francis was having none of it. When the English ambassadors attempted to sound out the French king, he replied coldly that 'he did not intend to make any fresh agreement' and that Charles should 'abide by the promise already given him,' as he himself had done. His mother, Louise of Savoy, and the French treasurer, Florimond Robertet, made the same reply, and Francis added that he would be withdrawing to

Paris in eight days' time.[1] Francis maintained a dignified silence over Henry's interactions with Charles and continued to pursue his policy of Anglo-French friendship.

On Sunday morning, Francis took the initiative. He arrived at around 8, and unannounced, at Guisnes Castle, with a handful of attendants with him, some sources saying four, others as many as ten, as well as his mother. Depending upon the account, Henry either quitted his chamber with 'glad haste' to welcome Francis 'in a friendly manner' or the French King surprised him at breakfast, ran to his friend and embraced him. The Venetians Badoer and Giustinian relate that Henry embraced and thanked him, removing from his own neck a 'collar of precious stones' as a gift, which Francis repaid by taking off 'jewelled bracelets of great value' and giving them to Henry.[2] The Lescaille account adds that 'this action removed all suspicion from the minds of the English,'[3] which is confirmed by at least one other source, although neither clarify exactly what this suspicion comprised, nor why it had arisen.

Guisnes Castle hosted Francis and Louise that day, while Henry and Mary rode over to Ardres. Unusually, Hall draws attention to the behind-the-scenes business of the 'Lord Chamberlain, (Charles Somerset, Earl of Worcester) Lord Steward (George Talbot, Earl of Shrewsbury) and all other officials (who were) to make ready feast and cheer,' adding that it would take too long to rehearse all, 'for such a feast and banquet was then made that of long time before had not been seen.'[4] Catherine received Francis 'with all honour that was according' and led him into the banqueting hall of the pavilion, On display, there was a 'multitude' of silver and gold plates and vessels and the finest ingredients had been sourced, from local 'forests, parks, field, salt sea, rivers, moats and ponds'; men were well rewarded for finding great delicacies.[5] Francis was seated on a table alone, Catherine ate nearby, and Louise a little below her, on the left hand side, according to protocol, while the French Princes who had accompanied Francis were provided for by Wolsey.

A provisional menu survives for the occasion in the Rutland Papers and, although it does not represent the final order of service, it gives a fair idea of the kinds of dishes that were consumed that evening. The first of three courses contained boiled capon, cygnets, carpet of venison, pike, heron and hart, followed by pear pies, custard, cream and fruit. Secondly, kid, capon, sturgeon, peacock, pigeons, quails and baked venison prefaced similar sweet dishes, before a final course introduced storks, pheasants, egrets, chickens, gull, haggis, bream and green apples, followed by oranges, fruit, creamy towers and a cold banquet.[6] When the plates were cleared away, masked dancers performed and women were disguised as mummers.

Henry and his party were received at Ardres by Claude and the French lords with 'much honour'.[8] He was conducted to a chamber hung with blue velvet embroidered with fleur de lys of cloth of gold, where there was a great bed decked out in the same material, and through into another room which was dressed in the king's estate, hung with cloth of gold decorated with cordels and knots of silver, and a royal canopy. Tables were set out for feasting and two cupboards displayed gold and silver plate. Henry was seated with Constable Bourbon, Charles, Duke of Suffolk, Monsieurs de Vendôme and de Lautrec, and 'another English Prince',[9] whom Soardino did not know, perhaps a cousin of Henry's, such as the Marquis of Dorset, or Buckingham. At the head of the next table sat Admiral Bonnivet, with Claude and Mary, Duchess of Suffolk, close enough to still be under the royal canopy, both women wearing jewels and pearls. As Hall stated, 'To tell you the apparel of the ladies, their rich attires, their sumptuous jewels, and the goodly behaviour from day to day since the first meeting, I assure you, ten men's wits could scarcely declare it,'[10] but then, Hall was not there!

After the meal was complete, Mary led the first dance, perhaps to distract attention away from the king's secret plan. Henry retreated, in order to change his costume, reappearing masked with 'a handsome company' in a series of international-themed masks. There were six German drummers in silk, then four 'Eastlanders' in crimson velvet doublets, with stripes of gold brocade, short mantles to match, red hats and red and yellow hose in the German style, with yellow feathers. Following them were five couples in long gowns of murrey (maroon) satin, down to their feet, 'such as were worn of old by doctors in England,' embroidered with mottoes that the Venetians could not decipher.[11] Hall's version of this relates that Henry disappeared secretly to please the Queen, returning in a company of thirty, which began with ten young lords dressed in the manner of 'Ry and Revel in the Ruseland,' or far Estland, perhaps a reference to the far east, or Asia. He describes their hose as being made from a rich gold satin called 'aureate', rolled over the knee with scarlet, and Estland shoes with little peaks of white nails, their hats were in the Danish style, their purses of sealskin, faces covered with visors and their bonnets drawn with gold laces. Hall's long gowns 'in the ancient style' are blue, rather than murrey, and he had been informed that their golden embroidery read 'adieu juness' (*sic*) or 'farewell youth'. Their outfits were completed with black velvet cloaks and hats, violet caps, silk girdles and golden purses, with old-fashioned visors.[12]

Henry appeared in the next masque of ten performers. The Venetians described it as being comprised of five couples dressed in Milanese gowns, chequered with hoods of gold brocade and tissue, and caps instead of hats.[13] Hall has them dressed in pale, rich cloth of gold robes of state, over gowns lined with green taffeta and tied with silver knots, and wearing beards of fine gold wire.[14] The Venetians interpreted these costumes as being in the 'Greek and Albanian cavalry fashion'.[15] A group of musicians including the 'Drunslad Players' paraded through the streets of Ardres, playing their instruments and summoning revellers from the town, bringing them up to greet the French queen. After having greeted them, Claude permitted them to dance with her ladies, 'passing the time right honourably', before removing their visors and partaking of jellies, spices, fruits and banquet delicacies.[16] Afterwards, Henry took his leave of Claude and her court, before the revellers secretly replaced their masks, so their identities remained anonymous, then thirty horses in white and yellow damask, were brought out for them to make their way home.

The following morning, Monday 18 June, a company met at the lists, including the two kings, and various English and French ladies, but not the queens. Hall relates that 'there blew such storms of wind and weather that marvel was to hear' but that 'for which hideous tempest some said it was very prognostication of trouble and hatred to come between princes.'[17] This wording sounds very similar to that delivered by Bishop John Fisher in a sermon that November, which may well have coloured Hall's version. Henry and Francis did not seem perturbed. Neither of them tilted but passed the time among the company, and on horseback, watching as 'many spears were shivered, most especially by the challengers.' At the close of the lists that day, Francis gave Henry six horses, including the dappled 'Mozaurcha' mare and 'Monsieur Ludovico's sorrel horse', the latter showing itself to particularly good advantage when 'Thomaso put them all through their paces.' Reputedly Henry was 'much pleased with them' because his stable 'is not well stocked',[18] Another source has Francis visiting Henry again early in the morning, and dining with him at Guisnes, although this may be a conflation with events of the previous day. The same writer also has Wolsey entertaining again upon the Monday, giving a banquet to a total of twenty bishops, abbots and foreign ambassadors of the courts of England and France. The guests were served with plates and vessels of gold, and after the meal Wolsey was persuaded to sing a mass, and also to do so in the valley at the conclusion of the event It was agreed that both countries should contribute to the building of a chapel dedicated to 'Notre Dona de l'Amistà,' or Our Lady of Friendship. Wolsey apparently gave a gift to Louise, of a small cross of precious stones, 'containing wood of the true cross' and backtracked upon his efforts to reconcile Francis with Charles, speaking of the love between England and France, declaring that 'the Emperor must not aspire to greater power in Italy,' nor 'molest' Francis, 'whom he praised vastly'.[19]

Tuesday 19 June was the last official day of the jousting. Both kings and queens were present at the Balinghem lists, with Soardino stating that Francis had again ridden ahead to

Guisnes to intercept Henry, who gave him 'good greeting' and accompanied him, taking their seats to watch proceedings but not tilting in person. 'The whole court of France rejoices,' he wrote, 'for until now no mark of confidence had been displayed by the English king; nay, in all matters he invariably evinced small trust,' but that Francis 'compelled him to make this demonstration, having set the example by placing himself with such assurance in his hands last Sunday in the Castle of Guisnes.'[20] This statement, coupled with that of the Lescaille account concerning Francis' early arrival on 16 June, suggest the continuing undercurrent of uncertainty that is likely to have arisen as a result of Henry's meeting with the Emperor, and Wolsey's attempts to negotiate on Charles' behalf.

Vergil's account expands upon the tension, but it was published after Wolsey's fall from grace, and thus finds in him a convenient scapegoat for any dissent. However, it also does pick up on the long-standing xenophobia of the English:

And so for many days everything resounded with the voices of merrymakers, but it was possible to see that not all Englishman were looking on the French with happy eyes. What are we to say of the fact that there were some freer spirits who could not even control their words? And so the French king easily saw that he and his subjects were being held in bad odour, and, taking a suitable occasion to expostulate, is said to have addressed Henry and Wolsey: 'I am eternally grateful to you Henry, for I can read in your face (as they say) that you match my affection with your own. And I confess to you, excellent prelate, that I am greatly in your debt, since you uniquely love me and by your work you have made Henry my friend and close intimate. For the rest of the English, as I can see with my eyes and mind, are so far from loving us that they cannot even look upon us gladly. But I think that nature's faults must be forgiven. For I have chosen to mention this, not because I want you to regard your subjects as less dear and beloved for this, but lest you imagine I am unaware of how kind you are being to me.' Henry aptly excused this thing by a joke, since in the absence of humour he could not have done so.[21]

The challenger in the lists upon that final day was Monsieur 'Bonyual', as Hall records him, or 'Bonavalle' as he is described elsewhere, probably meaning Bonnivet, who appeared with a company of fourteen. They wore black velvet and cloth of gold, with 'fair plumes' upon their heads, first doing their observance to the queens before riding about the lists and taking their place at the far end. Although Soardino is very clear that neither king tilted that day, Hall has both Henry and Francis riding against this company, 'course after course' and 'lost no course' until 'Bonyual' and his riders were defeated. The next challenger was Charles, Duke of Bourbon, in white, black and tawny velvet, bordered with cloth of gold, with matching coloured plumes, and a company of seventeen men. Hall attempts to turn the kings' responses into legend, with Henry so successful that 'all men there that him beheld reported his doings, (so valiant were his facts) ever more in honour to be renowned' and Francis deserving 'ever to be spoken of.'[22] However, none of the men that beheld the kings at the lists that day confirm Hall's version of events, suggesting his account is accurate more in the laudatory intention, than the day-to-day reality of those three weeks.

Where Hall and Soardino agree, is that on 19 June the jousting gave way to tournament fighting, particularly wrestling and swordfighting on foot. Francis dressed his band in purple satin, with gold and purple velvet, embroidered with white satin and pansy flowers, while Henry's silver tissue and russet velvet featured the motif of a lady appearing from a cloud and striking a knight with a deadly blow, and the legend 'In love, whoso mounteth, passeth in peril.' The queens took their places, as did the judges, and the heralds were poised to record the event, when the combatants took arms. At the sound of trumpets, a band of 'divers noble and well-armed men' took to the field, led by the Duke d'Alençon and

Bonnivet, on horseback, with naked swords drawn. The two kings put down their visors and rode to the encounter valiantly, beating their counter parties into disarming, after which the men fought in pairs.[23] The Mantuan account claims that on the Tuesday, 'the most Christian Queen (Claude) went to Guisnes with the Queen of England and banqueted there,' although no other source verifies this.[24]

On Wednesday, 20 June (which Hall has as Thursday) Soardino merely records that the bands fought again with swords. The Lescaille account is similarly brief, stating that 'on the following Monday, Tuesday and Wednesday the jousts continued. Jerningham was nearly unhorsed by one of Tremouille's band.'[25] Hall's description of Wednesday's encounter is fuller, beginning with the arrival of the two queens at the camp 'in royalty like unto their estates', and the kings 'armed and apparelled' in the field. Francis had chosen purple satin and velvet, while Henry's entourage dressed in cloth of silver and damask, embroidered with little mountains and sprigs of basil, bordered with gold letters, which read 'break not these sweet herbs of the rich mount, doubt for damage.' The challenger that day was Henry's cousin, Henry Courtenay, Earl of Devon, with sixteen men, and the answerers were Monsieur Florange with twelve men, followed by Bonyval, or Bonnivet, the Duke of Bourbon, Monsieur de Rambeurs and Monsieur de Pyns, each with between nine and seventeen men apiece, 'all well and warlike horse and armed... their devices apparelled right richly.' Francis rode against Devon and Henry against Floranges, breaking his weapon and disarming him, which action was much praised by the spectators. Then the combatants put down their visors and took up swords for hand-to-hand fighting, 'fervently, battle after battle and none ceased till (sic) they all that would enter were delivered of their pretence in challenge.' Such close combat could be dangerous, and Sir John Neville, Francis Bryan, Richard Jerningham and Sir Rowland were appointed 'as aides for the hurt persons'.[26] The account for the following day states that men were throwing spears 'the one to the other, ready or not ready'[27] while others threw darts, so it is little surprise that injuries may have occurred. Afterwards, the kings rode about the field, and heralds proclaimed the end of the tournament.

On Thursday 21 and Friday 22, more 'combats at the barriers were performed on foot, with thrusting and casting lance and two-handed swords,' concluding the two weeks' entertainments.[28] A barrier was erected for the fighters, as was an English hall, upon which work must have been swift and relentless, possibly even taking place overnight. Decorated with blue clouds out of which the sun rose, the hall bore Henry's motto of 'Dieu et mon Droit,' in which the combatants armed themselves while the queens took their places to watch. Dressed and ready, the fighters hurried to the barrier, each holding up a puncheon spear, engaging with whoever was there, 'two for two as the lot fell.' When the spears were broken, they took to swords, and fought with such force that 'the fire sprang out of their armour.' Despite the random throwing of spears and darts, Hall relates that the 'two kings, safe in body and limbs', drew the battle to a close with great honour. It may have been at this point that Claude presented Henry with the 'prize and honour of the joust', which was a diamond and a ruby in two rings, which Catherine matched with a similar gift to Francis.[29]

Lescaille provides a list of those who 'have deserved prizes'.[30] Predictably, the two kings were named first, followed by Charles Brandon, the Comte St Pol, the Marquis of Dorset, Francis Bryan, Anne de Montmorency, and the Duke of Guise. Several knights were also singled out from the various entourages, including Oliver de la Vernade, Sir William Carey, Sir Anthony Brown, Lord Edmund Howard, Rauf Broke and Richard Jerningham. And with that, the lists at Balinghem fell silent.

17

SATURDAY, 23 JUNE –
MONDAY, 25 JUNE

Overnight between Friday 22 and Saturday 23 June, the builders were busy in the valley at Balinghem. A large timber frame was constructed, a fathom and a half high, on pillars, standing opposite the stage, or gallery, from which the jousts had been viewed. It had a 'lofty tribune' on which stood the altar, and was hung with richly embroidered cloths, satins, silks, and cloth of gold. The altar was 'most sumptuously furnished, with ten very large silver-gilt images of saints and two golden candlesticks, all exquisitely wrought' and 'a large jewelled crucifix entirely of gold, and a gold basin and two golden vases, the one for the wine and the other for the water'. Two canopies of estate were hung, and chairs set out beneath for royalty on each side.[1]

At nine on the morning of the Saturday, the English chanters sang the canonical hour of terce, after which they changed into 'very rich vestments'.[2] Henry and Francis were seated inside a special royal enclosure, made in two parts, side by side, and hung with tapestries and cloths of gold. Francis knelt on the right and Henry on the left, with the Duke d'Alençon, Charles, Duke of Bourbon, Charles, Duke of Suffolk, the Duke of Lorraine, Monsieur de Vendôme and Henry, King of Navarre. In another enclosure were the two queens, their positioning mirroring that of the kings, with Mary, Duchess of Suffolk, Louise of Savoy, Marguerite of Alençon and two other important ladies. Wolsey sat under a canopy on the right of the altar, attended by ten English bishops in mitres and a second canopy a little further down marked the seat of the Cardinal and Papal Legate, Adrien Gouffier de Boissy, in his red camlet robe and cape. One step further down sat the Cardinals of Vendôme, Albret and Lorraine, then twelve French bishops with their mitres, and then all the ambassadors resident with the two kings, 'of the Pope, the king of Spain, the Venetians and others'.[3] Between the chapel and enclosure were the chanters of each king and, above them, two oratories, one for the kings, the other for the queens. Soardino observed that 'the platforms and galleries, which contained great numbers of people, were so well arranged that everyone could see,'[4] which was a considerable feat for a building that was erected overnight.

Around noon, Henry and Francis, Catherine and Claude, mounted the platform and knelt at the oratory. Wolsey began the high mass De Trinitate, with the first part sung by English chanters and the second by the French, then Pierre Mouton played the *Kyrie*, and the English played the Gloria in Excelsis, the Patrem sung by Francis' band of sackbuttes and fifes, the Sanctus by the English and the Agnus Dei by the French. They were accompanied by an organ, with trumpets and cornets. One source states that it was Cardinal Bourbon who carried the Gospel forward to the kings to kiss, presenting it first to Francis, who deferred to Henry, who 'refused the honour'. Soardino, presumably seated among the ambassadors known to be present in the chapel, says it was Wolsey who offered them the Gospel and the Pax, which Francis, Henry and Claude kissed, presumably Catherine too, and that it was offered to Louise, who declined 'out of respect for the queen'. The Lescaille account also has Bourbon doing the honours, and the queens, 'after many mutual respects, kissed each other instead.'[5]

At this point, the proceedings were interrupted by a strange sight, incongruous and carnivalesque amid such piety. There appeared in the sky from the direction of Ardres a 'great artificial salamander or dragon', four fathoms long 'and full of fire', which passed overhead in the direction of Guisnes. It travelled 'as fast as a footman can go' and 'as high as a bolt shot from a crossbow'.

Many of those watching were afraid, 'thinking it a comet, or some monster, as they could see nothing to which it was attached,'[6] and the logistics of what may have been an early hot air balloon are still uncertain. The direction of travel, and the choice of the salamander as Francis' personal device, point to him as the instigator of a final flourish to the proceedings, or an attempt to outshine or outwit the English, although it appeared at a very inopportune moment. The flying salamander is captured in the top left corner of the 1545 painting, white and gold with touches of dark green to the wings and neck, a long line of red down its back and along the length of its coiling tail. In this respect, it appears similar to the visual representations of Francis' device in stained glass and carvings at Fontainebleau and Chambord. What became of it is unknown, with its fiery insides, as it is not mentioned again, but was presumably grounded and safely dismantled out of sight.

When the service was resumed, Wolsey gave the benediction and the bishops 'observed all such ceremonies as could possibly have been used with the Pope.'[7] When the Mass was complete, Wolsey's secretary, Richard Pace, addressed the kings from the stage, saying that indulgences were issued for all those who had been present, and then delivered a speech in Latin, which began:

Certain is it that friendship may be easily contracted in absence, but subsequently it increases through presence, and, by means of colloquies and familiar conversation, becomes greater. Then again, it augments when accompanied by the prayers and blessings of the servants of God who have authority to bless, such as the Right Reverend Legate, not only in the realm of England, but in all places where his most serene King lays claim to jurisdiction. He therefore now blesses the two most potent princes, and, by the authority of our Lord Pope Leo, grants plenary indulgence, absolution, etc., to all present, beseeching each individual to pray God to maintain the friendship contracted between the two sovereigns, to the praise of the Christian faith, and for the stability of the holy Apostolic See.[8]

Then, the first stone was laid for the foundation of the church that Henry and Francis had agreed to build in the valley, to mark the place where they had met. It was to be named 'Our Lady of Friendship' and furnished with sacerdotal ornaments at the expense of the two kings, who pledged to visit it every year on the anniversary of the Field of the Cloth of Gold.[9]

Afterwards, the kings and their immediate circle dined together; they 'washed and sat to meat under their cloths of estate,' both on the same side, with Francis at the top. The Queens, Mary, Louise and Marguerite ate in another chamber, while the legates, cardinals and prelates in a third, and the princes, princesses, lords and ladies in others, including some of the additional tents that had been erected around the chapel. In his typical style, Hall declines to elaborate in order to express his praise, as 'the royalty of fare and the richness of vessel, plate and jewels, surmounteth the wit of man to express' and 'to tell you the apparel of the ladies, their rich attires, their sumptuous jewels, their diversities of beauties, and the goodly behaviour of day to day since the first meeting, I assure you ten men's wits can scarce declare it.'[10]

When the meal was finished, the final feats of combat took place. Two knights entered the lists and fought first, followed by a battle, in which Hall claims 106 people took part, before the two kings concluded the event.[11] The Lescaille account has both parties returning home to the sound of trumpets, with the traditional bonfires being lit in the lists and guns fired, to celebrate the night before the feast day of St John the Baptist, which was also Midsummer Night's Eve.[12] 10s was paid to the pages of the Hall, for making and tending the fire.[13] Hall describes masques taking place that evening, but these are more likely to have taken place on the following evening, as Lescaille records.

On Sunday, 24 June, the final encounter of the Field of the Cloth of Gold took place. For the third time, Henry went to Ardres and Francis went to Guisnes, for 'sumptuous banquets' and 'disguisings in costly apparel', hosted by the queens. Henry alone had four companies with him, and each one containing ten courtiers.

The first masque was led by the figure of Hercules, dressed in a shirt of silver damask embroidered in purple with the message 'en femes et infantes cy petit assurances, (sic)' or 'in women and children there is little assurance,' a strange choice possibly intended to emphasise the masculine bond between the kings. Hercules wore a hood which was crowned by a garland of hawthorn and vine leaves, and carried a club of green damask covered with spikes. He wore a lion's skin upon his back, made out of cloth of gold, with hairs of crinkled gold wire, and gold buskins on his legs.[14]

Three others in the company wore the costumes of Hector, Alexander and Julius Caesar in Turkish costumes of green cloth of gold, with bonnets of silver rolled in Cyprus and gold tissue, and gold girdles with pendants cut in the shape of flames. Others were dressed as David, Joshua and Judas, in long gowns of russet tinsel satin with wide sleeves lined with cloth of gold, details of gold and green damask, and gold beards set upon their visors. The final three were Charlemagne, Arthur and Godfrey of Boulogne, in long gowns of purple and purple cloth of gold, with matching hoods and caps.[15] Sadly, Hall does not relate why these individuals were chosen, nor how they were considered to relate to each other, or the story or message they enacted. Similar to Tudor pageants, they may have been randomly selected because of qualities they represented, or as personal favourites of the performers, rather than as part of any consecutive narrative. What they do reflect is the idiosyncratic nature of the Tudor vision of the world, drawn from travellers' tales, imports and visitors, part fact, part legend, mingled with history, and packaged to represent the message of Henry's power in 1520.

All ten of the next company were dressed in coats of crimson satin covered with quatrefoils of gold and silver tissue, each one tied to the other with gold laces. Over these, each had a large robe of crimson satin embroidered with gold figures, matching hoods as well as bonnets with gold damask work and the visors with beards. Ten more ladies wore costumes in the Genovese style, of white satin diapered with crimson and gold, with square gold bonnets rolled with loose gold that hung down their backs, and kerchiefs of fine Cyprus. The final group followed Milanese fashions, in rich silver tissue, with parted, ruffled sleeves, knit with points of gold, and crimson satin bonnets drawn with gold laces.[16]

Among these revellers were Henry and Mary, mounted on horses trapped in white and yellow velvet, although Hall doesn't specify which roles they took. They rode out of Guisnes to the accompaniment of minstrels along the road to Ardres, where they met Francis coming the other way in a chariot, with his company of disguisers. Upon arriving at Ardres, Henry was conducted into a rich chamber where he was received by Claude, at whose insistence all masks were remove before the banquet was served. They were 'nobly served with strange meats' and after dinner, 'began the dances in passing the time joyously' and much 'solace'[17] before the time came for him to replace his mask, quit the French court and ride home through the streets of Ardres. Other members of the English court were feasted by Admiral Bonnivet, the Constable Bourbon and the Dukes of Lorraine and Vendôme, before rejoining the royal party.

Francis' entourage were also dressed in several different styles, 'of divers silks, some cut, some broached, some had plumes that were very fair' and the overall sight was 'very beautiful'. They were met by Catherine at Guisnes and, similarly, all unmasked, after which she did them 'greater reverence' and 'great was the cheer that was there then.' After dinner and dancing, Francis retired to a secret chamber, where he took off his costume and put on his 'apparel of usuance', which was set with many emeralds. Then he reappeared, looked over the court with a 'high countenance',[18] bid the Queen farewell and departed, accompanied by Wolsey and Buckingham.

Henry and Francis did not return home at once. They headed for the valley of Balinghem, the scene of their two-week friendship and rivalry, for one final meeting. The two kings 'embraced and amiably together communed' before exchanging gifts.[19] Soardino goes into some detail about what was given, and to whom, although he doesn't specify whether the queens 'made presents to each other'[20] in person, or through their husbands, as the accounts suggest they did not meet upon this day. Claude gave Catherine a litter of cloth of gold, with its mules and pages, while Catherine presented very beautiful palfreys and hobbies, well trapped. Louise of Savoy gave Wolsey a jewelled crucifix worth 6,000 crowns and Francis gave him gold vases costing 20,000 crowns. To Bonnivet, Henry gave a jewel that he had worn in his cap, worth around 4,000 crowns and a further 10,000 crowns-worth of vases, while San Severino received 1,000 crowns-worth of jewels and 1,800 crowns of gold vases. He gave a crucifix worth 2,000 crowns to Madame de Chateaubriand, a gown of cloth of gold and sable to Monsieur de l'Escu and a gold cup studded with beautiful jewels to Charles, Duke of Bourbon. Wolsey gave Bonnivet a 'very large salt-cellar, all of gold, studded with a number of very beautiful jewels, and surmounted by a St George'. Soardino recorded that other presents of horses were given, and that Henry gave 2,500 crowns to the French household, although he did not know what gift the English king received in return.[21] Hall believed a collar of Balas rubies with pearls and diamonds was given to the French king, and a bracelet of great price was the return gift for Henry, although this detail appears to be taken from their meeting on 17 June.[22] Soardino relates that Henry and Francis were sad at their parting, 'both being in tears, as were well nigh all the others' as a result of 'the tender love contracted by them reciprocally' and were both 'not a little anxious still to remain together.'[23] Lescaille adds that they 'seemed to leave each other with regret'[24] and that Henry liberated those gentlemen who had been hostages at the English court since early in 1519. Three of the Venetian ambassadors placed the farewells at evening time, and commented that they had been told by Louise of Savoy that 'they did so with tears' and that besides the chapel they intended to build, they also intended to visit each other 'frequently' there.[25] The Field of the Cloth of Gold had been a great diplomatic success. As remarked by Martin du Bellai, the spectators believed they had witnessed 'an amity so entire that nothing could ever alter it.'[26]

On Monday, 25 June, Francis and his court left their tents at Ardres and headed south, while Henry and his court deserted

Guisnes for Calais. Just before his arrival, Henry made an offering of 6s 8d at Our Lady of St Peter's, a church situated outside the town walls, although it was later incorporated into the lower town. Some of the older members of the English entourage may have visited the location twenty years before, when Henry's parents entertained the Duke of Burgundy there, transforming the building into a tapestried banqueting venue. Henry and Catherine headed back to the Chequer Inn for a period of rest, before the final phase of their diplomatic intrigue.

AFTERMATH

Drinking a toast at the Field of the Cloth of Gold.
The wine bill was massive.

18

SETTLING THE BILL

With the departure of the English and French courts, Guisnes, Ardres and Balinghem were left with a huge clean-up operation. The tents and temporary halls, the ovens, forges and stables, the Pavilion and the chapel, were dismantled. What happened to the building materials, and any provisions or items left behind, is not fully recorded; valuables were probably shipped back home and reused in the Tudor tradition of adapting clothing, artefacts and even architectural features to new purposes, but some of the perishables may have been sold off to local residents or those who could use them. Payments were received by Wolsey from Thomas Rawlins for salt, Lord Mongey for wood, Edward Ap John for a horse, from John Bryan, a brewer in Calais for malt, from Thomas Cooke, for beer sold on in Canterbury, and from John Newton 'for poultry sold at the King's departure from Calais.'[1] The two weeks that Henry rested in Calais provided him with an opportunity to examine the expense accounts and settle outstanding bills. To keep costs low, he summoned the gentlemen in his entourage, asked them to send half their servants home to England, and bid them to live 'warily', which Hall states was resented after the extravagance of the past few weeks, and the gentlemen 'sore disdained'.[2] The surviving bills allow us to look at the Field of the Cloth of Gold from the service end:

Payments for Wages and Recompense for Gifts Given

Remaining behind as the resident French ambassador, Richard Wingfield was paid £100 for his 'diets and rewards' for the 50 days ending on 12 June, and another £100 for the next 50.

The wages were paid of Sir Griffiths Rhys and his 60 servants, Sir William Bulmer's 20 men, 30 servants employed by the Earl of Essex, Sir Richard Tempest's 20, Sir William Parr's 20 and 5 in the service of Nicholas Marland. The knights received 2s a day and the men 6d or 9d, while the masters were recompensed 4s for each livery coat they provided.

Sir William Fitzwilliam was paid £105 6s for providing victuals on the ships, and for a month's wages.

Wages of cooks, pastlers, &c., 164l. 17s. 2d. Wages out of court, 11l. 2s. 1d. Board wages, 63l. 6s.

To John Rycroft, wages of cooks and pastlers, at 20d. a day. Laborers in the Larder, privy kitchen, scalding house, hall kitchen, and boiling house, at 4d. a day.

Wages out of court to Robt. Constantine, groom of the kitchen, John Alumbye, groom of the boiling house, Peter Gold, Geo. Nelson and others, 6d. a day.

Wages of John Nicolls, breadbearer, June and July, 20s.

Robert Amadas, the king' goldsmith, received £305 1s for three chains that were given to the bailey of Caen, and a further £101 for another single chain

£101 to Sir Andrew Windsor for giving one gold chain to a Frenchman named Brosse.

To Sir Richard Weston, recompense for giving three chains to Moret the Frenchman valet

To Wolsey for a chain given to a Frenchman called Buckehalf, was valued at £55 16s 8d

To Francis' gentleman Rochepot for £200

To de la Batye for £133 6s 8d

To Bryan, a gentleman of Francis' court, £100

To the 'gentlemen of the Equite,' £333 6s 8d

£20 to one of the king's gentlemen called Parker, who was 'hurt at the camp.'

Wages of John Williams, Thos. Vaux, John Welche, Jas. Sutton and Thos. Bone, 6d. a day; Stephen Cope, 12d.

John Pellam, John Repyngton, Thos Sawer, Thos. Clydrowe, John Hunt and Wm. Antony, cutters of meat for the poultry. 6d. a day

William. Barton, William. Farnett, Roger Barowe, Alexander Story, and other feeders, 4d. a day

Jane Boneford and Adrian Story, 12d. a week

Agnes Alonbon, 2 weeks, 20d.

Reward to the Emperor's clerk of the kitchen, who brought some fowls as a present to the King, 4l. 6s. 8d.

To John Copeland, riding into Flanders for poultry, and into the Vale for rabbits, 11s. 6d.

6s to Margery Bennett for fanning and washing hempseed.

Wages of Ric. Williams, and 5 others, in the Salsery, (making sauces) at 4d. a day.

To Thos. Hungerford, for going from London to Calais, to St. Omer's and to the lady Margaret, for wheat, from 11 April to 2 May, with a man to speak the language, 45s.

Costs of John Christopher and another soldier riding with Hungerford, to speak the language, 8s

To Edward ap John, chief overseer of the brewhouse, 8d. a day. William Andrew, under overseer, 6d. a day; William Donkerman, chief brewer, 10d.; Selas Johnson, under brewer, 8d.; other brewers, 6d. To Edward Portalen, for his reward for making Hippocras in the cellar, 20s.[3]

Payments for the Hiring of Property

John Van Standley, a house hired at Guisnes for the clerk of the kitchen, 2s. 8d.

House hire, 28s. 4d.

To Mychell Bynde, hire of a house at Newnam Bridge, for a butchery, 6 wks., 10s.

To Mr. Whetell, John Cokson and Mr. Peche, for pasture hire £60 6s 9d

To Margett Goldsmith, for a butchery at Guisnes, 3 weeks, 13s. 4d.

To Nicholas Mychell, William Rice and William Mumbre, for their houses, hired for Mr. Cofferer, Mr. Myklowe, and the countinghouse at Guisnes.

To Cornelius Baker and Mary Thomas, for their house, hired for a bakehouse at Calais, 26s. 8d

Rent of houses used for the Controlment, the Spicery, the Chaundry and the Wafry at Calais and Guisnes.

Hire of a wool house from Mr. Yerforde, for the pantry, 10s.[4]

Payments for the Provision of Food

John Shurley, the cofferer was paid £1,000 for providing food,[5] but specific payments were also made to suppliers of particular goods in the departments of fish, flesh, poultry, dairy etc Some individuals listed were professional fishers, butchers or grocers, but the quantities required were such that a number of purchases were also made from individuals. Henry's observance of the Catholic calendar required large quantities of fish for Wednesdays, Fridays and Saturdays, when it was decreed that no flesh would be eaten, although this was not always strictly followed. The occurrence of Trinity Sunday, Corpus Christi and the Feast of St John the Baptist during the event would have required special dishes, though.

To William Wolverston, the King's sea fisher, for five dories, 8s. 8d. 48 mullets, 31s. 8d.; 21 basses, 26s. 8d.; 30 turbots, 66s. 4d.; 9,100 plaice, 36l. 11s. 8d.; 7,836 whiting, 7l. 12s.; 6 halibuts, 20s. 4d.; 700 conger, 49l. 12s.; 288 cod, 4l. 4s. 8d.; 5,554 soles, 28l. 0s. 8d.; 1 dolphin, 40s.; 300 breams, 102s. 8d.; 1,890 mackerel, 66s. 7d.; 3 porpoises, 4l.; 11 haddocks, 3s.; 3 crabs and 1 lobster, 16d.; 4 trout, 10s.; 2,800 doz. (?) crayfish, 35s. 4d.; 1 fresh sturgeon, 4l. 13s. 4d.; 3 fresh salmon, 13s.; carriage, 53s, 4d.

Fish from William Honyng and John Fenne: 2 trouts, 4s. 4d.; 1 fresh salmon, and 3 great trouts, 13s. 4d. To Hen. Berd, for 111 carp, 11l. 17s. 8d.; 223 tench, 116s. 4d.; 316 perch, 28s. 8d.; 36 bream, 37s.; 218 pike, 6l. 16s. 2d.; 3,300 roach, 66s.; 250 shallows, 23s. 8d.; 160 crabs, 6s. 4d.; 1 basse, 16d.; 600 flounders, 12s.; 1 trout, 5s. 4d. To Thos. Tylley, for 40 bream, 4l. 18s. 4d.; 6 trout, 10s. 8d.; 494 tench, 11l. 13s. 6d.; 276 pike, 11l. 12s. 4½d.; 450 perch, 73s.; 2,900 roach, 73s. 10d.; 2,600 flounders, 45s. 10d.; 217 carp, 15l. 18s. 8d.; 22 roasting eels, 16s. 2d.; 200 'pimple,' 4s.; mussels, 2d.; 380 crabs and lobsters, 12s. 8d.; 116 shallows, 15s. 4d.

78s 8d to John James, of Antwerp, for 2 fresh sturgeons

To William. Honyng, 373 oxen, at 29s. 10½d. a-piece; 4 were sold to the lord Steward. 2,014 muttons, at 3s. 7d.; 20 sold to the lord Steward. 86 veals, from 2s. 4d. to 3s. 8d. a-piece.

To William. Stafford and Thomas Raven, for 756 veals, from 31 May to 17 July; 18 hogs of grease, at divers prices. 2,014 sheep, £360 16s. 10d, 842 veals, £156 13s. 5d, 18 hogs of grease, £15 6s. 8d, 51 pigs, 33s. 8d, 16 lambs, 22s. 101 flitches of bacon, 117s. 10d.

To John Newton, for 30 doz. capons of grease, 2s. 4d.; 75 doz. and 1 capons 'K,' at 12d.; 6 doz. and 10 pheasants, at 2s.; 203 doz. and 9 quails, at 4s. a doz.; 42 doz. and 2 geese, at 7d.; 2 peacocks, 5s. 4d.; 16 doz. and 7 gulls, at 16d.;

7 doz. and 8 cygnets, at 5s.; 30 doz. and 9 pigeons, at 10d. a
doz.; 11 doz. and 7 mews, at 10d.; 26 doz. and 1 herons, at
2s.; 5 doz. and 5 shovellers, at 2s.; 6 doz. and 4 storks, at 3s.;
7 doz. and 2 bitterns, at 2s.; 4 doz. brewes, at 20d.; 11 egrets,
at 20d.; 36 gal. oil, 36s.

To John Byrling, of St. Omers, for 13 doz. and 4 quails, at
2s. a doz.

To Stephen Cope, 7 partridges, 12d.; 17 plovers, 12d.;
7 lapwings, 4d.; 21 doz. pigeons, 18s. 10d.; 41 doz. hens, 6l.
16s. 10d.; 27 doz. and 3 pullets, 62s. 2½d.;

To Basteau Albright, 26 doz. and 7 herons, 26l. 11s. 8d.

To Thos. Wudroffe, 13 swans, 30s. 4d.

To John Copland, for 9 dozen and 10 conies, 39s. 4d.

To John Forde, 137 doz. rabbits, at 2s. 6d. the doz.

To John Leyland, for 1365 lambs at 19d.

To Julyan Palyard, for 46 doz. 6 quails, at 2s. 2d. a doz., and
2s. 2d. for a cage for them.

To Edw. Brysley, 33 doz. and 7 rabbits, 6l. 14s. 4d.; 12 kids,
12s.; 1 carp, 10s.

To Thomas Seryven, for a hogshead of white vinegar, 23s. 4d.;
3 hhds. red vinegar, 50s.; a pipe of verjuice, 20s.

6 bunches onions, 12d. and onions, 18d.

4 bush. mustard seed, 10s and a mustard querne, 7s. 3d.

12 cheeses, 8s. 1d.

To John Rogers, 432½ gal. cream, 14l. 8s. 4d.

562 gal. milk, 7l. 0s. 7½d.

20s 10d to Thomas Tayllor for cream for the King's cakes

To John White, 195 dishes butter, 30s and 214 lbs. butter, at
2d. a 1b.

30,700 eggs, at 12d. a 100 and 67,350 eggs, 24l. 9s. 8d

To John Fenne, for 2 doz. bread at Guisnes, 2s.

2s for a casket for wafers

1s for two pairs of wafer irons

4,000 wafers for 'soteilties,' 16s. 8d

9s 1d for fourteen sticks of sugar candy

To John Rogers, 5s for two hundred pippins (apples)

To John Busshe, 25s for strawberries and junkets

1,000 pepins, 3s. 4d.

5,500 oranges, 4l. 10s.

8,300 pippins, 8l. 2s.

200 lemons, 2s. 8d.

4 gal. gooseberries, 2s. 2d.[6]

Payments for Drink

To Allen King, for 2 butts Malvesey, at £4.

To Jas. Spence, 1 butt Romeneye, 53s. 4d.; 3 butts Muscadel, at 100s.; 2 butts Camplett, at 53s. 4d.; 15 fats of Rhenish wine, at 6l. 8s.

To Richard Prowe, Richard Harton, Robert Colyns, Edward Burlacy, William. Courtman and Richard Gittons, for Gascon wine, from £4 to £4. 13s. 4d. a tun; French wine, at 72s. 7½d. and 100s. a tun.

To Thomas Knight, John Plesauns, Elizabeth Harte and Robert Flaxton, for ale, at 39s. 3d. a tun.

To John Swete of Melton, for 1 tun of beer of the King's drinking, 32s.

To Adrian Bereman, of London, and Wm. Antony, for beer at 20s. a tun.

To William Skerne, carriage of 100 tuns empty foists to the ship at London, 23s. 8d.

To Davy Miller, freight of 87 tons, empty foists and 2 loads of hoops from London to Calais, 8l.

To John Mace, Thomas Lancastre, Edward ap John, Adrian Hole and Thomas Cooke, for empty hogsheads at 6d. each, and carriage of foists from Calais and St. Peter's to Medelweye and other places.

To Roger Moore, Edmund Pekham and John Bryan, malt at 6s. 8d. the qr.

To John King and William Coterell, oats for the brewhouse at Medlewey, 3s. 6d. a qr.

To William Antony and Edward ap John, for beer hops at 9s. the hundred.

To Henry Wright and William Ruge, ashen cups at 3s. 8d. the 100.

To Edward Skele, for pint and quart earthen cruses, pottlers and galloners.

To Roger Dell, for carriage of wine at wine at Wulkey and Botall wharf, at 2d. a tun. 5 fats Rhenish wine from Bruges to Calais, 40s. 8d.

Grinding 145 qrs. wheat and oats at 3d. a qr.[7]

Payments for Transport

An immense number of items needed transporting to Dover from various locations in England, across the Channel, to Calais, and on to Guisnes. The roads in the short stretch from the coast to the English camp must have been in constant use, with the bad weather influencing their condition for the worse.

To the mayor of Dover, for carriage of venison from parks in England, 116s. 6d.

Freight of 2 bucks powdered from Dover to Calais, 2s

17 bucks from Essex to Guisnes, 52s.

Costs of Edmund Sampson, sent from Calais to Sussex to my lord Arundel for venison, 40s.

Carriage of bucks from Walden Park in Essex, Hithe, Bowghton Park, Arundel, Eltham, Ledys, Donemowe and Bradfield.

Carriage of 3 doz. venison pasties from Dover to Calais, 12d.

To my Lady Tachett, for carriage of venison from Calais to Guisnes, 12d.

To John Boylinger, carriage of 2 great leads from Calais to Guisnes, 5s. 2d.

Carriage of kitchen stuff, 19s. 7d.

To Wm. Rawson and others, carrying bay-salt, 1d. a load.

To Thos. Judd, waiting upon the offal, between Guisnes and Calais, 6d. a day.

carriage of 200 lings from Canterbury to Calais, 9s. 8d.

To Robt. Lark and Geo. Mawkes, carrying 600 ling from the ship to the Garner.

To John Alen, carriage of 9 qrs. 4 lb. bay-salt from Calais to Guisnes, in 3 wagons, 20d. a wagon.

To Margett Goldsmith, carriage of 84 loads of flesh from the butchery in Guisnes to the larder, 4d. a load.

Adrian Sprete, carriage of offal from Guisnes to Calais, 2s. 8d. a day.

To Wm. Honyng, freight of sheep from Hithe to Calais, 4d. a-piece; oxen, 2s.

Carriage of poultry from Brugges to Calais, 12l. 14s. 8d.; toll at Gravelines, 40s.

To Julyan Loder, carriage of a load of poultry from the Haven to the Poultry in Calais, 3d.

To Adrian Johnson, carriage of poultry stuff from Calais to Guisnes, 23 days, at 2s. 8d. a day.

Carriage of 715 lambs from Newman Bridge to Guisnes, 44s

To Robert. Wilkinson, carriage of water from Medelwey to the poultry at Calais, 11d. a day.

To Stephen Cope, carriage of 40 doz. quails from Antwerp to Calais, 4s.

To the carrier of St. Omer's, for a quarter of hempseed, 6s.

To Ric. Gressham and Ric. Blagrave, for Holland cloth at 20d. an ell.

To Ric. Harton, camerik at 4s. an ell; diaper at 4s. 8d. and 1s. 6d. a yd.

To John Mace, for diaper of damask work, 7s. 6d. a yard; 8 barrels of white lights, each containing 12 doz., 6l.

To Thos. Longe, carriage of 2 hogsheads and 3 barrels of wax from London to Calais, 3s. 4d.

To John Carter, carriage of Mr. Myklowe's and Mr. Byrk's stuff from St. Antony's to the ship, 8d.

To John Smith and his fellows, carriage of wood, rushes and salt from Calais to Guisnes, from 5 June to 15 July, 25l. 1s. 4d.

To Laurence Chaundler, carriage of wheat meal, &c. from the haven to the bakehouse at Boulogne Gate, 20s.

To Thomas Rutton, carriage of 16 loads torches from the chaundry to the storehouse in Watergate, 10d.

To William. Bitler, carriage of 8 loads of jewelhouse stuff from the chapel without Watergate to the Cheker, at 3d. a load.

To Antony Carleton, carriage of 2 loads of the Queen's wardrobe from Guisnes to Calais, 5s. 4d.

To Jasper Cope, 4 loads of the same from Guisnes to the camp, 8s.

To John Pate, carriage of the King's Wardrobe of Beds, with 8 carts, from Guisnes to the camp, 16s.

To Dr. Rawson, carriage of the King's closet stuff from Dover Castle to the ship, and from Calais Haven to St. Nicholas' Church, 3s. 8d.

To Thos. Betberd, carriage of 52 loads of the King's wardrobe from Calais to the ship, 13s.[8]

Payments for Art and Material Supplies

1 lb. blue bice, 5s

1½ lb. vermillion, 20d

sponge, 8d.;

16 doz. thin paper, 13s. 4d. 2 lb

3 lb. 'grene arabik,' 16d

4 lb. glue, 10d

4 lb. 'vergresse,' 2s. 8d

2 lb. red lead, 4d.

1 lb. white lead, 2d

1 lb. yellow ochre, 1d.

½ lb. sanguis draconis, (dragon's blood) 5s. 4d.

½ bundle brown paper, 6d.[9]

Payments for Tools and Repairs

To John Alumbye, for mending two wagons, and for a laborer who helped the leads up into the cart which broke between Calais and Guisnes, 2s.

To Robert Whitelok, for soldering the boiling leads, 6s. 8d.

To William Company, for 3 flesh axes, 5s.

6 dressing knives, 10s.

3 mincing knives, 5s.

10 lashing knives, 3s. 4d.

16 'conyssances' upon glasses for the King's arms, 10s. 8d.

41 score 'fanys' of the King's and others' arms, 6d. a score; 60 moulds, 6l.

24 lamps, 2s. 8d.

2 doz. glasses, 9s.

2 panes of copper tinned for ovens, 8s.

To a joiner at Calais, for a cage with joined work, 2s. 2d.

12d to Mr Dosson for making a lock and key for the spicery door.

14d to Robert Constantin for supplying line and cord to hang the quails' cages.

To John Thompson, Thos. Lane, Ric. Nashe, Wm. Hall, Ric. Moriff, Edw. Billing, Thos. Dercye, Alex. Nashe, Wm. Rogers and Stephen Ward, for white wax at 12d. and 14d. a lb.

Pollen wax provided by Belknapp and Thos. Knight at 4l. the 100;

Torchstaves, 16d. a doz.; wick, 2d. a lb.; links, 2d. a lb.

2,200 treen platters for the torches at the banquet, 13l. 15s. To Pase Mewe. cooper, a great tankard for the Ewery, 12d.

To Thomas Lane, the hire of 100 moulds of wax, 6 May, 6l. 13s. 4d.

White wax, 4,702 lb. 1½ qr., 301l. 11s. 3d. and white lights, 17l. 3s. 10¼d.

Yellow wax, 7,914 lb., 317l. 13s. 8½d.

Torch staves, wicks and links, 30l. 8s..

To Thomas Ustwayte and Laurence Ascleyn, pewterers, for 10,654 lb. pewter vessels, at 46s. 8d. the cwt.

To William Ruttor, for 16 glasses for 'soteilties,' at 3½d.

To Roger Norrys, for 2 great coalbaskets, 8d.; 12 white baskets, 3s.; 11 doz. and 6 great flaskets, 57s. 6d.

To Nicholas Pynson, for 8 skimmers, 13s. 4d.; 5 laten ladles, 8s. 4d.

To Philip Fewacre for 6 treen peels, 2s.; 2½ doz. great bowls, 20s.; 2 doz. hippocras bowls, 10s.; 5 doz. trays, 25s.; 3 doz. great treen pestles, 60s.; 18 coalstaves, 3s.; 6 coal shovels, 18d.; 12 drinking bowls, 9d.; 2 great bread graters, 4s. 8d.

To Robert. Thosen, for 18 cowls, 21s.; 2 close cowls, 3s. 4d.; 13 stowpes, 3s. 3d.; 12 small padlocks, 18d.; 3 jaging irons, 12d.; a pair of water bowges, 33s. 4d.; empty pipes for powdering tubs, 14s. 8d.; 6 stock locks with keys, for woolhouses, at 8d.

To Jasper Wading, hire of a great kettle to boil beef in, for 6 weeks, 10s.;

Hire of pots, pans, spits, &c., from London cooks, 17l. 7s. 8d.; Wm. Lowyn, Thos. Allen, and other 'brenners,' colliers, and hewers, 6d. a day.

To John Ap Rice, sent from Calais to London, for pewter vessels for the banquet, 10s. 8d.

To Matthew Page, 450 doz. sent from London to Calais, 23l. 6s. 8d.; for mowing and gathering rushes, 14 days, 6s. 8d.

To Richard. Wales, 4 loads straw, 2s. 8d. a load.

1½ hundred paving stones, 2s. 10d. To a bricklayer and his men for laying them, 8d[10]

Payments for the Stables

To William Cotton, 2 loads hay, at 5s.

To Cornelius Williams, freight of hay from London to Calais, at 7s. 6d. a load, over and above 40s. paid by Edw. Weldon.

To Laurence Townley, 1 load, 16s. 5d.

To William Cottill and John Candisshe, freight of oats from Greenwich to Calais, 8d. a qr.

To John King, of Aldren, in Essex, 82 qrs. oats, 3s. 6d. a quarter with freight.

258 loads hay, 204l. 11s. 1d. 1092 qrs. oats, 194l. 7s. 6d.[11]

At the same time as the bills for the Field of Cloth of Gold were being settled, Henry was incurring new costs in advance of his meeting with the Emperor. Many of the officers who had just fulfilled their roles at Guisnes were tasked with the preparation and supply of another costly event. Henry ordered that a new pavilion be built for the entertainment of his Imperial guests, more food, drink and necessaries were ordered, the town cleaned and prepared and in addition to the English entourage already present, lodgings, with stabling, needed to be found for up to 150 more people. Just as he had at Guisnes, Henry set about transforming Calais.

19

INTERIM, 25 JUNE – 10 JULY

After the kings parted, some of the old doubts resurfaced. In spite of the gaudy tents and pavilions, the feasts and jousts, gifts and promises, absence bred suspicion in an Anglo-French friendship which was already predisposed to fragility. Arranging a lavish reception for Charles at Calais, Henry was aware of this, and dispatched Sir Richard Wingfield to pursue the French king. Francis had not headed immediately to Paris, as he had previously suggested. Instead he travelled west towards Crécy, to hunt in the surrounding forest. It was in the nearby monastery that Wingfield found him and delivered two letters from Wolsey and one from Francis Bryan. Francis welcomed the English ambassador and thanked him for Bryan's 'cordial and loving' letter, which had 'dispelled his pensiveness for the new departure from him'. He was sure 'Henry in his intended meeting with the King Catholic (Charles) would not listen to any proposal to his prejudice' and that an observer had noticed how 'a great amity had arisen' between the English and French kings. Francis confirmed this, 'saying that he honoured Henry for his high virtues, and had such trust in him that... he would have ridden in post to Calais to see him, if he had not failed on provision of horse,' before adding that not only would he visit Henry in Calais, but 'upon the least desire which he can make me, go to him into his city of London.' Francis issued orders that all his ports should treat English merchants well and made 'pleasant and loving devices… very cordially towards Henry' and would be 'to him the most faithful friend in Christendom'.[1]

Francis was as keen to woo Wolsey as Charles had been, both recognising him as the true architect behind Henry's foreign policy. Wingfield wrote to the Cardinal, expressing the French king's 'delight at the love and friendship' he had been shown, and that Francis 'did not doubt that neither at this interview now shortly to be had, nor in none other place where… your grace shall be, he nor any of his affairs can take any harm.' Francis stated that he and Henry were 'two of the happiest princes of this world, the one to have such a subject and servant as your grace was, and he to have of you so perfect a friend and prudent a counsellor.' As both kings' causes were being 'managed and organised' by Wolsey, they could not fail to have 'glorious and prosperous success'. He concluded by promising Wolsey a 'much greater recompense than any remembrance he had yet made him for the trouble he had taken to effect the amity.'[2]

Wingfield also met with Louise of Savoy and appealed to her directly to always be a friend to Henry. Calling him her 'new acquested (sic) son', she promised with 'a joyful countenance' to keep him in remembrance, and that he 'did her the highest honour that ever lady received, to be mother to two of the most perfect and accomplished princes that were ever in the world at once.' She informed Wingfield that Francis was intending to travel into his Duchy of Milan, and was considering 'leaving the government of his realms in Henry's hands till his return, to show his confidence in him'.[3] Francis did not decide to make this gesture in the end, but his and his mother's interactions with Wingfield continued the hyperbole and friendship of the Field of the Cloth of Gold as a means of balancing their fears for Henry's forthcoming meeting with the Emperor.

As part of the new friendship, three unidentified French gentlemen travelled to London. They were greeted by the Lords of the Council and banqueted by the Lord Mayor in Cheapside, at very short notice, as Wolsey's letters of instruction informing the city of their arrival turned up on the same day.

They were conducted through the city the next day by Lord Barnes, and were taken by horseback to dine with the Mayor, visit the Savoy and Henry VII's chapel at Westminster. The Abbot entertained them with 'right goodly cheer' and one of the Sheriffs made them a 'goodly dinner' before they took a barge to Richmond where they visited Princess Mary. The four-year-old impressed them with her precocity at playing on the virgils and they were fed a banquet of strawberries, wafers, wine and hippocras, before returning to another 'goodly supper' with the Sheriff. On Sunday, 1 July, they dined with the Duke of Norfolk and the following day, visited the Tower of London before departing the city to return home. The Lords enclosed their grateful letters of thanks to Henry and reassurances that all was tranquil at home, and their hopes that his meetings were 'to the advancement and increase in honour to his realm'.[4]

Around the same time Wingfield was meeting Francis, the Venetian ambassador Surian wrote to the Signory from Calais. He reported the arrival in the town of an Imperial envoy, who announced that Charles' entourage would include his younger brother Ferdinand, his aunt Margaret, and 300 gentlemen, who required 150 chambers. This was felt by the English to be an excessive amount, so they 'hinted that it should be diminished' but, regardless, building of a new pavilion was underway and 'great preparations had been made and were still making for this visit.' Surian's detail indicates that Henry was hoping for a one-pavilion-fits-all style approach to European diplomacy, as this 'house of canvas and timber... hung with tapestry, (was) like the one made lately for the reception of the most Christian King,' Francis. He also reported that he had been told by Wolsey that he relied upon 'making peace between Spain and France'.[5]

The provisioning of the Emperor's visit began in earnest. John Shurley, Henry's Cofferer, issued £500 to Sir Richard Whethell, Miles Gerrard, Thomas Prowde and William Lelegrave to cater for the Emperor's visit to Calais, and Sir John Heron, Treasurer of the Chamber, likewise gave £550 to Robert Fowler.[6]

The search began again to find suitable quantities of people and food to sustain such a huge venture, especially given the recent amount spent, and local resources used, to supply the Field of the Cloth of Gold. Rewards went to John Snoton's wife for supplying 101 dishes of butter, milk, cream, a calf, pigs and chickens, the baker Robert Mase provided forty-five dozen loaves, flour, barley and bran, John Deswarke of St Omer offered seventy-five carp, fifty pikes and tench, William Matres for capons and butter, Catherine Deacon for peacocks and capons and Robert Ungle for nine ducks. Also on the shopping list were 4,000 eggs, 24lb of cherries, 1,250 herring, seven barrels of sturgeon, a barrel of Holland salmon, nine barrels of oysters, 38lb of bacon, 46lb of lard, 1,400 apples, 220 muttons, 171 lambs, twenty-six veals, four dozen sheep's feet and two barrels of charcoal. Sourcing all this required some travel, with 4s 4d paid to a man for sending to Lille for provision, 6d paid to eight labourers for 'bearing flesh and fish to the great men' and tolls were paid at various points along the road, at New Chateau, Abbeville and Newnam Bridge, to the amount of 5d.[7]

Back in May, when the timings had been uncertain, Henry had set out specifications for his meeting with Charles, if it were to take place across the Channel. Although the exact details were to change a little, the essentials and roles of those involved were the same. Henry considered that the best place to meet would be halfway between Calais and Gravelines, but no exact location had been specified. The first meeting had been planned for 4 July at 3pm, with both sides leaving their lodgings by 1pm, and returning there again afterwards. As the time passed, and greater preparations were needed, it looked increasingly likely that a first meeting would be delayed by a few days, and that the two main arenas of interaction would be the kings' bases at Calais and Gravelines. Richard Gibson was in charge of erecting the pavilion and George Talbot, Lord Steward, would provision it, with Sir Edward Belknapp creating a separate banqueting house. The Lord Chamberlain, Charles Somerset, was to appoint officers of the wardrobe to furnish the rooms in which guests would stay and assign servers for the king's chamber and banquet house. Sir Edward Poynyngs as Treasurer of the Household and Sir William Sandys, Treasurer of Calais were appointed to survey the area.[8] There was also a temporary theatre, over which the legendary figure of King Arthur presided, in the form of a statue in the vestibule, and the representation of a round table.[9]

Charles, Margaret and Chièvres, were to be lodged in the Staple Inn, Archduke Ferdinand was to be placed in a house owned by a Mr Banester and Chièvres' nephew and namesake, William de Croy, Bishop of Toledo, would stay with the Marquis of Dorset. The Lord Chamberlain was to appoint a substantial Master of the House to oversee every lodging where the Imperial noblemen were lodged. In addition to victuals and fuel, the guests' chambers must be provided with torches, fruit, wafers and hippocras, for the entertainment of the nobles. John van Oye was paid 7s 8d for supplying wine to the house of Bartholomew Brewer, where Monsieur Nassau and other lords slept, while Philip Van Broke supplied five lots of Rhenish wine at 10d each and John Demonyer brought 11 lots more for Nassau's residence. Robert Donnington received 12d a day for delivering spices 'at the great men's lodgings' and William Amore of Calais delivered 27 gallons of hippocras at 4s 4d, and 7,350 wafers at 3s the 1,000 'for the ambassadors of Flanders'. The church of Our Lady of St Peter was to be garnished by the Dean of Chapel, the devising of banquets and pageants left to William Cornish, and the filling of cupboards with plate assigned to Sir Henry Wyatt.[10]

Henry's original plan was that on Thursday, 5 July, he would leave Calais with 100 noblemen and 100 of his guard to visit the Emperor at Gravelines, and stay there for Friday and Saturday.[11] Soon after his return to Calais, though, Chièvres appeared in the town to ask Henry to meet Charles at Bruges, 'but this was refused, not being consonant to the conventions made at Canterbury… and being likely to hinder the amity between France and England.'[12] On the evening of Saturday, 7 July, it was planned that Henry, the Emperor, Margaret of Savoy and some of their nobility would return to Calais and dine at the Staple where Charles was lodged. Then, he had hoped, on the morning of Sunday 8 July, Henry, Catherine and Mary, Charles, Ferdinand and Margaret were to attend Mass at Our Lady's Church, sung by Thomas Ruthall, Bishop of Durham, and watchmen at the door were to ensure only noblemen and women were admitted. After Mass, the company were to dine at Henry's lodgings in the Chequer, Henry, Charles and Ferdinand together, Margaret and Catherine on another table, and the Cardinal, Chièvres and the others with Wolsey. On Sunday evening, there would be a supper, followed by a mummery, banquet, dancing and other sports. On Monday, Henry would dine with Charles at the Chequer. Afterwards Catherine would take her leave of her nephew, and Henry and Wolsey would accompany him a few miles until he was back in his own territory.[13]

However, the best laid plans of May had to adjust to a new timescale. On Tuesday, 3 July, Henry celebrated the feast day of St Thomas with a meal of fresh salmon costing 4s 4d,[14] and awaited news from the Emperor. It was not until early in the morning on Thursday, 5 July that Charles left Ghent. Spinelly wrote to Wolsey the following day to confirm his departure, and that he had spent the night at Odenborg, three leagues the other side of Bruges. He was expected to stop at Dunkirk that night and reach Gravelines on 7 July. It had also been suggested to Spinelly that Francis was still lurking nearby in 'some hope of being called to the meeting' and that the 'chief obstacle to peace is the French jealousy of the Emperor's going to Rome,' to be crowned by Pope Leo.[15] Francis had considered himself a special ally of the Pope since his visit in 1515, when they had agreed to stand together against Spain. Also on Saturday 7 July, Surian reported that the Emperor was to cross a 'boundary stream between the English and Flemish Pale, and that Henry and Charles were to host each other for four days.[16] By the following day, 8 July, Margaret of Savoy had reached Gravelines, from where she wrote to Henry that she was returning to him a letter of promise he had made her, presumably about his loyalty to

Charles, as she had 'such confidence in the king, that she requires no surety from him but his simple word.'[17] On July 9, Richard Wingfield wrote from the French court at Chantilly to confirm that Bonnivet had received the Cardinal's assurances that Francis would be 'advertised from time to time of all that shall be entreated'.[18]

Having sent a number of ambassadors to observe the Field of the Cloth of Gold, the Doge of Venice, Leonardo Loredan, wrote to congratulate Wolsey upon his success. One of the most important Doges in the city's history, who had previously allied with the French against the Pope, he is the subject of a now-iconic portrait by Bellini. He had, he wrote, 'long hoped for an interview between the two powerful sovereigns, his confederates, and rejoices it should now have been effected.' As well as affirming their friendship, it proved Wolsey's abilities and wisdom, as a man who could 'accomplish anything, however difficult, provided it were fair and laudable.' He also congratulated the Cardinal for the forthcoming meeting with the Emperor, 'devised by his skill to the advantage of the Christian commonwealth,' considering him a man 'who is deservedly considered his Majesty's second self.'[19] This was quite an accolade for a butcher's son from Ipswich. The Doge also wrote to Francis and Henry, having heard about the 'magnificence displayed' from his ambassadors, 'and the mutual graciousness, affection and insuperable feats of both Kings'.[20] Soon, the ambassadors would have even greater magnificence to report on.

As Henry readied to meet Charles, French eyes were watching. While preparations were being made in the Netherlands, the Duchess de Vendôme and her party arrived unexpectedly, and in Calais, Francis' Grand Chamberlain, Oliver de la Vernade, Seigneur de la Bastie, was present as the negotiations were being finalised, and accompanied Henry as he rode out to meet the Emperor. Loredan paired Antonio Surian with Francesco Cornaro as his eyes upon Henry and kept Giustinian and Badoer together as his team at Francis' court. As the final preparations were made in Calais, Henry gathered his entourage, donned another of his dazzling outfits and mounted the horse given to him by Francis, in order to meet the Emperor.

20

RETURN OF THE EMPEROR

On Tuesday, 10 July, Henry left Calais and rode eastward towards Gravelines. While Hall relates that he was accompanied by Wolsey, 'Dukes, Marquises, Dukes, Earls, Bishops, Barons, Knights and gentlemen', it was the Venetians in his company who observed that the king went masked, perhaps for his own safety when leaving English territory. Before he departed, he uncovered his face for the French ambassador, De la Bastie, 'and addressed the Frenchman publicly on the spot; so he chooses his understanding with France to be known.'[1] The actual size of Henry's entourage was considerable, as Wolsey alone took fifty horsemen and fifty men on foot, the Archbishop of Canterbury, William Warham, had ten horsemen and ten on foot, the Bishop of Durham eight horsemen, the other Bishops six each, the Dukes of Buckingham and Suffolk with ten each and the Marquis of Dorset with eight. 113 knights were named as attending and allocated two horsemen and one footman apiece, the eleven accompanying Earls had six horsemen, the eighteen barons, the three Knights of the Garter and four councillors all had two riders each, and the four chaplains were allocated one horseman per person. In addition, this vast company was protected by 100 of the king's guard. The total was given as 975 people, less than a fifth of Henry's company for the Field of the Cloth of Gold, but still a large group.[2]

Ludovico Spinelli, secretary to ambassador Surian, witnessed the meeting. Charles arrived first, riding a bay horse covered with crimson velvet, then changed to a dapple-grey horse trapped in cloth of gold and silver, which matched his own clothing. The nobility in his company, which Spinelli estimated at not above 200 men, also wore gold and silver, while his knights were dressed in black velvet. Henry wore a similar cloth of gold and silver checks and his dappled grey horse was covered in the same material. A few of his men wore gold but not many, and Spinelli guessed that there were more than 300 in attendance. The visit was 'very unceremonious and without pomp', as the two kings moved towards each other 'in advance of their attendants at no very quick pace'. Henry raised his hand in greeting, drew near and then embraced Charles, who welcomed the English party with 'such semblance of love' that he 'won the love of the Englishmen.' As they were still within the English Pale, the Emperor went on the right hand side, until the boundary which was marked by the 'bridge of boats,' after which they swapped positions and Henry went on the right, as the guest in Imperial territory.[3]

There were only around sixteen miles between Calais and Gravelines. Hall's Chronicle has Charles passing Gravelines water and meeting Henry at place called Waell.[4] No equivalent place exists on a modern map, unless this is Hall's phonetic spelling for 'Vielle' and refers to the village of Vielle-Eglise, at the junction of the modern D229 and D255 roads, nine miles east of Calais, and a likely central spot. From the meeting place, the two kings rode back to Gravelines, where Margaret of Savoy was waiting at the entrance to the palace, and after Henry had 'embraced and kissed her' both kings entered the palace, where supper had been prepared for them. Hall relates how 'the highest to the lowest were so cheered and feasted, with so loving manner that much they praised the Emperor's court.'[5]

On Wednesday 11 July, Henry and Charles dined at Gravelines, then, with Ferdinand, Margaret and their entourage, rode on to Calais. The banqueting hall, overseen by Sir Edward Belknapp, was a 'goodly device', eighty feet round, built using the masts of ships 'in such manner as I think was never seen.' Within it, the 'whole sphere was portrayed,' suggestive of a panoply of the earth or heavens, but it was unfinished, and 'could not be achieved' because of the strong winds.[6] Surian explains that 'a gale of wind carried away the canvas roof, so that the repast was of necessity served in a certain small house,'[7] which was probably the Staple Inn, where Charles was residing. Undeterred, Henry lead fifteen dancers all dressed in black velvet covered in cloth of gold, with the velvet slashed and tied with gold knots, on which hung gold spangles, matching bonnets and cloaks of crimson satin with gold details. They 'danced and revelled' in Charles' presence chamber and Henry only removed his mask when the Emperor requested to know which dancer he was.[8]

However, in conflict with Hall's timescale, the Venetian ambassador Spinelli does not mention Wednesday, but states that Henry remained in Gravelines until the Thursday, dining there with Charles before departing the town to ride back to Calais, with Margaret, Ferdinand and their entourage. Arriving at around seven in the evening, in bad weather, Spinelli has them entering by the Boulogne Gate, where Catherine was waiting. As it was late, Margaret then got into a black velvet litter, while Henry and Charles, dressed again in their gold and silver, presented themselves to the English Queen before all proceeded to their lodgings. That evening, Margaret visited Catherine and Henry went masked to the Emperor.[9] This reads so much like Hall's account, that it appears they are describing the same day, but that one of them was mistaken about the date. It seems most likely that these events took place on the Wednesday.

On Thursday, 12 July, Charles and Margaret visited the English court for supper, which was followed by masks with ninety-six dancers, divided into eight companies of twelve each. Dressed in gold, silver and velvet, they were 'richly apparelled'. With Henry based in the Checker, the change of venue did not do them justice, as 'the room was small' so the 'show was less.'[10] A woman brought the Emperor a portrait that had been made of him, and was rewarded with a chain worth 500 crowns. Hall adds that among this number were young French noblemen, unknown to Henry, acting as spies, so that they 'saw and much more heard than they should,'[11] no doubt reporting back to Francis. This was followed by a banquet, after which Henry accompanied his guests back to their lodgings.

On the same day, Badoer and Giustinian wrote jointly to the Signory of Venice from the French court to report that Francis had 'spoken of his great friendship for the King of England, who had reciprocated in most gracious terms.' Henry had, they said, been open about his intention to meet Charles and although the Emperor's plan was to invade Italy, Francis should 'not be apprehensive... for King Henry intended King Francis to retain all his territory, which would descend to Henry's daughter, as she was to marry his son.' Two days later, though, Henry and Charles agreed a treaty 'to the effect that they will make no treaty with the king of France for any closer matrimonial alliance than exists at present.'[12]

Charles had been due to return to Gravelines on Friday 13 July, but 'the counsel was such that he departed not that night.'[13] Whether this was due to the success of the interview, the weather, superstition or other matters, Hall identifies this day as the occasion when Charles and Henry agreed to renew the treaty of commerce they had made back in April. One other source suggests this may have been achieved as early as 10 July,[14] at Gravelines, although there would likely have been little time on that day, given the arrangements for travel, Henry's reception and supper. The terms reaffirmed their friendship and the nominal extension of their alliance to mutual friends and to stand against their common enemies, and insisted upon each seeking the other's approval before entering into treaties 'with any prince', which included Francis:

1. All former treaties renewed, especially that of 1516, in which prince Ferdinand is to be included. The same to extend not only to the actual possessions of the king of

England and to those which were then due to him, but to those which may accrue to him hereafter.

2. Both Powers to have the same enemies and the same friends. Offence or injury to the one to be repelled by the other as done to himself.

3. In case of invasion, neither party to desist until the aggrieved has recovered his rights.

4. If a captain or lieutenant of another state employed by the one do injury to the other, the one who employs him shall make satisfaction on demand within a month's time.

5. Neither party to enter into treaty with any prince without the consent of the other; and if any treaties exist or hereafter be made contrary to the effect of this, they shall be invalid without the consent of both.

6. Intercourse between the two states to be in conformity with the arrangements made on the 11th April.[15]

Henry was not immediately betraying Francis in the renewal of this treaty, which included the typical diplomatic clauses of most friendship agreements between princes of the time, but the fifth clause might have given the French king pause for thought. It was Wolsey to whom Francis turned, in the belief that the Cardinal would be his friend at the Gravelines meeting and not allow his cause to be weakened. He promoted La Bastie at Wolsey's recommendation, 'entirely out of respect' for him, and Bonnivet re-enforced the king's trust by writing to tell Wolsey of his master's 'great opinion' of him.[16] The Archbishop of Sens, Stephen Poncher, also informed the Cardinal that Francis had been 'very unwilling' to leave Henry's company, and that he, Louise and Marguerite, 'your daughter by adoption, as it is said,' wished to be commended to him. The French court was then at St Germain, and Francis intended 'now they are so far apart, to send frequent messengers and letters.'[17] It was clear that the French saw Wolsey as not only the architect of European policy, but their safeguard against the Emperor, and the equal of royalty. 'Christendom,' wrote Ponchers, 'owes much to you.'

Contrary to this, Hall believed that Henry's meeting with Charles was the beginning of the end for Anglo-French relations. Writing with hindsight, he claimed that when Francis and his nobility

> ...had knowledge of the meeting of the Emperor and the king of England... they were therewith greatly grieved, as by many things appeared, for after the Englishmen were in France disdained and in their suits there greatly deferred and had little right and much less favour [so that, over time] more and more began heartburning, and in conclusion open war did arise between the two realms.[18]

Open war certainly did not arise immediately, as is clear from Francis' correspondence, and his fears that Henry aligned himself more closely with the Emperor would not be justified for another year. For the time being, as Sir Richard Wingfield reported from Poissy, Francis continued in the amity established the previous month. De la Bastie had also communicated his impressions of the meeting of 10 July, which Wingfield had seen, including the detail that Henry rode upon Francis' charger, 'as his said good brother had sent him.' The ambassador had been told that Henry's face did not appear 'to be so replenished with joy' as when he had met Francis.[19]

The Imperial party departed about noon on Saturday the 14th, after taking leave of Catherine and Mary, and Henry rode with them back to 'Waell', presented the Emperor with two horses and doffed his bonnet upon taking his leave.[20] Henry returned to Calais, where he rested for a few days, while preparations were made for the return voyage home. The final expenses were cleared, such as 11s to the Emperor's footmen, fees to the stewards, servants and treasurers of visiting Dukes and expenses for the guests' horses, such as the Chancellor's horses being lodged at the George at 4½ d daily. Recompense was made to those who had lodged guests, such as John Cristoffer, who sheltered five horses belonging to Chièvres for six days, at 18s 6d daily, Thomas Wodnott, who received 27s 3 ¼ d for lodging the Bishop of Toledo's servants, Edward Malpas who housed the servants of Monsieur de Halwyn for 29s 6d and the publican of the Noble, John Loker, for having sixteen horses and eighteen servants at 78s. Henry had also forbidden anyone based along the route from Gravelines to Calais to accept any money for goods and services from the Emperor's company. Those businesses and individuals were compensated, such as Thomas Chapman's wife, for 'the expenses of the strangers at her house outside the gates,' Garard Lebar for grazing fifty-three horses, Jacquett Founten for grazing 150 horses and other supplies of beer, hay, bread and candles.[21] Leaving Wolsey behind to tie up the loose ends, Henry, Catherine, Mary, Brandon and the remaining members of their company sailed home on Wednesday 18 July.

21

ENDPIECE

For six months after the English departure from Calais, the delicate juggling act between the three monarchs continued. The first and most immediate danger was the French concern that Henry would make a new alliance with the Emperor and invalidate his new friendship with Francis. This was swiftly allayed by letters like that from Surian, who wrote to the Signory of Venice that Henry had sailed 'without having come to any agreement with the Emperor' because he, Henry, 'chooses to be French'.[1] Whatever Henry's inclination may have been, though, a latent element of francophobia still found expression in an unfortunate conversation between two English noblemen, one of whom was the brother of the Marquis of Dorset. They were overheard together as one of them said, 'If I had a drop of French blood in my body, I would cut myself open to get rid of it,' to which the other replied 'And so would I.' This was reported to Henry, who had them arrested, and as Surian stated at the time of writing, 'They are expected to fare badly unless the most Christian King (Francis) intercedes for them.'[2]

The next problem was Charles' impending coronation. The crown imperial was, at that point, located in Rome, miles out of reach of the new Emperor, whose relationship with Pope Leo was such that Charles believed he would have to invade Italy to retrieve it. At some point during his talks with the Emperor in

Gravelines or Calais, Henry intervened on behalf of the French king. Surian had heard 'on good authority' that he told the Emperor not to carry out his plans to invade Italy, by which Charles had hoped to obtain the crown and even force a reluctant Pope's hand. This would threaten the peace that had been established following years of conflict in Italy by the treaties of Brussels and Noyon, of 1516. Henry's advice to Charles that July was not to unsettle this balance, 'as it would displease him, because he means to be united with his brother the most Christian King,' and gave Charles 'a certain writing', which had also been sent to Francis for approval, presumably pertaining to this matter. Wolsey's influence is discernible, as the 'good authority', with Surian referring to conversations he had held with the Cardinal, who was secure in his belief that 'There is no fear of the Emperor's coming.'[3]

Thirdly, Surian made the worrying report that Charles' chancellor, Gattinara, and his chief advisor, Chièvres, had attempted to persuade Henry 'to break off the marriage between Charles and the French princess, making an offer' for Mary, who had been betrothed to the dauphin since the 1518 Treaty of London, newly ratified by both parties in June. The scheming pair had also offered to 'undertake to commence war against France four ways by land and sea' and assist Henry to pass through Italy and Milan to claim Francis' throne. This was deeply misjudged, as it ran counter to Henry's feeling in July 1520, yet he replied diplomatically but firmly. Finding their proposal strange, and believing they acted independently of Charles, he reminded the Emperor's servants that they were bound by their oaths to serve him, and in breaking his trust, they might not expect him to trust them in turn. He exhorted them to regard their master's conscience and 'desist from such practices.' No doubt, he thought, as they now dissembled with France, so they would dissemble with him in the future. He added that if they started a war with Francis, he would go to his friend's assistance, and 'showing them how disadvantageous it would be, considering the rebellious state of Spain, and the king's minority and want of treasure'. Surian wrote that Henry 'values the observance of his promise above all earthly things' so he 'could never listen to such proposals' and urged Chièvres to 'study the ways of honour and peace,' or else the love of the princes of the empire would 'soon be turned to enmity'. Henry made the point that if Charles marched an army through Milan, it would constitute an invasion, and Henry would be bound by treaty to assist Francis. After a long debate, with 'the advice of the lady Margaret and others', Charles agreed to follow Henry's counsel.[4]

The Bishop of Bayeux had also heard of this incident, but from Anne de Montmorency, who had been one of the original French hostages to England, and who 'was present at the late interview'. According to Montmorency, Henry was 'ready to declare way against anyone who would do France an injury,' praised Francis highly and said he and the French king were 'not only alike in mind and will, but in person', and showed off a doublet and cloak he was wearing that Francis had given him, so that 'the Spaniards departed ill pleased.'[5] On 27 July though, Thomas Spinelly wrote to Wolsey that he had seen Charles at Bruges, who said he 'should never forget his reception in England and at Calais, and was sorry he could not return' Henry's kindness at a better place than Gravelines.[6]

Reassured by news of Henry's intervention, Francis remained confident in his new friendship. Wingfield described finding the king on the evening of 18 July at St Germain, rising from a nap at eight, after spending the day hunting in intense heat. Francis told the ambassador of the 'high declaration' made by Henry to Charles, of the English 'amity with France,,' adding that Henry had 'showed himself his perfect friend, and that he should think the time long till he had an opportunity to requite his friendship.'[7] It would not be through Wingfield, though, whose tenure in France was drawing to a close, as he was scheduled to return to England, 'on private affairs'.[8] His replacement was Richard Jerningham, who had previously been marshal, treasurer and deputy of Tournai between its capture in 1513 and its return to the French in 1519.

Jerningham was issued with his new instructions early in August 1520, for the transfer of position between him and Wingfield,

Endpiece

and the information he was to impart secretly to Francis, Louise and Bonnivet alone. Henry was already sure Francis had been informed by Montmorency about the manner of his meeting with Charles, but that the ambassadors must inform Francis about the attempted double-dealings of Chièvres and his 'other practices':

Francis will have perceived by this account the entire love and affection that Henry bears towards him; and the King looks for no recompense but correspondence of semblable love, plainness and constant dealing, feeling sure that, according to his last courteous letter, he will take no new steps, either about the marriage of Charles with his daughter, or in arranging with him for the attaining of the imperial crown, without Henry's express knowledge and consent... The King has heard from Wingfield that Francis wishes his ambassador resident at Rome to associate in open places with the English ambassador, that the friendship between their masters may outwardly appear. Henry is quite agreeable to this; but as a similar request has been made by the king of the Romans, it would be better for the three to associate together openly. He is desirous, however, that there should be other secret intelligence between the English and French ambassadors, that the Pope may evidently perceive the mutual love of their masters. He will not take any steps in the matter till he hears Francis's pleasure.[9]

By early September, Antonio Giustinian had returned home to Venice and was able to report to the Senate that 'the King of France, since this last interview, is on such loving terms with the King of England that he does not suppose there is any service in the world which the King of England would refuse him.' Henry had informed Francis that 'should he die without male heirs he meant to leave him the regency of England,' resulting from the marriage of Princess Mary to the Dauphin. Giustinian also claimed that Charles had made overtures of friendship and 'many proposals' to Francis, which he declined, saying that 'when the Emperor went to Spain' upon his succession in 1516, he had received 'all favour' from the French, but that they were afterwards 'ill treated' and the articles of the Treaty of Noyon binding Charles to surrender Navarre had been ignored. The ambassador added that 'the character of the Emperor is not such as entitles him to much consideration, as he is ruled by Monsieur de Chièvres,' and that there was no peace between France and Spain, but that they 'hate each other very cordially'.[10]

That November, after considering Henry's advice, Charles was crowned Emperor at Aachen. In order to circumvent Francis and Milan, he asked the Pope to send a legate with the Imperial crown to conduct the ceremony. Thomas Spinelly described to Wolsey how he travelled with all the Electors and their horsemen and was met half a league from the city gates by 5,000 footmen and conducted into the city. Dismounting at the Cathedral, he gave thanks at the high altar, visited the chapel of the Three Kings and then went on to his lodgings. The next day Charles dressed as an Archduke of Austria to return to the Cathedral to hear high mass and swear the coronation oath to observe peace, and then changed into imperial clothing to host a huge banquet where the Bishop of Aachen danced. Spinelly's final observation was that the German people marvelled at Charles, and that he had the potential to become 'very powerful'. In the decade that followed the Field of the Cloth of Gold, Spinelly's prediction was to come true, with the Emperor thwarting both Francis and Henry.

Catherine of Aragon had written to Queen Claude after her return home, in response to the French Queen's 'good and affectionate letters'. Just six weeks after having left Ardres, Claude had been delivered of a daughter, named Madeline. Catherine had been 'very greatly consoled' to hear the 'good news, health, estate and prosperity in (which is my) very dear and most beloved good son, and yours, the dauphin.' She expressed the 'good love, friendship and fraternal intelligence and alliance which is now between the two kings our husbands and their kingdoms, which I hold inseparable and pray God that it may continue.'

However, the French betrothal proved even shorter than Catherine may have anticipated, being broken the following January in favour of Mary's betrothal to Emperor Charles. As Henry explained, 'our daughter will be of age before the French King's, and will be a more advantageous match than the other, by possibility of succession.' In opening Imperial negotiations, Henry was mindful of his daughter's worth: 'It is to be considered that she is now our sole heir, and may succeed to the crown; so that we ought rather to receive from the Emperor as large a sum as we should give with her if she were not our heir.' However, the King was still hopeful that Catherine would conceive again, two years and two months after her last delivery. Henry specified that 'if we have a male heir hereafter,' he was willing to give Mary as great a dowry as he had to his sister. In 1526, though, Charles grew tired of waiting for Mary to grow up and married Isabella of Portugal.

In 1521, the French were driven out of Milan by a joint Imperial-Papal army, beginning a new phase of the Italian wars. Henry did not feel obliged to come to Francis' assistance, as he had promised to do the year before. Francis' army was defeated by Charles at Bicocca in April 1522 and at Sesia in April 1524. Three months later, Queen Claude died at the age of twenty-four, having borne two more children, making a total of seven pregnancies in her short life. In February 1525 Francis personally led an army into Lombardy to try and recapture Milan but after his forces were decimated at the Battle of Pavia, he was captured by Charles and imprisoned in Madrid. The French king remained at the mercy of the Emperor until March 1526, when he was released, but only after offering his two sons as hostages in his place.

In around 1525, Henry fell in love with Claude's former lady-in-waiting, Anne Boleyn. Replacing her sister Mary in the king's affections, Anne refused to replace her in his bed, prompting Henry to request a divorce from Catherine in order to marry her. Kept in the dark about his master's true motives, Wolsey attempted to negotiate a match with Renée of France (who would become Duchess of Ferrara in 1528 on marrying Ercole II, Duke of Ferrara), before being taken into Henry's confidence. The new Pope, Julius III, was inclined to grant Henry's wish until the sack of Rome in May 1527, after which Julius was controlled by Charles, who sided with his aunt.

Blocked by the Pope and Emperor, Wolsey, the great architect of the Field of the Cloth of Gold, failed to achieve the king's divorce, was charged with praemunire, and died on his way to trial in November 1530. Henry sent Catherine away from court in 1531, never to see her again, and married Anne in January 1533, who bore his daughter, Elizabeth, that September. Marginalised, separated from her daughter and shifted from house to house, Catherine died in January 1536. Four months later, Anne Boleyn was executed for adultery.

Henry and Francis met once more. In October 1532, at the height of his passion for Anne, Henry took his beloved back across the Channel to meet the French king. Twelve years had passed since the colourful young men had jousted and feasted at Balinghem, and there had been bitter disappointments and losses on each side. The kings spent four days together at Boulogne before returning to Calais, where Anne awaited them. Francis' second wife, Eleanor of Austria, the sister of Emperor Charles, did not attend the event. Francis was lodged at the Staple as he and Henry conducted business, attended Mass and bull-baiting over the next two days. Francis and Anne met again on Sunday 27 October, when both kings dined at the Checker, in a chamber hung with cloths of silver and gold; a cupboard there bore seven shelves of gold plate. On Tuesday, 29 October, Henry and Francis exchanged gifts and said goodbye. Francis rode away, but Henry and Anne were delayed at Calais by bad weather for around two weeks. (See appendix 3.) The kings would never see each other again. Both died in 1547.

The final words go to John Fisher, Bishop of Rochester, who had attended the Field of the Cloth of Gold and preached a sermon which referred to it on 1 November 1520. Although the event had been dazzling, the very pinnacle of earthly beauty and achievement, Fisher reminded his flock of the moral and spiritual cost of such an enterprise. Typical of the early renaissance *memento mori* theme, he stresses that such splendour, magnificent as it had been, was now nothing but dust:

Our eyen hath seen many pleasures, many gay sights many wonderful things that hath appeared and seemed unto us joyous and comfortable. But yet all these were but counterfeits of the true joys, all these were but dull and dark images of the perfect comfort which the blessed saints have now above in the kingdom of heaven.

I doubt not but ye have heard of many goodly sights which were showed of late beyond the sea, with much joy and pleasure worldly. Was it not a great thing within so short a space to see three great princes of this world? I mean the Emperor, and the king our master, and the French king. And each of these three, in so great honour, showing their royalty, showing their riches, showing their power with each of their noblesse appointed and apparelled in rich clothes, in silks, in velvets, in cloths of gold, and such other precious arrayments. To see three right excellent queens at once together, and of three great realms. That one, the noble queen our mistress, the very exemplar of virtue and nobleness to all women. And the French Queen. And the third, Queen Mary, sometime wife unto Louis, French king, sister to our sovereign lord, a right excellent and fair lady.

And every of them accompanied by so many other fair ladies in sumptuous and gorgeous apparel, such dancings, such harmonies, such dalliance, and so many pleasant pastimes, so curious houses and buildings, so preciously apparelled, such costly welfare of dinners, suppers and banquets, so delicate wines, so precious meats, such and so many noble men of arms, so rich and goodly tents, such jousting, such tourneys and such feats of war. These were assuredly wonderful sights for this world, and as much as hath been read of in years done, or in any Chronicles of Histories heretofore written, and as great as men's wits and studies could devise and imagine for that season. Nevertheless, these great sights have a far difference from the joys of heaven, and that in five points.

First, the joys and pleasures of this life, be they never so great, yet they have a weariness and fastidiousness with them adjoined, whereby men at length of time be weary of them, as thus: there is no meat or drink so delicate, so pleasant, so delectable, but if a man or woman be long accustomed therewith, he shall have at the length a loathsomeness thereof. Take the most delicate and pleasant fish that the heart standeth unto, and use it customably and none other, and thou shall be full soon weary thereof. And in like manner it was of those goodly sights which were had and done beyond the sea. I say not the contrary but that they were pleasant sights. But yet doubtless many were full weary of them at length, and had a loathsomeness and fastidiousness of them, and some of them had much liever (rather) be at home.

...Verily of such pleasures ariseth their own destruction at the end which did right well appear in the pleasant sights whereof I spake before. For by the reason of them, great money was spent, many great men's coffers were emptied and many were brought to a great ebb and poverty. This ebb caused a greater flow of covetousness afterwards in many men's hearts. Some of them were the sicker and weaker in their bodies, and divers took their deaths thereby. Some by reason of their sumptuous apparellment learned so great pride that hitherto they could not shift it from them. Never was seen in England such excess of apparellment before as hath been used ever since. And therefore also must needs arise much heart burning and secret envy amongst many for the apparel. They which had the least did envy the other which had richer apparel than they had or might reach unto. Thus, many for these pleasures were the worse, both in their bodies and souls.

...For that little while that we were there, sometime there was such dust, and therewithal so great winds, that all the air was full of dust. The gowns of velvet and cloth of gold were full of dust, the rich trappers of horses were full of dust, hats, caps, gowns were full of dust and briefly to speak, horse and men were so encumbered with dust that scantly one might see another. The wind blew down many tents, shaked sore the houses that were built for pleasure and let divers of them to be builded. Sometimes again we had rains and thunder so immeasurably that no man might stir forth to see no pleasures. Sometimes when men would longer have disported them at the jousts, came the night and darkness upon them and interrupted their pleasure.

In Heaven is no such interruptions...

Kings and Emperors all be but men, all be but mortal. All the gold and all the precious stones of this world, can not but make them mortal men. All the rich apparel that can be devised, can not take from them the condition of mortality. They be in themselves but earth and ashes, and to earth they must return, and all their glory well considered and beholden with right eyes is but very miserable.[11]

Thus, Bishop Fisher drew a line under the emptiness and temporality of the two weeks at Guisnes, glorious in its wealth and display, yet perilous to men's souls, and doomed to return once again to dust.

22

ALL THAT GLITTERS

Considering the reams of cloth of gold that crossed the Channel, the barrels of sturgeon, pounds of butter, jars of cream and boxes of strawberries; considering the hundreds of workmen who painted, carved, chopped and glazed, and the fingers that sewed, plucked, fashioned and created; considering the ships that sailed back and forth, the glorious buildings buffeted by the wind and dismantled after only a few weeks - exactly what was achieved by the immense spectacle of the Field of the Cloth of Gold? As the most expensive event of Henry's reign, and costing the already indebted Francis around £200,000,[1] its short-lived brilliance had not come cheap, but was it a long-term investment or a glorious flash in the pan? Was it mere dust, imperilling men's souls, as John Fisher described? Or a portentous deception of one king by another? With the passage of five centuries since the dismantling of the gold tents, what conclusions does hindsight allow to be drawn from the enterprise?

No doubt the event was glorious. Historians have analysed those two weeks in June in terms of its aesthetic, asking what meaning its symbolism had for those who attended, and how the material culture of the tents, costumes and jousting expressed contemporary social and political values. From the costumes, to the tree of noblesse, it reinforced the chivalric code and military values in a more mutually satisfying way than if Francis and Henry had met on the battlefield. In an interpretative sense, the Field of the Cloth of Gold teeters on the boundary of the medieval and modern worlds. It was a paradox of old and new, reviving ancient codes of chivalry and piety alongside new renaissance 'spy systems and secret instructions'. It represented 'the attempt at rekindling a departed chivalry (which) was irrelevant to the problems of a nationalistic Europe.'[2] Perhaps it is perceived as achieving little because it was essentially pulling in two directions. Its dominant aesthetic was at odds with its diplomatic undercurrents.

The Field of the Cloth of Gold was essentially about rivalry. Undoubtedly, it achieved its foremost aim for Henry and Francis, of staging a display of majesty to impress, and outdo, one another. Since the French king's accession in 1515, and given the similarities in their ages, characters and tastes, it was inevitable that he and Henry were fiercely competitive and mutually curious before they met, questioning ambassadors about each other and vying to achieve greater military glory. Henry's successes at Tournai and Thérouanne in 1513 paled in comparison with the grand victory achieved by Francis at Marignano in 1515, and nor could Henry claim the more impressive English victory against the Scots at Flodden, as it had taken place while he was out of the country. The shadow of Marignano was still felt three years later, when the two kings agreed to meet. Thus, the intent of the occasion was overtly personal and not political. The Field of the Cloth of Gold was not conceived as being a means of dealing with concerns of policy between the two nations, the focus was upon pleasure; feasting, jousting and tournaments in the best tradition of entertaining foreign allies, in order to secure friendship. In this aspect, as the most spectacular and costly paean to friendship of the century, it proved a great success, passing off remarkably smoothly for two countries that had traditionally been enemies.

The most important factor in enabling this new amity was the lead taken by the two kings. Henry and Francis embraced an openness and desire for friendship, displaying generous hospitality and a willingness to place trust in each other, often when the boundaries of their own control were challenged. This represented a huge leap of faith and was warmly repaid on both sides. Gestures of friendship, from gifts, physical embrace, talks, shared space, ritual and protocol, shared pleasures such as jousting and attending mass, and impromptu visits and marks of affection, were key to establishing the relationship between the two kings in person, and were prefaced and followed up by the exchange of letters and messages by ambassadors. This was the result of natural inclination felt by Henry and Francis, who recognised their similarities and formed a genuine attachment. According to Wolsey, although Henry was bound to Charles by 'good peace, fraternal love and consanguinity, yet there were such great concordances… in personages, appetites and manners' between Henry and Francis, that the Anglo-French alliance was, for Henry, 'the most principal, and imprinted in his heart and affection.'[3]

The Field of the Cloth of Gold established not just a personal friendship between the kings of England and France, but was successful in dampening much national antagonism and suspicion. The long-standing xenophobia and particularly francophobia in England was matched by an equally entrenched French hatred of the English, as a result of the Hundred Years' War. Although the wars technically ended in the 1450s, open hostilities continued for at least two decades, and the royal marriages arranged during Henry VII's reign fostered a continuing culture of mutual suspicion. This had been noted by the Venetian visitor in 1500, who characterised the English as proud bordering on arrogant, elitist in their belief in their own superiority and wary of all foreigners. Although there were anti-French murmurings before and after the meeting at Balinghem, tensions concerning numbers and expressions of distaste afterwards, these were relatively few, and were dealt with swiftly. The amity and comradeship displayed at the Field of the Cloth of Gold was successful in easing decades of cross-Channel animosity.

In the opinion of some historians, the Field of the Cloth of Gold had 'little practical significance',[4] leading them to question 'How much is left of its glory when we pierce the golden veil to discover the harsh reality of achievement?'[5] It is still perceived as a deception, a golden bubble or 'golden mountain (which) brought forth a mouse'.[6] Phyllis Mack saw Henry's subsequent meeting with Charles as undermining 'whatever personal links had been established during the kings' dinner parties and embraces'.[7] Yet this overlooks Henry's rejection of Chièvres' scheming and his advice to Charles not to invade France or Milan in July. Henry could not hold back the growing tide of the Emperor's power and, as the situation in Europe evolved, he had little choice but to play the diplomatic game and shift his goals. This was political pragmatism: but the personal links and friendship that Henry and Francis forged at Balinghem had been genuine. In 1532, when Henry was desperate to marry Anne Boleyn, it was to Francis he turned as a personal ally, after years of obstruction and threats from the Emperor. The reality of the Field of the Cloth of Gold, and its achievement, through all its aesthetic glory, proved to be personal.

The Field of the Cloth of Gold was not the 'most portentous deception on record' as claimed by A J Pollard,[8] or 'little more than an immense charade', as stated by J. J. Scarisbrick.[9] It may have been short-lived, but it represented an ideal of peace and friendship, and the very best of kingly intentions and aspirations, which were dazzlingly achieved. In its apoliticism and focus on friendship, it briefly transcended banality, temporality and fear, through an almost Bakhtinian sense of carnival and role play. Marot's poem illustrates the allegorical shift from the roles of mortals to the highest level of literary abstraction, with the triumphs of Amour, or Venus, quenching the fires of Mars and guarding the camps. This spiritual elevation of the brief, earthly aesthetic experience does not diminish the Field of Cloth of Gold, or expose its weaknesses. Rather, it elevates the players to abstract ideals, allowing them to achieve a brief perfection before returning to the world. Ideologically, it was a goal achieved, just as much as any victory on the battlefield. The dynamic in Europe may have altered afterwards, but the month of June 1520 represents Francis and Henry at their best. Its contribution to history was to mark a standard, a pinnacle and culmination of chivalric achievement to which European monarchs might aspire; the last golden hurrah of the pre-reformation world.

'What more shall I say,' concludes Marot. 'Such signal richness demonstrates, and shows, to all people, the great power of the two parties.'

Appendix 1

TIMELINE

1485, December 16, birth of Catherine of Aragon at Alcala de Henares, Spain.

1491, July 28, birth of Henry VIII at Greenwich, England.

1494, September 15, birth of Francis I, at Cognac, France.

1496, March, birth of Mary Tudor at Sheen, England.

1499, October 13, birth of Claude, at Romorantin, France.

1500, February 24, birth of Charles V, at Ghent, Netherlands.

1501, October, Catherine of Aragon arrives in England to be married to Prince Arthur Tudor.

1502, April, Princess Catherine widowed upon the death of Arthur.

1509, April 21, succession of Henry VIII.
  June 11, Henry marries Catherine of Aragon
  June 24, joint coronation of Henry and Catherine

1511, October, Henry and Ferdinand of Aragon join Pope Julius' Anti-French Holy League.

1513, June 30 Henry invades France and takes Therouanne and Tournai. Henry and Brandon
  are entertained by Margaret of Savoy.
  Catherine is Regent of England, while the Scots are defeated at Flodden.

Anne Boleyn is resident at Margaret of Savoy's court in Malines, Netherlands.

1514, January 9, death of Anne of Brittany.

May 18, Francis marries Claude.

October 9, Mary Tudor marries Louis XII of France at Abbeville

1515, January 1, death of Louis XII. Succession of Francis I.

September 13-14 Battle of Marignano.

1516, January, death of Ferdinand of Aragon. Succession of Charles I.

1516, February 16, birth of Princess Mary.

August 13, Treaties of Noyon and Brussels end the third phase of the Italian Wars.

1518, October 2, Treaty of London.

1519, January, death of Emperor Maximilian

February 12, the English leave Tournai after it was surrendered to the French.

June 28, Charles elected as Holy Roman Emperor Charles V.

1520, April 11, Treaty of Commerce between Henry and Charles signed at Greenwich.

May 4, Charles waits at Coronna to embark for England.

May 5, Claude arrives in Paris.

May 7, Francis arrives in Paris.

May 8/9 Francis and Claude depart for Abbeville

May 13, at Greenwich, Henry decrees that a joust will be held and gives instructions for the creation of costumes and props.

May 21, Henry, Catherine and Mary, Duchess of Suffolk, depart from Greenwich towards Canterbury.

May 26, Charles lands at Dover.

May 27, Henry rides to meet Charles at Dover. Henry and Charles ride to Canterbury and meet Catherine and Mary.

May 31, Charles sails from Sandwich to Flanders. Henry, Catherine and Mary sail from Dover and arrive at Calais at 11pm.

Friday, 1 June, the English party are unwell after a turbulent crossing. The intended meeting of the kings is postponed. Wolsey rides to Ardres to meet Francis.

Saturday, 2 June, Wolsey returns to Calais or Guisnes. Francis rides to Marquise, which Claude and Louise have reached.

Sunday, 3 June, Trinity Sunday, a day of devotion. Henry makes an offering after Mass.

Monday 4 June, preparations are made for the English court moving from Calais to Guisnes.

Tuesday 5 June, the English Party reaches Guisnes. Claude and Louise arrive at Ardres.

Wednesday 6 June, Henry rides to Balinghem valley. The Anglo-French treaty is ratified by Wolsey. French visitors dine at Guisnes Castle.

Thursday 7 June, the feast of Corpus Christi. First meeting of Henry and Francis at the Val d'Or at Balinghem.

Friday 8 June, Henry and Francis meet at Balinghem for four hours. The tree of noblesse is erected.

Saturday 9 June, Henry and Francis ride out to inspect the lists at Balinghem and prepare for the start of the tournament the following Monday.

Sunday 10 June, Francis visits Guisnes early, before Henry is up. The kings swap courts for dinner; Francis is entertained by Catherine and Mary at Guisnes, while Francis is welcomed at Ardres, by Claude, Louise and Marguerite.

Monday 11 June, the jousts begin. Both courts spend the day at the lists. Catherine and Claude meet for the first time.

Tuesday 12 June, the jousting continues despite bad weather. The kings attend, but not the queens. Wolsey entertains members of the French nobility. An English party performs a masque for the French at Ardres.

Wednesday 13 June, bad weather prevents jousting, so wrestling takes place instead. The Treaty of London is ratified for a second time.

Thursday 14 June, both kings and queens attend the lists, Henry and Francis joust. Charles writes to Henry from Brussels.

Friday 15 June, more bad weather means that the kings do not joust, but some of their gentlemen do.

Saturday 16 June, day of rest.

Sunday 17 June, Francis rides to Guisnes at 8am. Francis and Louise dine with Catherine at Guisnes, Henry and Mary dine with Claude at Ardres, then Henry participates in a masque.

Monday 18 June, Henry and Francis attend the lists despite the bad weather, and watch others tilt. The queens do not attend.

Tuesday 19 June, last official day of the jousting, attended by both kings and both queens. Swordfighting.

Wednesday 20 June, the kings and queens attend the swordfighting.

Thursday 21 June, combats on foot.

Friday 22 June, final combats, prizes may have been distributed on this occasion, and the lists at Balinghem were closed. Over night, a chapel is constructed in the valley.

Saturday 23 June, both courts attend chapel where Mass is sung by Wolsey and indulgences are issued. Half way through, a giant salamander appears in the sky overhead. The royal party dine at Balinghem, before a few more feats of combat take place. Trumpets sound and bonfires are lit to celebrate the eve of St John the Baptist's Day.

Sunday 24 June, feast day of St John the Baptist. Henry goes to Ardres and Francis goes to Guisnes for feasting and disguising. The two kings meet on the return journey and part with regret.

Monday 25 June, The English Party leaves Guisnes for Calais, the French leave Ardres for Paris.

Tuesday 3 July, feast day of St Thomas.

Thursday 5 July, Charles leaves Ghent.

Saturday 7 July, Charles arrives at Gravelines.

Sunday 8 July, Margaret of Austria writes to Henry from Gravelines.

Tuesday 10 July, Henry and Charles meet midway between Gravelines and Calais, at a small place Hall names 'Waell.' Henry returns to Gravelines with Charles.

Wednesday 11 July, Henry and Charles dine together at Gravelines, then depart for Calais, arriving about 7pm.

Henry visits Charles and Margaret at the Staple, where he participates in a masque.

Thursday 12 July, Charles and Margaret dine at the Checker, after which a large mask takes place, comprising 96 dancers.

Friday 13 July, Charles was scheduled to leave Calais, but decides to remain for an additional day. Charles and Henry ratify the treaty they made in April.

Saturday 14 July, Henry accompanies Charles and his party to Waell, before returning to Calais.

Wednesday 18 July, the English sail from Calais to Dover.

August 10, Claude gives birth to Princess Madeline.

October 26, Charles is crowned as Holy Roman Emperor in Nuremburg, Germany.

1521, French driven out of Milan, fourth phase of the Italian Wars begins.

May 17, execution of Edward Stafford, Duke of Buckingham.

May 28, death of William de Croy, Lord of Chièvres, reputedly by poison,

1525, February 24, French defeated by Charles at the Battle of Pavia. Francis was captured and held in Madrid until March 1526.

1526, March 11, Charles married Eleanor of Portugal.

1527 Henry makes public his intention to divorce Catherine
May 6, Charles sacks Rome.

1532, October 21-29 Henry and Francis meet again in Calais.

1547 January 28, death of Henry VIII
March 31, death of Francis I.

Appendix 2

SOURCES

Much of our knowledge about the Field of the Cloth of Gold is to be found in contemporary letters. These were written by the participants, Henry and Francis, Catherine, Claude and Mary, Bonnivet and Wolsey, Margaret and Charles, as well as their servants. A number of letters survive from each, particularly from the kings and Wolsey, which chart the stages of the process and the public reassurances they made each other. Occasionally, hidden among the secret instructions to ambassadors, or between those who trusted their correspondents, an individual's private feelings can be glimpsed, such as Catherine's disapproval or Henry's ambition.

An official account of the event was created by Jean Lescaille and printed for Pierre Vidoue, a Parisian bookseller active from 1516 and located in the Rue Perdue, beside the Place Maubert. This is likely to have been printed as a pamphlet, in a limited run, and circulated amongst a comparatively small audience, perhaps being used as the official, authorised account of the meeting. Such works were often dispatched to other ruling heads of state, and one copy is included in the State Letters and Papers of Henry's reign. In addition, two anonymous plaquettes, or booklets, were produced, one in French and another in Latin. Another French account was given in the chronicle written by Robert de la Marck, Seigneur de Florange, whose closeness to the king makes him a first-rate witness.

The fullest version of the occasion from the English chroniclers is that of Edward Hall, a lawyer whose vast chronicle spans the accession of Henry IV in 1399 through to the reign of Henry VIII. It was completed after his death by printer Richard Grafton, who published the work in full in 1548. Born in 1497, Hall was twenty-three at the time of the Field of the Cloth of Gold, and there is no evidence to suggest he attended the event in person in an official capacity. He had graduated from King's College, Cambridge in 1518 and had entered Gray's Inn by 1521, so his presence cannot be ruled out entirely, perhaps in a role of service, or as a clerk or official. Whilst his account is full of unprecedented detail, the occasional confusion over specific dates might suggest he was gaining his material second hand. Grafton also went on to produce his own *Abridgement of the Chronicles of England*, which he published in 1563 and provides an overview of the event.

The Field of the Cloth of Gold is also mentioned in the chronicle of Polydore Vergil, although in far less detail, more as a summary than an account. Born in Urbino, he travelled to England in 1502, was commissioned by Henry VII to write a history of the country and was naturalised as an Englishman in 1510. Initially, his *Anglica Historia* was drafted in 1513 and its first two imprints did not go beyond this. The third version, though, published in 1555, in the year of Vergil's death, extended the narrative to 1537 and covered the Field of the Cloth of Gold. This was very much a retrospective narrative, reflecting subsequent events such as Wolsey's fall, which coloured the depiction of the Cardinal in the text. It is almost certain that Vergil did not attend the Field of the Cloth of Gold. By 1515, he had fallen foul of Henry as the result of criticisms of the king in an intercepted letter, which led to his imprisonment in the Tower. The Pope wrote on his behalf to Henry and he was granted his liberty at the end of the year, although he never recovered his former position.

A number of ambassadors attended the Field of the Cloth of Gold in order to record their first-hand observations for their employers.

Some were already placed at the French or English courts, or else arrived as soon as they could. The majority of letters which survive were written by attendees from the various Italian states, from Venice, Mantua and Genoa, among whom were the prolific Giovanni Badoer and Antonio Giustinian, Venetian ambassadors to France, writing to the governing body of their home city, the Signory.[1] Giustinian was already resident at the French court when Francis headed to Ardres, and dispatched three letters before the arrival of Badoer on 4 June, after which they wrote seven more together.[2] Badoer was 55 in 1520, a doctor of philosophy from Padua University, a celebrated poet, Roman Senator and formerly ambassador to Spain, Poland and Hungary. His relative, Andrea Badoer, was Venetian Ambassador to England.

Less is known about Antonio Giustinian, in comparison with the well documented career of his brother, Sebastian Giustinian, who was Venetian ambassador to Henry's court. Sebastian had been in England since early in 1515, when the Doge Leonardo Loredano issued him with credentials to support his mission. Departing Venice on 10 January with a newly raised salary of 140 ducats a month, he was described as a 'knight'.[3] He was at Lyon on 27 February, after a difficult journey, from where he was already writing that Francis was 'negotiating for a conference' and that 'it was settled (that) the most serene kings should meet at Calais,' a whole five years before the Field of the Cloth of Gold took place.[4] On 20 March he was in Paris, reached Boulogne on 4 April and reached Dover on 11 April 1515 after being 'mercilessly buffeted at sea 24 hours.' A week later he was in London, where he was writing on behalf of Badoer, who 'wanted money' and had delivered his arrival speech in front of Henry.[5] From the start, Giustinian had worked in favour of the Anglo-French alliance, 'exhorting' Henry to continue the alliance, use it to work against the Empire, and help Venice regain its lost territory. Of Henry and Catherine in May 1515, Giustinian wrote:

He is very expert in arms, most excellent in his personal endowments, so adorned with mental accomplishments of every sort, he has few equals in the world. He speaks English, French and Latin; understands Italian; plays almost every instrument; sings and composes; and is free from all vice. On visiting the Queen, Pasqualigo addressed her in Spanish, knowing it would please her. The Queen talked to them in Spanish on the state of Spain.[6]

Also based in the English entourage at Guisnes was the prolific Antonio Surian, Venetian ambassador, writing eight times alone to the Doge and Signory, and once in conjunction with Badoer and Giustinian.[7] Little is known about Surian, but he may well have been the son or relation of his namesake, a former Patriarch of Venice, who had died in 1520. In May 1519, Surian was at the French court at Poissy, where Thomas Boleyn described him as 'the Venetian ambassador who is coming to England.' There, he presented Francis with a 'great letter in parchment, sealed with lead'.[8] By 21 June Surian was in London, where Sebastian Giustinian described him as the 'Magnifico Surian', being flattered by visiting privy councillors who arranged for him to attend court at Windsor the following day, where he made a Latin oration about his arrival. He was apparently intended to replace Giustinian, who had been appointed Councillor of Venice, and whom Henry declared he would miss, as he had 'ever loved him like a father'.[9] In June 1520, the 'ambassadors of Venice' were allowed to take 23 servants and 11 horses, in comparison with the 20 servants and 23 horses allocated to the ambassadors from the Emperor.[10]

The Mantuan ambassador Soardino is even more of a shadowy figure, whose forename does not even appear in the records. His six detailed letters were written to Federico II Gonzaga, Marquis of Mantua since 1519[11]. Equally mysterious is Gioan Joachino, secretary of Octavian Fregoso, the Governor of Genoa, and usually resident at the French court. He wrote a single report of the event, in detail and at length.[12] The final Italian ambassador, Paolo Camillo Trivulzio, Duke of Boiano, had been expelled from his native Milan for rebellion after falling foul of the Sforza family, so in 1516 entered the service of the king of France. He was rewarded with an annual pension of 1,200 ducats after his attendance at the Field of the Cloth of Gold. It is possible that he was, or was related to, the Governor of Lyon, to whom Clement Marot dedicated his poem 'The May Tree; planted by the printers of Lyon in front of Seigneur Trivulse's (sic) house.' At the time, Lyon was a city that sheltered many Italian exiles and became a centre of poetry. A number of other letters were held in a collection made by Venetian historian Marino Sanuto, written either by anonymous or private individuals, such as the single one from 'Della Croce' (Delacroix?) or Count Alexandro Donato's two missives to Giovanni Francesco Griti. Contemporary letters also survive from Alvise Marin, the Venetian secretary at Milan, to the Signory and Francesco Cornaro, the Venetian ambassador to the Emperor.

Original accounts and payments survive in the Letters and Papers of Henry VIII that provide insight into the practicalities of the event. From lists of supplies and provisions, warrants for attendance, costings of materials and predictions of quantities, the catering for the English court can be revealed in its various phases. These are also to be found in the Rutland Papers, a collection of documents from the mid nineteenth century, which lists those in attendance in the departments of the king's and queen's household, including the kitchens, stables and other necessaries, such as the estimations of quantities that would be consumed along with the costings.

Appendix 3

THE SECOND MEETING, HENRY AND FRANCIS IN 1532

Twelve years after the Field of the Cloth of Gold, Henry and Francis met again. The youthful, daring French king had been broken by defeat at Pavia and imprisonment by the Emperor. He was then thirty-eight, Queen Claude had died, and he was remarried to Eleanor of Austria. Henry was forty-one and had banished Catherine of Aragon and their daughter Mary from his court in order to marry Anne, daughter of Sir Thomas Boleyn. Wolsey had tried, and failed, to achieve the king's wish, and had lost his head as a result. After years of prevarication from the Pope and resistance from Charles, Henry was approaching the point when he would just push ahead with the ceremony, and sought to balance Imperial hostility with the approval of the French king. In preparation, he elevated her to the title of Marquis of Pembroke and requisitioned Catherine's crown jewels to adorn her person.

In early October, Henry and Anne left Greenwich by barge and sailed down the Thames to Gravesend. They stayed at nearby Stone Castle, home to Sir Richard Wingfield, then at Mote Park in Maidstone, formerly owned by Henry's Woodville relations, before using the barge again to reach Shurland Hall at Eastchurch, on the north-east tip of the Isle of Sheppey. Afterwards, Henry and Anne travelled to Canterbury, staying there the night of 10 October, before the final leg of the journey down to Dover. They embarked for Calais aboard *The Swallow* at five the following morning, arriving the same day, at around ten.[1]

An official account of the visit was published by Henry's private printer, Wynkyn de Worde, who had taken over William Caxton's press at Westminster. They were lodged at The Exchequer, where Henry and Catherine had stayed in 1520, and where they awaited the arrival of Francis. It was Anne's uncle, the Duke of Norfolk, who rode out to meet Anne de Montmorency, one of the hostages to England in 1520, to devise a suitable place for the two monarchs to meet. The date was fixed for 21 October. Dressed in a coat of riches, 'in braids of gold laid loose on russet velvet and set with trefoils full of pearls and stones', Henry met the equally gorgeously attired French king, who had chosen a coat of crimson velvet, with the gold lining pulled through the slashes. 140 gentlemen in velvet coats rode with him, and forty guards, accompanied by around 600 horsemen.[2] The two men came face to face near Sandingfield Abbey, or La Maison de St. Ingelvert, twelve years after they had first met at Balinghem. It was located nine miles to the south-east of Calais, on the border, before the village of Maquise. The official account related that the kings felt great pleasure upon their reunion, with 'the lovingest meeting that ever was seen, for the one embraced the other five or six times on horseback' and rode hand in hand, 'with great love the space of a mile'.[3]

Etiquette dictated that Anne was unable to join Henry and Francis, owing to the absence of a corresponding household from the French queen, so she remained behind in Calais awaiting their return, with thirty of her ladies. Privy purse records include supplies of grapes and pears that were brought to her by a servant of Montmorency, as well as others who provided her with red deer pasties, carp and porpoise for her table. The time was whiled away playing dice, dominoes and other games.[4] Anne waited from Monday until Friday, while the Kings stayed in Boulogne, preparing for their return. She would have heard as they drew near, with the guns of Calais shooting 2,000 rounds, prompting the servants in their tawny coats and the soldiers in red and blue to line the streets in welcome.[5] Back in 1520, Francis had declared himself willing to cross into English territory and meet Henry in Calais; twelve years later the kings rode into the town together.

Francis was lodged in the Inn of the Staple, a 'princely house', in rooms hung with tissue and velvet, embroidered with flowers, where he dined on 'all manner of flesh, fowl, spice, venison, both of fallow deer and red deer, and as for wine, they lacked none.'[6] Francis sent Anne a diamond as a gift of friendship and welcome, but they would not meet again for another forty-eight hours, attending mass and council meetings on the Saturday, before the Sunday was spent watching bull-baiting. Henry also made payments to Francis's minstrels and jester, suggestive of more leisure pursuits that weekend. On Sunday, 27 October, Francis came to dine with Henry at the Exchequer in a chamber hung alternately with panels of silver and gold tissue, with seams covered with embroidered gold, full of pearls and gems. A cupboard with seven shelves displayed plate of gold and gilt, while white silver branches bore chains from which were hung wax lights.[7] Three courses were served, totalling a hundred and fifty dishes of 'costly and pleasant' food, with the meat dressed in the French style for Francis and in the English style for Henry. Then Anne entered the chamber with seven ladies including Mary Carey and Jane Boleyn, all masked, wearing crimson tinsel satin with cloth of silver 'lying lose' and caught up in gold laces.[8] Richard Gibson was paid £11 3s 1d for 'masking gear', while much larger sums, exceeding £8,000, were spent on jewels for the occasion.[9] Every lady 'took a Lord', with Anne partnering Francis, before her mask was revealed. They talked 'for a space' before the French King retired for the night, without revealing the subject of their conversation.[10]

On 29 October, after exchanging gifts, Henry and Anne bid farewell to Francis and prepared to leave Calais. The weather though, was terrible, with storms making it dangerous to cross the Channel and 'such a winde, tempest and thunder that no man could conveniently stir in the streets of Calais.'[11] Waiting for two weeks at the Exchequer in their fine rooms, linked by a connecting door, this may well have been the moment that Henry and Anne consummated their love. They finally left Calais at midnight on 12 November and, after a terrible crossing, sailed into Dover early in the morning of 14 November, St Erkenwald's day. According to accounts by Hall and others, they were married secretly the same day, probably in the chapel or their apartments at Dover Castle.

Their progress back to London was steady. They were at Sandwich on 16 November and then at Canterbury from 17-19 November, where the expenses of the fool were paid, as were the Canterbury waites, or musicians, and the Abbot of St Augustines was rewarded for bringing the king a book.[12] They stayed one night at The Lion in Sittingbourne, probably the Red Lion, an old coaching inn in the High Street, reputed to also have housed Henry V on his return from Agincourt. There, rewards were given to the wife of the owner, to a poor woman who brought the king pears and to a sailor.[13] It may have been the use of the royal barge again, avoiding the plague-ridden Rochester, that allowed them to sail from Faversham's harbour to reach Stone on 20 November, moving on by road to Eltham Palace soon afterwards. Henry and Anne were officially married on 25 January 1533, by which point Anne may well have already been pregnant with the future Elizabeth I.

Appendix 4

LIST OF ENGLISH ATTENDEES AT THE FIELD OF THE CLOTH OF GOLD, AS TAKEN FROM THE RUTLAND PAPERS AND STATE LETTERS AND PAPERS

Servants for the King

The cardinal of York, with 300 servants, of whom 12 shall be chaplains and 50 gentlemen, with 50 horses.

One archbishop with 70 servants, of whom 5 shall be chaplains and 10 gentlemen, with 30 horses.

2 dukes, each with 70 servants, 5 to be chaplains.

10 gentlemen, with 30 horses.

1 marquis with 56 servants, 4 to be chaplains and 8 gentlemen; 26 horses.

10 earls, each with 42 servants, 3 to be chaplains and 6 gentlemen; 20 horses.

5 bishops, of whom the bishop of Winchester shall have 56 servants, 4 to be chaplains and 8 gentlemen; 26 horses.

Each of the others, 44 servants, 4 to be chaplains and 6 gentlemen; 20 horses.

20 barons, each to have 22 servants, 2 to be chaplains and 2 gentlemen; 12 horses.

4 knights of the order of St. George, each to have 22 servants, 2 to be chaplains and 2 gentlemen; 48 horses.

70 knights, each to have 12 servants, one to be a chaplain; 8 horses.

Councillors of the long robe; viz., the King's secretary, the vice-chancellor, the dean of the Chapel, and the almoner, each to have 12 servants, one a chaplain, and 8 horses.

12 King's chaplains, each with 6 servants and 3 horses.

12 serjeants-at-arms, each with 1 servant and two horses.

200 of the King's guard with 100 horses.

70 grooms of the chamber, with 150 servants and 100 horses among them.

266 officers of the house, with 216 servants and 70 horses.

205 grooms of the stable and of the armories, with 211 horses.

The earl of Essex, being earl marshal, shall have, beside the number above stated, 130 servants and 100 light horses.

Sum total of the King's company, 3,997 persons and 2,087 horses.

Servants for the Queen

The Duchess of Buckingham with 4 women, 6 servants and 12 horses.

7 countesses with 3 women and 4 servants, and 8 horses each:
  Countess of Stafford.
  Countess of Oxford.
  Countess Dowager of Oxford.

Countess of Westmorland.
Countess of Shrewsbury.
Countess of Devonshire.
Countess of Derby.

12 baronesses, with 2 women, 3 servants and 6 horses each:
Lady Fitzwalter.
Lady Hastings.
Lady Boleyn.
Lady Montague.
Lady Willoughby.
Lady Daubney.
Lady Bergavenny.
Lady Mountjoy.
Lady Cobham.
Lady Grey, Lord John's wife.
Lady Elizabeth Grey
Lady Anne Grey, widow.
Lady Broke.
Lady Morley.
Lady Scrope.
Lady Guildford the elder.

20 knights' ladies, with 1 woman, 2 servants and 4 horses each:
Lady Vaux.
Lay Guildford the younger.
Lady Fettiplace.
Lady Selinger.
Lady Parr, widow.
Lady Parr, wife.
Lady Rice.
Lady Compton.
Lady Darrell.
Lady Finche.
Lady Hopton.

Lady Wingfield, Sir Richard's wife.
Lady Wingfield, Sir Anthony's wife.
Lady Tilney.
Lady Clere.
Lady Owen.
Lady Neville.
Lady Boleyn, Sir Edward's wife.

25 gentlewomen, each with one woman, 2 men servants and 3 horses:

Mistress Carew.
Mistress Cheney.
Mistress Carey (Mary Boleyn)
My Lord Fitzwarren's daughter.
Mistress Courtney.
Mistress Coffyn.
Mistress Morris.
Mistress Parker.
Mistress Fitzwarren.
Mistress Jerningham, widow.
Mistress Wootton.
Mistress Bruce.
Mistress Brown.
Mistress Danet.
Mistress Finche.
Mistress Pointz, Sir Anthony's daughter.
Mistress Cornwallis.
Mistress Coke.
Mistress Paris.
Mistress Katherine Mountoria.
Mistress Laurence.
Mistress Victoria.
Mistress Aphard.
Anne Wentworth.
Bridget Hugan.

Chamberers with 1 servant and 2 horses each:
  Mistress Kemp.
  Mistress Margery.
  Mistress Margaret.

The Earl of Derby, with 42 servants, 3 to be chaplains and 9 gentlemen; horses 20.

The Bishops of Rochester, Llandaff and Hereford, to have 44 servants, 4 to be chaplains and 6 gentlemen; horses 60.

Barons Mountjoy, Willoughby, Cobham and Morley, with 22 servants, 2 to be chaplains and 2 gentlemen; horses 48.

30 knights, each with 12 servants, 1 of which would be a chaplain, with 240 horses in total:
  Sir Robert Pointz.
  Sir Edward Darrell.
  Sir Thomas Tyrrell.
  Sir Thomas Fettiplace.
  Sir John Lyle.
  Sir George Foster.
  Sir Adrian Fortescue.
  Sir Walter Stoner.
  Sir Edward Greville.
  Sir Roger Wentworth.
  Sir Symond Harecourt.
  Sir Thomas Trenchard.
  Sir John Hampton.
  Sir Thomas Lynde.
  Sir John Villers.
  Sir John Kirkham.
  Sir Matthew Brown.
  Sir Miles Bushey.
  Sir John Ashton.
  Sir Marmaduke Constable.
  Sir Ralph Chamberlain.
  Sir John Shelton.
  Sir Henry Willoughby.

Sir Ralph Verney the younger.
Sir Robert Clere.
Sir Philip Calthrop.
Sir William Walgrave.
Sir Robert Jones.
John Heningham.
John Morden.

Parys of Cambridgeshire.

6 chaplains with 3 servants and 2 horses each.

Grooms, 50.

Officers of the King's chamber, 50, with 20 servants and 30 horses.

Officers of the King's stable, 60, with 70 horses.

Sum total of the Queen's company, 1,175 persons and 778 horses.

Ambassadors
The Emperors Ambassadors, 20 servants with 23 horses.
The Ambassadors of Venice, 23 servants with 11 horses.

Chaplains
The Dean of Sarum (Winchester).
The Archdeacon of Richmond.
Doctor Taillour.
Doctor Knight.
Doctor Felle.
Master Stokesley.
Master Higgons.
Doctor Powle.
Doctor Rawson.
Doctor Cromer.
Every chaplain 6 servants and 4 horses.

Secretaries
Jean Meautis, French secretary, with 5 servants and 6 horses.
Bryan Tuke, Master of the Posts, 3 servants, 4 posts and 8 horses.

Two clerks of the signet.

Two clerks of the privy seal.

Each clerk with 3 servants and 4 horses.

Names of those appointed to attend the King of England at the Congress

Commissioners appointed to oversee those who shall accompany the king of France: The Earl of Essex, Lord Abergavenny, Sir Edward Ponynges, Sir Robert Wingfield.

To give orders to the gentlemen: Sir Edward Belknapp, Sir Nicholas Vaux, Sir John Peche, Sir Maurice Berkeley.

To give orders to the foot soldiers: Sir Weston Browne, Sir Edward Ferrers, Sir Robert Constable, Sir Ralph Egerton, Sir Thomas Lucy, Sir John Marney.

To ride with the king of England at the embracing of the two Kings: The Legate (Wolsey), William Warham Archbishop of Canterbury, Dukes of Buckingham and Suffolk, Marquis of Dorset. Bishops of Durham, Armagh, Ely, Chester, Rochester, Exeter, Hereford. Earls of Stafford, Northumberland, Westmoreland, Shrewsbury, Worcester, Devonshire, Kent, Wiltshire, Derby, Kildare. Barons Maltravers, Montagu, Herbert, the Grand Prior of St. John of England, Roos, Fitzwalter, Hastings, Delavare, Dacres, Ferrers, Cobham, Daubney, Lumley, Sir Henry Marney, Sir William Sandys, Thomas Boleyn, Lord Howard.

List of Noblemen and Others
(Some already assigned specific roles above.)

The King's Council.

My lord Cardinal.

The Privy Seal.

The Bishops of Lincoln, Norwich, Hereford and Rochester.

The Dukes of Norfolk and Buckingham.

List of English Attendees at the Field of the Cloth of Gold

The Marquis Dorset.

The Earls of Surrey, Shrewsbury, Worcester, Derby, Northumberland, Essex and Wiltshire. The Lords of St. John, Burgevenny, Devonshire, Montague, Mounteagle, Cobham, Ferys, Fitzwalter, Dudley, Dacres of the South, Darcy, Conyers, Audeley, Broke and Fitzwarren. The Deans of the Chapel and of Paul's.

The Archdeacon of Richmond.

The Dean of Salisbury.

Dr. Syxtyne.

Dr. Clark.

The Abbots of Glastonbury, Westminster, Bury and Winchecombe.

All knights and others of the King's Council.

The secretaries in Latin, French and English.

The clerks of the Privy Seal and Signet.

The heralds.

The officers of the household.

The minstrels.

Those Representing Counties
Bedford: Sir John St. John, William. Gascoyn, Robert Spenser, Lenthorp, William Fitzjeffrey, George Harvey.

Buckingham: Sir Andrew Windsor, Sir Rauf Verney, junior, John Cheynye, Sir William. Hampden, John Gyfford.

Warwick: Lord Dudley, Sir Gilbert Talbot, junior, George Throgmorton, Sir Edward Belknapp, Edward Greville, Sir John Burdute, Sir Thomas Lucy, Sir Edward Ferrers, Edward Conway.

Lincoln: Lord Willoughby, Sir Christopher Willoughby, Sir John Husey, Sir Geoffrey Paynell, Sir Miles Bushe, Sir Robert Sheffield, Sir William Tirwytt, William Askew, George Fitzwilliam, Sir Robert Dymocke, William. Hansard.

Essex: The Earl of Essex, Lord Fitzwalter, Sir Henry Marny, Sir John Raynysford, Sir Thomas Tyrell, Sir Richard Lewys, Sir Roger Wentworth, William Pirton, Sir Whistan Browne, John Marnye.

Sussex: The Duke of Norfolk, the Earl of Surrey, Lord Maltravers, Sir Thomas West, Lord Dacre, Sir David Owen, Sir Godard Oxynbridge, William Ashbornham, Sir Edward Lewkenor, Sir John Dawtry.

Berkshire: Sir George Forster, Sir Thomas Fettyplace, Sir William Essex, Sir Richard Weston, Henry Bridges, John Cheyny, Richard Norris, Richard Hampden.

Hertford: Lord Barnesse, Sir Edward Benstede, Thomas Clyfford.

Gloucester: The Duke of Buckingham, Sir Maurice Berkeley, William Denys, Sir William Kyngston, Sir Christopher Baynham, Sir John Hungerford, Sir Edward Wadham, Sir John Brydges.

Cornwall: Lord Broke, Sir John Arundell, Sir Piers Edgecombe, Sir Roger Graynefeld, Sir John Trevenyan.

Suffolk: Sir Thomas Boleyn, Sir Robert Brandon, Sir Robert Drury, Sir Anthony Wyngfeld, Sir William Walgrave, Sir Richard Wentworth, Sir John Shelton, Sir Arthur Hopton, Sir Robert Courson, Sir John Audley, Thomas Felton, Branzton, Sir William Sidney.

Stafford: Sir John Feryes, Sir Louis Bagot, Sir John Gifford, Sir John Asheton, John

Egyrton, Sir John Braycot, Sir John Stanley, John Blount.

Devonshire: Lord Fitzwaren, Sir William Courtney, Sir Edmund Owen, Sir John Basset, Sir Nicholas Kyrkeham, Sir Edward Pomery.

Oxford: Sir Adryan Fortescue, Sir Edward Chamberlayn, Sir William Rede, Walter Bulstrode, Sir John Daunce.

Shropshire: The Earl of Shrewsbury, Sir Richard Laykyn, Sir Thomas Blount, Sir Thomas Leighton, Sir Robert Corbett, Sir Thomas Cornwall.

Somerset: The Earl of Wiltshire, Sir John Trevelyan, Sir Nicholas Wadham, Sir John Rodney, Sir Richard Ware, Lord Daubney.

Dorset: Henry Strangwyshe, Giles Strangwyshe, John Horsey, Sir Thomas Trenchard.

Wiltshire: Sir Edward Hungerford, Sir John Seymour, Sir Edward Darell, Sir John Dakers, Sir John Newport, Sir Maurice Barow, Sir John Scrope, Sir Thomas Long.

Yorkshire: The Earl of Northumberland, Lord Darcy, Lord Lumeley, Sir John Constable, Sir Robert Constable, Lord Conyers, Sir George Fitzhugh, Sir Rauf Ellerkar, Sir William Gascoigne, Sir Richard Tempest, Sir William Skargill, Sir Guy Wolstrope, Sir Rauf Evers, Sir William Evers, Sir William Bulmer, Sir John Bulmer, Sir Edward Pickering.

Westmoreland: Sir Thomas Parr.

Hereford: Lord Ferrers, Sir Cornewall.

Hampshire: Lord Audeley, Sir William Sandys, Sir John Lyle, William Pound, John Pawlet, junior, Sir John Lye, Sir George Putenham, Sir William Gyfford, Robert Walop, Arthur Plantagenet, Sir Maurice Barrow.

Kent: Lord Bergavenny, Lord Cobham, Lord Clinton, Sir Edward Ponynges, Sir William Scot, Sir John Peche, Sir Edward Guildford, Sir Henry Guildford, Thomas Cheynye, Sir Rauf St.Leger, Sir John Darell, Raynold Pymp, Sir John Scott, Sir William Crowner, Sir John Fogge, Sir John Norton.

Leicester: The lord Marquis, Lord Hastyngs, Sir John Digby, Sir Edward Fieldyng, Sir Richard Sacheverell, Lord John Gray, Lord Leonard Gray, Lord Richard Gray, Sir William Skevyngton, Sir John Villers, Hasylrygge.

Cambridge: Sir William Findern, Sir Robert Cotton, Sir Rauf Chamberlain, Sir Giles Alyngton.

Northampton: Sir Nicholas Vaux, Sir William Parr, Sir Thomas Lucy, Thomas Empson.

Nottingham: Sir William Pierpoint, Sir Thomas Sutton, Sir Brian Stapleton, Robert Clifton, Humphrey Hersy, Rowland Dygby, John Beron, Sir William Meryng, Sir Henry Willoughby.

Norfolk: Lord Edmund Howard, Sir Philip Calthorp, Sir Robert Clere, Sir John Haydon, Sir Thomas Woodhouse, Sir Thomas Wyndham, William Paston, Sir Robert Lovell, John Shelton, Sir Thomas Benyngfeld, Nicholas Appelyard, Edward Knyvet.

Derby: Sir Henry Sacheverell, Sir John Montgomery, Sir Godfrey Fulgeham, Thomas Cokyn.

Middlesex: The lord of Saint John's, Sir Thomas Lovell.

Surrey: Sir Henry Wyatt, Sir Matthew Brown, Sir John Yardby, Sir Edward Bray.

Cheshire: Sir John Warberton, Sir William Both, Sir John Warren, Sir George Holford, Sir John Lye of Bagley, Sir William Brereton.

Those who Would Be with the French King when he Met the King of England

The King of Navarre.

The Dukes of Alençon, Bourbon, Vendome and Lorraine.

The Count of Saint Pol.

The Prince de la Roche Suryon.

The Count of Dreux and Rhetel.

Sieur Dorval.

The Governor of Champagne.

The Count of Benon.

Sieur de la Tremoille, first Chamberlain, admiral of Guyenne and governor of Burgundy; Count of Estampes and Caravats.

Sieur de Boissy, Grand Master and governor of the Dauphin.

Bonnivet, Admiral of France.

Lautrec, La Palisse and Chastillon, Marshals.

Count of Guise, brother of the Duke of Lorraine.

The bastard of Savoy, count of Villars and Beaufort, governor of Provence.

The Count de Laval.

Monsieur de Chasteaubriant.

Count of Harcourt.

Princes of Orange and Tallemont.

Monsieur de Nevers.

Monsieur d'Esparrox, lieutenant of Guyenne, and count of Montfort.

Mess. de Lescun and Montmorency.

Le Grand Escuyer.

Counts de la Chambre, Tonnerre, Brienne, Joigny, Bremie and Mont Reuel

Monsieur d'Albret.

Other knights of the Order.

200 horse.

English Knights to Attend Upon Henry in the Field
Duke of Buckingham.
Duke of Suffolk.
Marquis of Dorset.
Earl of Northumberland.
Earl of Essex.
Earl of Devonshire.
Earl of Worcester.
Earl of Wiltshire.
Earl of Shrewsbury.
Earl of Kent.
Earl of Westmorland.
Lord of St Johns.
Lord Ross.
Lord Fitzwalter.

Lord Bergavenny.

Lord Montague.

Lord Hastings.

Lord Ferrers.

Lord Herbert.

Lord Edmund Howard.

Lord John Grey.

Lord Mountjoy.

Sir Edward Poynings.

Sir Henry Marney.

Sir Nicholas Wadham.

Sir William Parr.

Sir Edward Guildford.

Sir William Sandys.

Sir Thomas Boleyn.

Sir Edward Guildford.

Sir Nicholas Vaux.

Sir Edward Neville.

Sir Maurice Berkeley.

Sir Edmund Walsingham.

Sir Ragland

Sir John Peche

Sir John Hussey

Sir Richard Weston.

Sir Thomas Cornwall.

Sir Ralph Egerton.

Sir William Fitzwilliam.

Sir Edward Wadham.

Sir John Hungerford.

Sir William Compton.

Sir Gilbert Taillour.

Sir Henry Guildford.

Sir William Askew.

Sir William Hussey.

Sir Christopher Willoughby.

List of English Attendees at the Field of the Cloth of Gold

Sir Thomas Broughton.
Sir William Hansard.
Sir Thomas West.
Sir Edward Hungerford.
Sir John Seymour.
Sir Richard Sachaverell.
Sir Giles Capel.
Sir John Neville.
Sir Edward Ferrers.
Sir John Burdett.
Sir John Talbot.
Sir Richard Norris.
Sir Thomas Cheney
Sir William Carey

Challengers
Sir Henry Jerningham.
Sir William Kingston.
Sir Giles Capel.
Antony Knyvett.

Appendix 5

EXTRACT OF THE ACCOUNT OF THE FIELD OF THE CLOTH OF GOLD, AS PRINTED BY JEAN LESCAILLE

State Letters and Papers Henry VIII, June 1520, 870. All spellings in context.

The French king, Queen and Madame spent Whitsuntide at Monthereul, where the cardinal d'Albret and the ladies of Navarre met them. The king of England was meanwhile at Canterbury with the King Catholic, who arrived at Dover on the 26th of May. After his departure the King and Queen embarked for Calais, and then proceeded to Guisnes, to meet the French king and queen, who were waiting for them at Ardre. This town being old and in decay, the fosses and ramparts were repaired by the French king, and a brick house was built for this meeting, but not perfectly completed. The tents and pavilions, numbering 300 or 400, made of cloth of gold and silver, and velvet, emblazoned with the arms of their owners, were pitched near a small river outside the town. The King had three middle-sized and one large pavilion. At the top of the large one was a figure of St. Michael, gilt, with a blue mantle powdered with gold fleur de lis, holding in his right hand a dart, in his left a shield with the French arms. They were covered with cloth of gold, inside and out. The pavilions of the Queen, Madame, Mons. d'Alençon, the Constable, Messieurs de Lorraine, de Vendosme, de Guise, St. Pol and others were all very fine. The large pavilion of the King was afterwards blown down and the mast broken. The princes and gentlemen lodged in their tents, and in the castles and villages around. There was good order everywhere, and abundance of provisions at reasonable prices. The king of England, on his arrival at Calais with his Queen and all their train, sent an embassy to the French king, consisting of the cardinal of York and others, as follows:—First, before the Legate, 100 archers of the Guard, in doublets of crimson velvet, with cloaks (*chamarres*) of fine scarlet; then 50 gentlemen of the Household, their bonnets in their hands, with cloaks of crimson velvet, and great chains of gold. They rode with their lances on their thighs, but went no further than the gates of Ardre. Next came the gentlemen and servants of the Legate, with their bonnets in their hands, all in crimson velvet, mostly wearing gold chains scarfwise, and their horses trapped in crimson velvet. Next, the Legate's crossbearer, in a scarlet robe, and a crimson velvet hood, with a short *cornette*. He carried two crosses till he was past the territory of Guisnes, where he left one. Next, round the Legate were four lackeys, in paletots of crimson velvet, with his device in goldsmith's work, bearing gilt bâtons and poleaxes (*bees de faulcon*). Then came the Legate, on a richly caparisoned mule, with gold frontstall, studs, buckles and stirrups, the footcloth of velvet figured on crimson velvet, the rochet of fine linen over all, and a red hat with large hanging tassels. After him, five or six bishops, the grand prior of Jerusalem, and several prothonotaries, in crimson and black velvet, and wearing great gold chains. Last, were 50 archers of the King's guard well mounted, their bows bent, and their quivers at their side, in red cloth jackets, with a gold rose before and behind.

The French king sent to meet him La Tremouille and Chastillon, with a great number of gentlemen, and 50 archers of the Guard. They met the Legate at two bowshots from Ardre, and joined the procession, marching behind the Legate and before the bishops.

The King met him, riding on his mule, at the gates, where he arrived about two hours after dinner. The princes, gentlemen, archers and Swiss were arranged on both sides of the street, from the gate to the King's house; the trumpets, fifes and other instruments played most melodiously, and the artillery made such a noise you could not hear. At the King's lodging, the Legate dismounted, and the King embraced him, with great signs of affection, bonnet in hand; then led him to his lodging, where they talked together for a long time with the other princes and lords, all magnificently dressed. Meanwhile good cheer was made to all the Legate's company. That done, the Legate returned to Calais.

The Saturday following, 2 June, the Legate revisited the King with a small company, at Ardre, and remained about 7 hours. Friday and Saturday, the Archbishop of Sens, the Admiral and other French lords visited the king of England at Calais. After supper on Saturday the king of France went to Marquise, between Ardre and Boulogne, where the ladies were, returning on Monday evening. Tuesday, 5 June, the king and queen of England, with their train, went to Guisnes. On their arrival, artillery was fired both there and at Ardre. Their tents were pitched near the castle, and those of the train in the field near the town. All necessaries were brought by sea from England. The King built a banqueting house, the most sumptuous that has long been seen. The foundations are of stone, the walls brick, and the rest wood; surrounded by cloth painted like brick; the covering painted *à l'antique*. Inside was tapestry of cloth of gold and silver, interlaced with white and green silk, the colors of the king of England. It contained four great *corps de maison*, eight saloons, chambers and wardrobes. The chapel was painted blue and gold, with hangings of gold and silver, and rich cupboards of plate. The gates were like those of a great castle, guarded by armed men above. At one door were two gilt pillars, bearing statues of Cupid and Bacchus, from which flowed streams of malmsey and claret into silver cups, for any to drink who wished. Between one of the gates and the castle of Guisnes was a winding alley, covered with verdure, like the house of Dædalus or the garden of Morganna la Fée, of the days of the knights errant.

Wednesday, 6 June, the archbishop of Sens, La Trimouille, the Admiral and other great lords, went to Guisnes, and were conducted by the Deputy (Milort de bittes) of Calais. The king of England sent Tallebot, his steward, to conduct them to the castle of Guisnes, with the sound of artillery and music. They were received and feasted by the English as if they were their brothers.

Thursday, 7 June, *la feste Dieu*, the Kings met in the Val Doré, a little valley between Ardre and Guisnes, in English ground, about vespers. The French king left Ardre, accompanied by the Constable, who carried the naked sword before him, and the Grand Escuyer, with the royal sword, powdered with gold fleurs de lis. After them came the king of Navarre, the dukes of Alençon, Lorraine and Vendome, the counts and lords of Guise, Laval, Lautraic, Dorval, La Tremouille and St. Pol, the marshals and lords of Chabannes, Chastillon, Lescun, Desperrault, Grand Master, the princes de la Roche Suryon, Tallemont, &c., in cloth of gold, wearing their order about their necks, and richly mounted. Then followed the archers of the Guard, with jackets of goldsmith's work; the gentlemen of the Household were on the left, without harness, according to their articles. The King was mounted on a beautiful charger, and clothed with a cassock of cloth of gold frieze, a mantle of cloth of gold, richly jewelled, the front and sleeves set with diamonds, rubies, emeralds and large pearls, hanging loose; his *barette* and bonnet of velvet, set with plumes, and resplendent with jewelry. Before him marched the Swiss, in his livery, with white feathers, led by Floranges, gorgeously arrayed, with fifes and all kinds of musical instruments. The trumpets and heralds marched near the King with banners displayed. Mountjoye, Bretaigne and Normandie heralds, went next him. The cardinals de Boissi, Legate in France, de Bourbon, d'Albret, de Lorraine and several bishops, with the ambassadors of the Pope, the King Catholic and others, marched in the King's company to near the Val Doré, where bounds were set which none but the Kings should pass. On the other side the king of England, accompanied by the dukes of Rotingan (Buckingham) and Suffolk, the marquis Dorset, the earls Northumberland, Talbot, Salisbury, the Grand Chamberlain, 'les contes Devonshire et Kent,' with numerous gentlemen and archers, wearing gilded hocquetons of white and green velvet, and a number of gentlemen not armed. The king of England was dressed in cloth of silver, richly jewelled, with white plumes. When the two companies approached, the Kings descended the valley, gently, with their constables bearing naked swords. On coming near, they gave their horses the spur like two combatants about to engage, but instead of putting their hands to their swords, each put his hand to his bonnet. They then embraced bareheaded, dismounted and embraced again, and took each other by the arm to a fine pavilion all like cloth of gold, which the king of England had prepared. After a dispute which should go last, the two Kings entered together. The Admiral and Wolsey entered before them. After some conversation within the pavilion, each king embraced the lords of the other's company, whilst the trumpets and other instruments sounded on each side, so that it seemed a paradise. At night they took leave of each other.

Saturday, the 9th, the two kings came to the lists. The camp was on high ground, about half-way between Ardres and Guisnes, surrounded with fosses like a town, the houses and galleries on each side long and spacious, and well hung with tapestry; and there was a chamber, well hung and glazed, for the Queens. At each entry to the park and lists was a guard of 12 French and 12 English archers, but they did not refuse entry to any person honorably apparelled. The Kings caused their shields to be attached by the kings-of-arms to the *perron* and tree of noblesse planted at the foot of the lists with the triumphal arch; the foot of which tree was covered with cloth of gold, and the *carrure* with green damask, and the leaves were of green silk. There was a dispute among the heralds which shield ought to be hung first and to the right. The Constable and others on the part of Francis, and the Marquis and others for the king of England, were appointed judges; but, finally, the king of England caused the French king's arms to be placed on the right, and his own on the left, equally high. After several feats that day, the Kings took leave of each other.

Sunday, the 10th, the French king and several of his gentlemen went to dine at Guisnes with the queen of England, and the king of England dined with the Queen at Ardre, accompanied by several English princes. The French king's mother went before him to the entry of the great court of the house, dressed as a widow, and did him reverence. They walked together to the room where they dined, which was well hung with cloth of gold from top to bottom. On the table the dishes were only set on one side. The king of England sat down first, the Queen next him, then Madame, the duchess of Alençon, her daughter and Madame de Vendome. Each had a service apart in vessels of gold. Among the entremets were salamanders, leopards and ermines, bearing the arms of the French king and queen, 'qui estoit une chose triumphante.' At the third service, largesse was cried by the heralds, who had a great golden goblet. And there was cried by Mountjoy, in the name of the king of England, 'Largesse to the high, mighty, and most excellent prince Henry, &c., largesse, largesse!' Then the heralds came to the *salle haute*, where were the duke d'Alençon and other lords entertaining the princes of England, and Bretaigne cried largesse, and then to the pavilion, &c. After much music, dances, songs, &c., the king of England took leave at 5 p.m., and returned to Guisnes. The reception given by the queen of England to the French king was not inferior.

Monday, the 11th, the jousts commenced. The kings of England and France, Vendosme, Suffolk, Dorset, Saint Pol and others held the lists, and were assailed by d'Alençon, the Admiral and others. This day the wind was so strong as to prevent the lances being couched. The Queens, who had not met before, were both present with their ladies, richly dressed in jewels, and with many chariots, litters and hackneys covered with cloth of gold and silver, and emblazoned with their arms. They sat together in a glazed gallery, hung with tapestry, and talked together about the tourney. Many persons present could not understand each other, and were obliged to have interpreters.

Wednesday, the 13th, the Kings and many of the ladies came to the camp, where were dancing, wrestling and other pastimes, but no jousting, on account of the high wind. Thursday, the 14th, the Kings and their aids tilted with the bands of Trimouille and Lescun, 25 men in all. The king of England and Suffolk did marvels. All returned home about 7. Friday, the 15th, the Kings did not run, but the other challengers received the bands of Vendosme and the marquis of Sallusses. The Marquis, out of 8 courses, broke 6 lances, *de droict fil.* Sunday, the 17th, the king of France and his mother dined with the queen of England in the palace which the King had built. Francis hearing that the King, who intended to dine with the Queen at Ardre, was still at Guisnes, went to see him, with only 4 companions, and finding him at breakfast, ran and embraced him. This action removed all suspicion from the minds of the English. The King, as was mentioned, dined with the queen of England, and after dinner there were masks and *damoiselles encornetées*, disguised as mummers. The king of England and his sister Mary dined at Ardre. The King dined apart, and sent for the Constable and others to dine with him. The Queen and the queen Mary dined together. After dinner there were dances, and the King retired to the Admiral's tent, where he and 30 gentlemen disguised themselves in the costumes of lanzknechts, Albanians, &c. On the following Monday, Tuesday and Wednesday the jousts continued. Jerningham was nearly unhorsed by one of Tremouille's band.

Friday and Saturday, the 22nd and 23rd, the combats at the barriers were performed on foot, with thrusting and casting lances, and short and two-handed swords. Sunday, the 24th, the Kings closed the lists with the Constable and his band. Saturday, the 23rd, a platform was built in the camp, and near it a chapel, a fathom and a half high, on pillars. It contained an altar and reliquaries, and at the side were two canopies of cloth of gold, with chairs for the legates of England and France, and the cardinals of France, and seats below for the French bishops. On another side were seats for the ambassadors of the Pope, the king of Spain, the Venetians and others. Between the chapel and the platforms for the Kings and Queens were the chanters of the Kings, each with his *popistre*; and above the platform, two oratories, one for the Kings, the other for the Queens, and other chambers; from one of which the Legates and Cardinals started at 10 o'clock to go to the chapel, all in red camlet, and seated themselves under the canopies; while the archbishop of Sens, and the bishops of Verdun, Lizieux, Angoulesme and others, sat below the canopy near the altar, and De Boysy under another. The English bishops were round the altar, to act as deacons and subdeacons, except the archbishop of Canterbury, who sat apart, near the French bishops. The English chanters began by saying *tierce*, which done, the English legate and the deacons, &c. changed their dress, and put on very rich vestments. The two Kings mounted the platform, and kneeled at the oratory, Francis on the right, and Henry on the left. The Queens did the like. There were with the French king, Alençon, Bourbon, the Constable, the king of Navarre, St. Pol, the King's confessor and the Grand Almoner. With the English king there were only two chaplains, who said mass at an altar at the oratory. About noon the English legate commenced the high mass *De Trinitate*. The first introit was sung by the English chanters, the second by the French. They had arranged that when the French organist played, the French chanters should sing, and *vice versâ*. Pierre Mouton played the *Kyrie*, then the English the *Gloria in Excelsis*; the *Patrem* was sung by the French, with the King's band of *cors de sabuttes* and fifes, the *Sanctus* by the English, and the *Agnus Dei* by the French, who concluded with several motetts. The cardinal de Bourbon, who brought the Gospel to the Kings to kiss, presented it first to Francis. He desired Henry to kiss it first, but he refused the honor. While the preface was being said, a great artificial salamander or dragon, four fathoms long, and full of fire, appeared in the air, from Ardre. Many were frightened, thinking it a comet, or some monster, as they could see nothing to which it was attached. It passed right over the chapel to Guisnes, as fast as a footman can go, and as high as a bolt shot from a crossbow. 'And when God was shown at the said mass, which was with great honour, reverence and devotion,' at the *Agnus Dei*, the *Pax* was presented to cardinal Bourbon to take to the Kings, who observed the same ceremony as before; then to the two Queens, who also declined to kiss it first, and, after many mutual respects, kissed each other instead. The benediction was given by the English legate, and one of the English secretaries made a Latin oration at the bottom (*fons*) of the chapel, turning to the royal personages, enlarging on the blessings of peace, and stating that those who assisted at the mass should have plenary remission; a privilege granted by the Pope to the English legate whenever he celebrated mass *in pontificalibus*. The platforms and galleries, which contained great numbers of people, were so well arranged that everyone could see. After mass the Kings dined together in a chamber on the high galleries. They sat on one side under a canopy of cloth of gold, the king of France at the top. The Queens dined in another chamber, and with them the queen Mary. The French queen was in the middle, under the canopy, and the duchess of Alençon at the end. The Kings and Queens always dined at home before coming to the banquets, and only conversed while admiring the service and the meats. The legates, cardinals and prelates dined in another room, and drank and ate *sans fiction*. The princes, princesses, lords and ladies dined in other chambers. After dinner the combats on foot were finished. Then the Kings and Queens returned home, the trumpets sounded, and in the evening, bonfires were made in the lists, and at Guisnes, Ardre and Calais guns were fired for it was the vigil of St. John.

Sunday, the 24th, the King went, masked, to Guisnes, to dine with the queen of England, and the king of England went to dine with the French queen. The Kings met in the lists, and bade each other farewell; and they seemed to leave each other with regret. The Constable, Lorraine Vendosme, the Admiral and others gave great banquets to the English princes and noblemen. The Kings, Princes and Princesses interchanged presents, as horses, litters, necklaces, &c. The Kings determined to build a chapel in the Val Doré, where they first met, for the daily performance of one mass, to be called 'La Chapelle de nostre Dame de la Paix.' The English king returned some French hostages who had been given for the affair of Tournay. 'Dieu par sa grace permette la paix estre durable. Amen.' (By God's Grace, this peace will last. Amen.)

Appendix 6

LIST OF ROYAL HALLS, TENTS AND PAVILIONS

This list is in the hand of Richard Gibson and was compiled before 1519, probably in relation to the 1513 expedition to France. All spellings are in context.

The pertecular namys of the halys, tentts and pavyllyons:

Each of these 12 ft. wide, 24 ft. long. Pomegarnet, Flowerdelyee, Whytte hart, Harpe, Gollod Stok, Castell, Crowne, Greyhound, Estereche fether, Gardyvyance.

30 ft. long, 15 ft. wide: Mone, Mounteyne, Mounde, Hynd of Golld, Braser, Leserd, Septer, Golld yok, Sonne beame.

45 ft. long, 15 ft. wide: Red Rose, Red Rose and Whytte, Lebard's Hed.

60 ft. long, 15 ft. wide: The Crownys, The Lyon, The Golld Cros, The thre Flourdelyces, The Cope of Golld, The Port Kolece, The Wheete Sheff.

22 ft. wide, 52 ft. long: The Mare, The Myhyll, The Gerne Shellde, The Fyer Ierene, The Manshe of Golld, The Hewytt,

The Red Shelld, The Blew Shelld, The Breket, The Golld Shelld, The Whytte Shelld, The Blak Shelld.

Of divers contents: The Annew of Golld, The Whytte Stavff (with my Lord Chamberlain), The Red Sword, The Whette Ere, The Gaunttlet, The Flagon, The Yellow Face, The Egyll, The Feshe, The Lylly Pott, The Combe, The Bedes, The Challys, The Fownteyne, The Swallow, The Marlyon, The Hamer, with tresans and inner halls.

Of several contents: The kitchen (perished), the knight harbingers hall, the Provost Marshall and the Master Cook's hall (perished).

The King's lodging, containing a porch, 10 ft. wide, 15 ft. long; a pavilion, 18 ft. wide; a tresans, 10 ft. wide and 30 ft. long; a hall called the first chamber; a tresans to the great chamber; a tresans thence to the King's house of timber; two cross tresans at the end of either tresans; a pavilion; all double walls of canvas.

Two square halls, 60 ft. long, 20 ft. wide.

Old store: The 8 pavilions of 16 ft. wide; the buttoned hall, 60 ft. long and 20 ft. wide; the 8 pavilions, 17 ft. wide.

NOTES

Introduction

1. The modern spelling is 'Guines' but hereafter in the text the sixteenth-century spelling 'Guisnes' will be used.
2. Pollard, A F *Henry VIII* Dodo Press, 2008 and Scarisbrick J.J *Henry VIII* University of California Press 1968

1. The World in 1520

1. Sneyd, Charlotte Augusta *A Relation, or Rather a True Account, of the Island of England... About the year 1500* Camden Society, London 1847
2. Ibid
3. 'Incunabla' being any book printed before the year 1500.
4. Sneyd

The English

2. Henry VIII

1. SLP Henry VIII November 1501
2. Ibid
3. Hall, Edward *Chronicle* J.Johnston, London 1809
4. SLP Henry VIII June 1509
5. Ibid
6. Ibid
7. Ibid
8. Ibid
9. Ibid
10. Hall
11. SLP Venice June 1509

12. Hall
13. Ibid
14. CSP Venice July 1517
15. Ibid
16. Ibid
17. Ibid
18. Ibid
19. Ibid
20. SLP Henry VIII October 1518
21. Ibid
22. Ibid
23. SLP Henry VIII February 1519
24. Ibid
25. Ibid
26. SLP Henry VIII May 1519

3. Catherine of Aragon
1. SLP Henry VII March 1489
2. Nichols, John Gough *London Pageants* J B Nichols and Son, London, 1831
3. Ibid
4. Hall
5. Thomas More
6. Hall
7. Ibid
8. CSP Spain Dec 1509
9. SLP Henry VIII July 1513
10. Ibid
11. SLP Henry VIII September 1513
12. SLP Henry VIII May 1515
13. Ibid
14. Ibid
15. Hall
16. Ibid
17. SLP Henry VIII May 1517
18. Hall
19. SLP Henry VIII April 1520

4. The English Party
1. SLP Venice June 1515
2. SLP Henry VIII March 1520
3. *Rutland Papers: Original documents illustrative of the courts and times of Henry VII and Henry VIII* Camden Society, J B Nichols 1842

4. Dictionary of National Biography
5. SLP March 1520
6. Rutland
7. Ibid
8. Ibid
9. Weir, Alison *Mary Boleyn: Mistress of Kings* Ballantine Books 2011
10. SLP Henry VIII March 1514
11. SLP Henry VIII October 1514
12. SLP Henry VIII December 1514
13. SLP Henry VIII March 1520
14. Sadlack, Erin A *The French Queen's Letters: Mary Tudor Brandon and the Politics of Marriage in Sixteenth Century Europe* Springer 2011 Thank you to Sarah Bryson for drawing this to my attention.

The French

5. Francis I
1. Knecht, R.J *Francis I* Cambridge University Press, 1981
2. Ibid
3. Ibid
4. Armstrong, Alistair *France 1500-1715* Heinemann 2003
5. Seward, Desmond *Prince of the Renaissance, The Life of Francois I* History Book Club, 1973
6. Ibid
7. Ibid
8. Ibid
9. SLP Henry VIII December 1519
10. Ibid
11. Knecht
12. SLP Henry VIII February 1519
13. Ibid
14. Knecht
15. Ibid

6. Claude
1. Knecht
2. Ibid
3. Ibid
4. Ibid
5. Ibid
6. Ibid
7. SLP Henry VIII March 1519
8. Ibid
9. Ibid
10. SLP Henry VIII April 19

11. Ibid
12. Ibid
13. Ibid
14. Ibid

7. *The French Party*
1. SLP Henry VIII March 1520
2. SLP Henry VIII February 1520
3. SLP Henry VIII May 1519
4. SLP Henry VIII April 1520
5. Ibid
6. Durant, William *The Lessons of History* Simon and Schuster 1968
7. Kolk, Caroline zum 'The Household of the Queen of France in the Sixteenth Century' in *The Court Historian* Volume 4, Number 1 June 2009
8. Ibid

The Planning

8. *Negotiations*
1. Hall
2. SLP Henry VIII March 1520
3. SLP Henry VIII March 1519
4. Ibid
5. SLP Henry VIII June 1519
6. Ibid
7. Ibid
8. SLP Henry VIII July 1519
9. SLP Henry VIII November 1519
10. SLP Henry VIII January 1520
11. SLP Henry VIII February 1520
12. Ibid
13. Ibid
14. Ibid
15. SLP Henry VIII March 1520
16. Ibid
17. Ibid
18. Ibid
19. Ibid
20. Ibid
21. Ibid
22. Ibid
23. Ibid
24. SLP Henry VIII April 1520

9. Preparations

1. SLP Henry VIII June 1520
2. Ibid
3. SLP Henry VIII April 1520
4. Ibid
5. SLP Henry VIII July 1520
6. SLP Henry VIII April 1520
7. Ibid
8. Ibid
9. SLP Henry VIII July 1520
10. SLP Henry VIII April 1520
11. Ibid
12. Ibid
13. Ibid
14. Ibid
15. SLP Henry VIII May 1520
16. Ibid
17. Ibid
18. Ibid
19. Ibid
20. Ibid
21. Ibid
22. Ibid
23. SLP Henry VIII April, May 1520
24. Ibid
25. Ibid

The Emperor

10. Charles V

1. See Licence, Amy *Anne Boleyn* Amberley 2018
2. Ibid
3. Vergil
4. SLP Henry VIII March 1520
5. SLP Henry VIII April 1520
6. Ibid
7. Ibid
8. Ibid
9. Ibid
10. SLP Henry VIII May 1520
11. Ibid
12. Ibid
13. Ibid
14. Ibid

15. Ibid
16. Ibid
17. Ibid
18. Ibid
19. Hall
20. Ibid
21. Holinshed, Raphael *Holinshed's Chronicles*, London 1577
22. Vergil
23. CSP Venice May 20
24. Ibid
25. SLP Henry VIII May 20
26. Ibid

The Field of the Cloth of Gold

11. The Encampments

1. CSP Venice June 1520
2. Hall
3. Ibid
4. Venice June 1520
5. Ibid
6. Ibid
7. Ibid
8. Hall
9. Ibid
10. Rutland
11. Venice June 1520
12. Ibid
13. Ibid
14. Ibid
15. Hall
16. Venice June 1520
17. Ibid
18. Ibid
19. Ibid
20. Ibid
21. Ibid, Hall
22. Rutland
23. Venice June 1520
24. Ibid
25. Ibid
26. Ibid

12. Friday, 1 June – Wednesday, 6 June
1. CSP Venice June 1520
2. Ibid
3. Ibid
4. Ibid
5. Hall
6. Venice 1520
7. Ibid
8. Ibid
9. SLP Henry VIII June 1520
10. Venice June 1520
11. Hall
12. Ibid
13. SLP Henry VIII June 1520
14. Ibid
15. Vergil
16. Grafton
17. Venice June 1520
18. Ibid
19. Ibid
20. Ibid
21. SLP Henry VIII June 1520
22. Venice June 1520
23. Ibid

13. Thursday, 7 June
1. CSP Venice June 1520
2. Ibid
3. Ibid
4. Ibid
5. Ibid
6. Ibid
7. Ibid
8. Ibid
9. Ibid
10. Ibid
11. SLP Henry VIII June 1520
12. Venice June 1520
13. Ibid
14. Ibid
15. Grafton
16. Ibid
17. Venice June 1520

18. Ibid
19. Ibid
20. Ibid
21. Ibid
22. Ibid
23. Ibid
24. Ibid
25. Hall
26. Venice June 1520
27. SLP Henry June 1520
28. Venice June 1520
29. Ibid
30. Hall
31. Ibid

14. *Friday, 8 June- Sunday, 10 June*
 1. SLP Henry May 1520
 2. Ibid
 3. SLP Henry VIII June 1520
 4. Rutland
 5. SLP Henry VIII June 1520
 6. Ibid
 7. SLP Venice June 1520
 8. Ibid
 9. Rutland
10. Venice
11. Hall
12. Venice
13. Ibid
14. SLP Henry VIII
15. Ibid
16. Venice
17. Hall
18. Ibid
19. Venice
20. Ibid
21. Hall
22. Ibid
23. Venice
24. Ibid
25. Ibid
26. Hall

15. Monday, 11 June – Friday, 15 June
 1. Hall
 2. Ibid
 3. Ibid
 4. CSP Venice June 1520
 5. Ibid
 6. Ibid
 7. Ibid
 8. Ibid
 9. Vergil
10. Hall
11. Ibid
12. Rutland
13. Venice
14. Ibid
15. Ibid
16. SLP Henry VIII June 1520
17. Ibid
18. Ibid
19. Ibid
20. Venice
21. Ibid
22. Hall
23. Venice
24. Hall
25. Venice
26. Ibid
27. Hall
28. Ibid
29. Knecht
30. Hall
31. Grafton
32. Venice
33. Venice
34. Ibid
35. Hall
36. Venice
37. SLP Henry VIII
38. Venice
39. Hall
40. SLP Henry VIII June 1520

16. *Saturday, 16 June - Friday, 22 June*
1. SLP Henry VIII June 1520
2. CSP Venice June 1520
3. SLP Henry VIII
4. Hall
5. Ibid
6. Rutland
7. Hall
8. Venice
9. Ibid
10. Hall
11. Venice
12. Hall
13. Venice
14. Hall
15. Venice
16. Hall
17. Ibid
18. Venice
19. Ibid
20. Ibid
21. Vergil
22. Hall
23. Ibid
24. Venice
25. SLP Henry
26. Hall
27. Ibid
28. Ibid
29. Hall
30. SLP Henry VIII

17. *Saturday, 23 June - Monday, 25 June*
1. Hall
2. Ibid
3. Ibid
4. CSP Venice June 1520
5. SLP Henry VIII June 1520
6. Ibid
7. Ibid
8. Venice
9. SLP Henry
10. Hall
11. Ibid

12. SLP Henry
13. Ibid
14. Hall
15. Ibid
16. Ibid
17. Ibid
18. Ibid
19. Ibid
20. Venice
21. Ibid
22. Hall
23. Venice
24. SLP Henry
25. Venice
26. Knecht

Aftermath

18. Settling the Bill
1. SLP Henry VIII June 1520
2. Hall
3. SLP Henry
4. Ibid
5. Ibid
6. Ibid
7. Ibid
8. Ibid
9. Ibid
10. Ibid
11. Ibid

19. Interim, 25 June - 10 July
1. SLP Henry VIII
2. Ibid
3. Ibid
4. Ibid
5. CSP Venice June 1520
6. SLP Henry
7. Ibid
8. Henry VIII May 1520
9. Anglo, Sydney 'The British History in Early Tudor Propaganda' in the *Bulletin of the John Rylands Library* 44 (1) 17-48 1961
10. Ibid
11. Ibid

12. SLP Henry VIII June
13. SLP Henry VIII May
14. SLP Henry VIII July
15. Ibid
16. Venice
17. SLP Henry VIII July
18. Ibid
19. Ibid
20. Ibid

20. *Return of the Emperor*
  1. CSP Venice July 1520
  2. Ibid
  3. Ibid
  4. Hall
  5. Ibid
  6. Ibid
  7. Venice
  8. Hall
  9. Venice
  10. Hall
  11. Ibid
  12. Venice
  13. Hall
  14. Venice
  15. SLP Henry July
  16. Ibid
  17. Ibid
  18. Hall
  19. Venice
  20. Hall
  21. SLP Henry

21. *Endpiece*
  1. CSP Venice July 1520
  2. Ibid
  3. Ibid
  4. Ibid
  5. SLP Henry VIII July 1520
  6. Ibid
  7. SLP Henry
  8. Ibid
  9. Ibid
  10. Venice
  11. Reynolds, E E *St John Fisher* 1955 (Mediatrix 2015)

22. *All that Glitters*
  1. Norwich, John Julius *Four Princes: Henry VIII, Francis I, Charles V and Suleiman the Magnificent* John Murray 2017
  2. Mack, Phyllis 'Political Rhetoric and Poetic Meaning in Renaissance Culture: Clement Marot and the Field of the Cloth of Gold' in *Politics and Culture in Early Modern Europe: Essays in Honour of H G Koenigsberger* Cambridge University Press 1987
  3. Scarisbrick J. J. *Henry VIII* University of California Press 1968
  4. Mack
  5. Russell, Joycelyne G. *The Field of the Cloth of Gold: Men and Manners in 1520* London 1969
  6. Ibid
  7. Mack
  8. Pollard, A F *Henry VIII* Dodo Press, 2008
  9. Scarisbrick

Appendix 2: The Sources
  1. CSP Venice 1520
  2. Ibid
  3. SLP Henry VIII October 1532
  4. CSP Venice February 1515
  5. CSP Venice April 1515
  6. CSP Venice May 1515
  7. CSP Venice June 1515
  8. SLP Henry VIII May 1519
  9. SLP Henry VIII June 1520
  10. Rutland
  11. SLP Venice 1519-20
  12. SLP Venice June 1520

Appendix 3: The Second Meeting: Henry and Francis in 1532.
  1. Hall
  2. Ibid
  3. SLP Henry VIII October 1532
  4. SLP Henry VIII Privy Purse expenses 1532
  5. Hall
  6. Ibid
  7. Ibid
  8. Ibid
  9. SLP Henry VIII October 1532
  10. Hall
  11. Ibid
  12. SLP Henry VIII October 1532
  13. Ibid

SELECT BIBLIOGRAPHY

Anglo, Sydney 'The British History in Early Tudor Propaganda' in the *Bulletin of the John Rylands Library* 44 (1) 17-48 1961

Anglo, Sydney *Spectacle, Pageantry and Early Tudor Policy* Clarendon Press, 1969

Armstrong, Alistair *France 1500-1715* Heinemann 2003

Calendar of State Papers for Spain

Calendar of State Papers for Venice, Volume 2, ed. Rawdon Brown, London 1864

Febvre, Lucian *Life in Renaissance France* trans. Marian Rothenstein, Cambridge, Massachusetts and London 1977

Grafton, Richard *Grafton's Chronicle* Volume 2 J.Johnson, London 1809

Hall, Edward *Chronicle* J.Johnston, London 1809

Holinshed, Raphael *Holinshed's Chronicles,* London 1577

Knecht, R.J *Francis I* Cambridge University Press, 1981

Letters and Papers Henry VIII, Volume 3, ed J.S.Brewer, London, 1867 HMSO

Licence, Amy *Anne Boleyn* Amberley 2018

Licence, Amy *Catherine of Aragon* Amberley 2016

Mack, Phyllis 'Political Rhetoric and Poetic Meaning in Renaissance Culture: Clement Marot and the Field of the Cloth of Gold' in *Politics and Culture in Early Modern Europe: Essays in Honour of H G Koenigsberger* Cambridge University Press 1987

Matusiak, John *Wolsey: The Life of King Henry VIII's Cardinal* The History Press 2014

More, Thomas *Collected Works* Luminarum http://www. luminarium.org/renlit/morebib.htm

Munby, Julian 'The Field of the Cloth of Gold: Guines and The Calais Pale Revisited' in English *Heritage Historical Review* Volume 9 2014

Nichols, John Gough *London Pageants* J B Nichols and Son, London, 1831

Norwich, John Julius *Four Princes: Henry VIII, Francis I, Charles V and Suleiman the Magnificent* John Murray 2017

Russell, Joycelyne G *The Field of the Cloth of Gold: Men and Manners in 1520* London 1969

Rutland Papers: Original documents illustrative of the courts and times of Henry VII and Henry VIII Camden Society, J B Nichols 1842

Seward, Desmond *Prince of the Renaissance, The Life of Francois I* History Book Club, 1973

Sneyd, Charlotte Augusta *A Relation, or Rather a True Account, of the Island of England... About the year 1500* Camden Society, London 1847

Vergil, Polydore *Anglia Historia* Royal Historical Society 1950

Weir, Alison *Mary Boleyn: Mistress of Kings* Ballantine Books 2011

ACKNOWLEDGEMENTS

My thanks go first to Amberley Publishing, to my editor Shaun Barrington, and all those who supported the writing of this book and their diligence in bringing it to a conclusion.

I would like to thank my mother, for her constant love and support, my husband Tom and my two sons, and our wider family, including my brother Tom, Ben, and my godmother, Susan. I have been blessed with some wonderfully kind friends. Thank you to Paul, Anne, Sharon and Kat, my wonderful comrades, and to all my friends and supporters, whose kind words have kept me going. Thank you particularly to Luke, for his enthusiasm about this book, and for sharing the journey through it.

INDEX

Micklowe, John, of the
Counting House 40, 101
Montemerlo, Pietro 137, 151,
163
Montmorency, Anne de, First
Valet of the Bedchamber to
Francis I 79, 88, 214
More, Sir Thomas, Master of
Requests 45, 68, 115, 117

Neville, George, Chief Larderer
48, 50, 149

Owen, Sir David 45
Owen, Henry 45

Pace, Richard, Wolsey's
secretary 30-1, 48, 115,
117, 130, 177
pageantry 33-4, 73, 74
Parr, Sir William 50
Paston, William 45
Peche, Sir John, Marshal of
Calais 49, 50, 101, 105,
149, 156, 159, 165
Percy, Henry, Duke of
Northumberland 44, 143,
157
Plaine, Gerard de, Master of
Requests to Charles V 114
Plantagenet, Sir Arthur 45
Poynyngs, Sir Edward, warden
of the Cinque Ports 44, 48,
50, 102, 157, 202

Rene of Savoy 152
Robertet, Florimond, French
Treasurer 80, 160, 166

Rohan, Charles de, Comte
de Guise, Grand Butler of
France 80
Ruthall, Thomas, Bishop of
Durham 44, 115, 117, 203
Rutland Papers 127, 130, 149,
167, 235

Sagudino, Nicolo, Secretary to
the Venetian ambassador
37, 41, 42
Sandys, Sir William, Treasurer
of Calais 44, 49, 88, 99,
107, 202
Sanseverino, (San Severino)
Galeazzo di, Grand Squire
to France 81, 141, 145,
157, 181
Sauche, Jean de la, Imperial
secretary 39, 113, 114,
115, 117
Savoy, Rene of, Comte de
Villars, Grand Master to
Francis I 78
Shurley, Sir John, Cofferer 49,
101, 127, 187, 200
Skevington, Sir William,
Master of the Ordinance
50, 99
Soardino, Mantuan
Ambassador 126, 127, 133,
141, 143, 145, 155, 157,
160, 163, 168, 170, 176,
180, 181, 234-4
Somerset, Charles, Earl
of Worcester, Lord
Chamberlain 44, 49, 88,
90, 98, 99, 101, 107, 116,
157, 167, 201

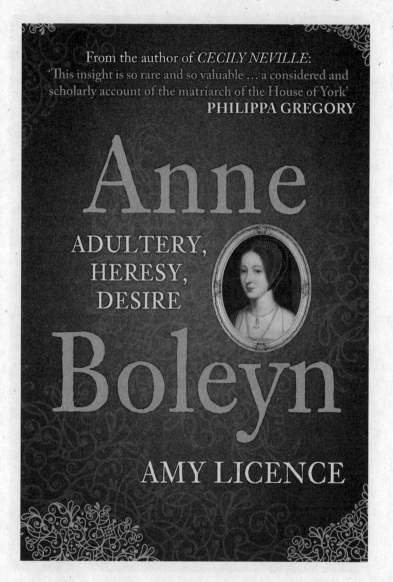

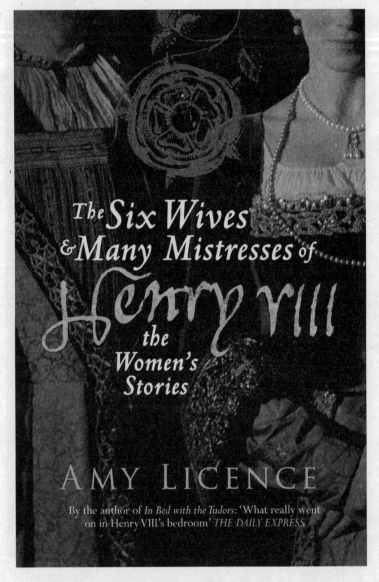